Praise for The Tr

" 'I'm not just sober, Judy gave me my
have heard many times over the years fro⸻⸻ ⸻⸻⸻⸻ ⸻⸻ked
with Judy. Most have had multiple residen⸻⸻ and outpatient treatment
episodes, racking up one disappointing relapse after another. That is,
until they learn from Judy and her staff the nature of the relationship
between their addiction and underlying trauma. Using state-of-the-art
approaches for accessing and processing the often long-suppressed material stored in body and mind, Judy's model offers people a safe way to see
in the mirror. They learn how to create and operate from a new, more
affirming story. At its heart, this book helps clients to learn that beyond
sobriety and survival, there is hope for a new life!"

—Brent Mruz, PsyD

"There's not a patient or family I've seen with substance abuse disorders who at the 'heart' of their suffering *hasn't* experienced trauma.
Whether incident-related or shame-based, if not treated as a core concept, trauma will only cause the cycle of suffering to continue. No one
understands this concept better than Judy Crane."

—Rob Waggener, LCSW, FACHE, Foundations Recovery Network

I have seen the whole world get better because of the work and writings of Judy Crane. Read this book! You will see the clarity, compassion,
and coherency Judy brings to use the wounded-ness in each of us to let
the light shine in, to allow growth, to become human, and to live fully.
Judy brings the awareness and wisdom to allow each of us to know, love,
and live the difficult and rewarding journey of 'becoming human.'"

—Ronald E. Smith MD, PhD,
Captain, Medical Corps, United States Navy

"Judy Crane has not only presented a beautiful story-picture of the
Trauma Heart's journey to hope, healing, and health, she has also cap-
tured a vital message for the hearts of those of us who are blessed to be
part of trauma heart journeys. Whether we're a family member, friend, or

a professional trauma therapist, that message is simply and powerfully...
the author's heart. As you read the pages you can't help but feel the heart
of Judy Crane; her love for and belief in people who have endured trauma.
That is perhaps the most impactful factor of this book; a moving and poignant example of who we need to be in our hearts in order to help trauma
survivors heal. I have seen Judy Crane's trauma heart in action as she
combines it in therapy intensive as well as in professional trainings with
me and our entire therapy staff at Capstone. When training therapists, she
integrates the research and therapy model into an experiential learning
process that's unmatched in its effect, much like she's done in this book
with her gift of storytelling. Nothing has impacted our team more than
the therapy approaches presented in this book and the heart that fuels it."

—Adrian Hickman, PhD, CTT, CSAT-S, CMAT-S,
AAMFT-S, LPC-S, LADAC, EMDR1
founder and CEO, Capstone Treatment Center

"Judy has an intuitive gift like no other, and this book explores the
power of finding meaning even in the darkest parts of our story, to discover the intricate beauty of the trauma recovery work! Whether you are
a survivor, a loved one, or a clinician, this book gets to the heart of what
trauma is and how to heal from it."

—Brennon P. Moore, CTT, CADC-II, LPC
trauma survivor and author of *Finding a New Tribe: Helping Young
Men Recover from Childhood Sexual Abuse and Addiction*

"Judy has taught me to identify my voice with my trauma, and I have
been able to use my voice to become a better person, both personally and
professionally. Judy is a true teacher of life skills in working with trauma."

—Rick Terzick MA, CTT

"The day I met Judy Crane my life changed forever. Judy's compassion, and innate genius as a trauma therapist has been the greatest gift in
thousands of her clients lives as well as mine. I am proud to call her friend,
mentor, business partner and colleague. She is a true gift to the world."

—John West, Co-Owner of The Guest House Ocala and
Managing Partner of Sober Companion Services

THE TRAUMA HEART

WE ARE NOT BAD PEOPLE TRYING TO BE GOOD, WE ARE WOUNDED PEOPLE TRYING TO HEAL

STORIES OF SURVIVAL, HOPE & HEALING

JUDY T. CRANE

Health Communications, Inc.
Deerfield Beach, Florida

www.hcibooks.com

Library of Congress Cataloging-in-Publication Data
is available through the Library of Congress

© 2017 Judy Crane

ISBN-13: 978-07573-1981-5 (Paperback)
ISBN-10: 07573-1981-5 (Paperback)
ISBN-13: 978-07573-1982-2 (ePub)
ISBN-10: 07573-1982-2 (ePub)

All rights reserved. Printed in the United States of America. No part of this publication may be reproduced, stored in a retrieval system, or transmitted in any form or by any means, electronic, mechanical, photocopying, recording, or otherwise, without the written permission of the publisher.

HCI, its logos, and marks are trademarks of Health Communications, Inc.

Publisher: Health Communications, Inc.
            3201 S.W. 15th Street
            Deerfield Beach, FL 33442–8190

Back cover artwork by Michelle Quinton
Color insert formatting by Larissa Hise Henoch
Cover design and interior formatting by Lawna Patterson Oldfield

*"You can accept or reject the way you are treated
by other people, but until you heal the wounds of your past,
you will continue to bleed. You can bandage the bleeding
with food, with alcohol, with drugs, with work, with cigarettes,
with sex, but eventually, it will all ooze through and stain your
life. You must find the strength to open the wounds, stick your
hands inside, pull out the core of the pain that is holding you in
your past, the memories, and make peace with them."*

—Iyanla Vanzant

❧

The Trauma Heart is dedicated to my family, to the present and to the past, the many generations of our family. There is wonderment in unraveling the many parts of our family tree; the roots, the trunk, the branches and the limbs. There still remains the mystery of more to unravel and, more importantly, the creation of fresh new limbs. These will carry the essence of our family forward, to grow and refine, to struggle and flourish with the resilience, compassion, sensitivity, innate talents and strengths, to build an ever-growing family tree where we can rest in the shade of our loving family.

We have our stories and whether glorious or painful, dark or light, the stories of our families are the architectural design of who we become and who we are.

To my father, who promised me I could do or be anything, even though I was a girl.

To my mother, who is the most courageous and resilient "rebel" I know . . . you were breaking the rules before I was born and I am so very grateful that you did.

To my godmother, Aunt Theresa, thank you for being such an important part of my life and for being the keeper of our history. I love you and send you Light.

To my three sisters, Linda, Kathleen, and Joan, thank you for loving me when I was so very unlovable. My love and prayers and hope are always with you. Always remember those crazy, wonderful summers in the neighborhood. Blessings to all my nieces and nephews.

To my most extraordinary children, Tom, Maria, and Michelle. I am so very proud of you all; you are amazing people and loving and incredible parents. In spite of the insanity that my addiction brought to your lives, you carry yourselves with grace and big, loving hearts. I love you beyond measure.

To my nieces and nephews in South Philly, I cherish our stories and our time together.

Grateful for Grandmom Rose, Grandpop Ralph, and precious Aunt Rita; and filled with love for our time with my husband Tommy, and Tommy the daddy of Tommy Jr., Maria, and Michelle.

And most importantly, Devyn, Delaney, Xander, AJ, and Marlee, the lights and joy of my life, the grandchildren who bring such excitement and pleasure as I enjoy your journey. Each of you are powerful in your uniqueness and you all SHINE so brightly. I'm thrilled to be your Yadda and I love you all totally and completely.

We are not bad people trying to be good;
we are wounded people trying to heal.

CONTENTS

ACKNOWLEDGEMENTS

There are people in this world who walk tall and find a life of purpose through their pain and redemption. These are the men and women who humbly and courageously offered their journey through trauma and trauma healing into the light; they have offered you their stories and their extraordinary experiential work.

These people have walked through the fire and shared their experiences with the hope that you may find a way through your own pain.

Many of these stories are from therapists who have had their own traumas, creating a space in their spirit that touches the spirits of the wounded who come to us for healing. We have lost many to the soul wounds of trauma and addiction. You live forever in our hearts and spirits, and this book is written in the hopes of saving those who also feel lost.

I would like to share my eternal gratitude to Tom Pecca, my son, for offering his help with many elements of *The Trauma Heart*. Tom is an extremely talented therapist who honed his skills as a little boy in a very dysfunctional family.

Many thanks to Stacy Maddox, who saved the day when I was ready to give up. Thank you from the bottom of my heart.

To Joan Nichols, thank you for you vital assistance with the early research and editing. It was a blessing to have a reader who was new to the field of trauma and addictions treatment.

I am filled with gratitude for my friends and colleagues—such a talented team—who created The Refuge in 2003 and, with great excitement and joy, The Guest House Ocala, in January 2017.

Thank you, John West, a wondrous young man who took a risk with me to build The Guest House Ocala, to create the finest trauma and addictions program in the world.

Finally, I have such gratitude for our partners who have supported The Guest House Ocala with more than your words. You know who you are; you are people who want to change the world.

We *can* change the world one story at a time!

PREFACE

This is not a textbook; I want to make that clear. I have been writing this book for a long time, four to five years, in the midst of creating and directing a world-class trauma, post-traumatic stress disorder (PTSD), and addictions treatment center; speaking and teaching about trauma; and writing pieces as I was whirling around in my life and the world. Friends and colleagues joked about "the" book, demanded that it be written, and lovingly chiding me that it was a ghost book, taking far too long.

The reality is this book wrote itself in the blood, snot, and tears of our beautiful alumni appropriately called Refugees. This is in honor of their completion of treatment at The Refuge, our treatment center in their forest. Their families and loved ones also shared their trauma histories, and many family members engaged in their own recovery process. These are the families that found real forgiveness, compassion, love, and intimacy, ensuring that the generations that follow are more capable of interrupting intergenerational maladaptive behaviors.

One gentleman admitted to treatment seven years ago as a result of turmoil created by trauma and alcoholism in his life changed dramatically because of his willingness to reach deeply into his soul wound. As a result of his example, thirty-seven other Refugees can be traced to him: family, friends, children of friends, neighbors, and even ex-spouses.

Twelve-step programs recommend that "it is through walking the walk" that people around us change, through "attraction, not promotion." As we change, the people in our life feel safe to reach out for help because they want what we have. These folks come from all over the world. These "survivors" courageously offered their own stories among their peers, exposing their wounds as they guided our clients into their story. This book wrote itself in the voices of those who desperately want to heal.

Initially I was writing gingerly, cautiously, so as not to expose people too deeply; however, these stories have been handed to me by folks who want their story told, who want to be the hope and healing for others to experience. The purpose of this book is to invite those who suffer into the circle of healing, which then synergistically changes the family, the community, the world—if we dream *big enough*.

So will you learn some "textbook things"? Yes, my prayer is that there are folks who will pick up this book and have "*Aha!*" moments, puzzle pieces falling-into-place moments, heart-gripping revelation moments, because you may recognize your story and your behaviors through someone else's work. Again, my prayer is that you will find hope and take a risk to explore *your* story.

This is my mantra:

When you unravel the trauma story, the behaviors make sense. When we

WHEN YOU UNRAVEL THE TRAUMA STORY, THE BEHAVIORS MAKE SENSE.

can make sense of our behaviors, the behaviors of our loved ones, the behaviors in the people around us, healing can take place. First, we must do the hard work of unraveling the story.

Here is an example, silly on the surface but not so silly in the unraveling. I have a closet *full* of shoes. I know I buy them when I am lonely, bored, or insecure. Buying shoes gives me relief. I am always alone when I buy shoes. When I find a pair that I love, I buy them in every color. I have a closet full of shoes, many that I haven't worn.

One day I thought about my favorite shoes as a kid. They were beautiful to me—I was probably ten years old. The shoes were brown with "peek-a-boo" toes and they had been given to me by a neighbor. I had one pair of shoes for school and a pair of sneakers and they both had holes in the bottom. I put cardboard in them to continue wearing them. This was pretty normal. We were a family of six: two parents and four sisters. I think my neighbor knew about my shoes! At least, that is the story I told myself.

Deprivation was my trauma and shoes were my solution, an expensive solution to assuage my shame about being poor and how others judge me.

So this is not a textbook; it's an experiential book.

It's been a good book for me to write: painful, gut-wrenching at times, joyful and satisfying at other times, and a revelation in so many ways. I've been doing my own work for years but writing this book has given me new information and incredible insights into my own life and my family. I was born in October of 1945 and I'm pretty sure I was responsible for the atomic bomb. I experienced

I WAS BORN IN OCTOBER OF 1945 AND I'M PRETTY SURE I WAS RESPONSIBLE FOR THE ATOMIC BOMB.

enormous guilt and shame from my earliest memories until several years into recovery. I felt responsible and great personal shame for everything that was wrong in the lives of the people in my life. And I felt responsible to "fix" those things—a huge burden for a young girl. I even apologized to walls and chairs I bumped into. The phrase I used the most was "I'm sorry."

Today I understand the concept of in-utero and intergenerational trauma, and realize that I felt that same shame and guilt that I carried oozing from my mother and aunt. I recognize clearly how those feelings and that energy impacted my vision of myself and my place in the world, just as it impacted so many others in my family tree.

My place in the world seemed so fragile and illusory that I searched for it in very desperate and lonely places. There was a divide between my immediate and extended family. We—my mother and father, three younger sisters and I—seemed to be the black sheep family. It was Gil, Ann, and "the girls." We visited my grandparents' house often, especially on family holidays. It seemed so big! There were four bedrooms and a huge room that used to be a plumbing supply store, as well as large family rooms, kitchen, dining room, living room, and a big backyard filled with blue hydrangea and roses. I have many photos of me and my sisters when we were very young, usually in a small wading pool, or in Easter outfits with cute bonnets and black patent-leather shoes. We were dressed for church, but we didn't attend because of the "family secret." The family secret was that my mother married my father against her family's wishes. Daddy was divorced and had another child, my half-brother Larry, *and* Daddy wasn't baptized. While "my" family remained home from church, all of my aunts, uncles, and cousins attended Mass and participated in the church rituals.

The guilt that permeated my mother and aunt centered on their choice of husbands. My mother was excommunicated from the Catholic Church. My Aunt Theresa was also my godmother, so at least, thank God, I was baptized. I may have been the family shame, born outside of the Catholic Church, but at least I was baptized.

I was the oldest grandchild. The energy in my grandparents' home was so uncomfortable, angry, and judgmental with grandmom and my grandpop, a silent, brooding Irishman. My uncles and their wives and children seemed to receive all the family grace. Those were my feelings, my experiences. I was highly attuned to feeling shame, guilt, and judgment, especially from my grandmother. I was also attuned to the role I perceived that we had as the "less-than" and "black sheep" family. I took ownership of being the black sheep child.

That dark energy seemed to ease up after my sisters were born so they didn't seem to experience life the way I did.

I didn't know my uncles or their families' very well. I often wonder how the rest of my family experienced this extended brood. I was close to my Aunt Theresa's children; my cousins and I experienced some of the joys and the pain of their lives. But I often wonder about the experiences and perceptions of other family members. Did they understand or know my grandparents more intimately? Were they driven by family messages? Did they feel more connected or part of a bigger family entity?

I also experienced the world around me in very visceral, sensory, and cellular ways. My world was in living Technicolor with vivid experiences of color, sound, taste, touch, and smells. I loved every new experience and worked diligently to fit in with the rest of the world (despite feeling as if I didn't belong), but this was often a place of loneliness. I learned about the world from movies and books. I remember visiting the Eiffel Tower in Paris many years later, and feeling as if I'd been there before because I had embraced and internalized the world as my very own. I had a voracious appetite to know, to experience everything. This was certainly a necessary attribute for an addict.

I could "fit in" by being a chameleon, but usually as a "mascot," an add-on, an outsider who charmed her way into the inner circle but never truly belonged. All of this history would become the cause, effect, and "cure" of my spiritual and internal pain, and would drive me to quite interesting solutions and adventures.

I grew up in a struggling blue-collar family in the 1950s and 1960s. I was a good girl with a spiritual connection who ached and yearned for human and emotional connection. However, deprivation was at the core of my spirit—emotional, physical, and economic deprivation. Thank God for my spiritual connection, my "God consciousness." I was searching for my tribe from the age of five, maybe younger.

As my sisters and I grew up, with very different feelings and perceptions, I am always fascinated when we share stories. Often the things that I felt devastated by, two of my sisters would find humorous, but that was their coping mechanism. Humor is still what they often use to deflect pain.

I was truly a child of the sixties; sex, drugs, and rock and roll; rebellion and strong social ideals. I worked my way through school and freshman and sophomore year of college.

I was engaged to an army warrant officer, a Huey helicopter gunship pilot who went to Vietnam. I was supposed to be groomed as an officer's wife. I didn't fit that model because I found myself against the war—totally incongruent with my fiancé. Therefore, we didn't stay engaged. (I know, but that was the insanity of the sixties.)

Yes, I was Jenny in *Forrest Gump* and this movie's soundtrack was the soundtrack to my life at that time. When I saw *Forrest Gump* I laughed and cried over and over again, in recognition and empathy of the insanity of my "quest for spiritual enlightenment."

My friends and I were arrested for our ideals, and, well, maybe a little pot. There was undercover law enforcement in our classes and I was really naïve. After that, my trust was truly broken. The establishment considered our ideals criminal. We were a bunch of idealistic, very bright college kids. Our arrest was in the newspapers from Valentine's Day through May of 1966, and we were unjustly connected with everything from robberies to counterfeiting. I was humiliated, dropped out of school, and moved across the bridge to the big city, Philadelphia. The Vietnam War impacted my generation in enormous ways. We lost many young men from Camden High School and Woodrow Wilson High School Class of '64, and many to the disease of addiction. Later, each of my sisters married Vietnam veterans; my second husband was a combat veteran as well. Ours was a wounded generation in many ways.

I continued to work two jobs and fell into experimenting with amphetamines. Of course, my reasons were justified: I needed to stay awake and have energy! As a result, I met the man of my dreams, a handsome Italian from South Philly. He invited me to his apartment and when he answered the door he was wearing knee-high jackboots, Jockey shorts, and a shoulder holster with a pistol. Suddenly, I was "in love!" Then I discovered he had a barrel of pharmaceutical-grade crystal methamphetamine, and I was truly and passionately in love—I'd found my soul mate.

Well, with my first "shot" of pharmaceutical crystal meth, the world changed. It was glorious, brighter, shinier—and so was I. I felt beautiful, brilliantly intelligent, taller, as though I was truly a unique and glorious being of infinite worth and potential, valued and loved beyond my comprehension. My soon-to-be husband felt that way too, powerful and invincible. It was a chemically induced illusion that hid the pain, loneliness, and fear. For twenty years I chased that feeling, never realizing that I was *already* a glorious being who needed to clear away the trauma shadows hiding that glorious being that I was. That we all are.

Tommy and I really were soul mates; we were two wounded individuals coming together to try and make sense of the insanity—and insane it was. Sometimes I look back and wonder who that young woman with all the broken dreams really was. I am horrified at the destruction of which I was capable. I have been shot, stabbed, and had many black eyes and broken bones. I've been arrested multiple times and been held physically and emotionally hostage. I spent three weeks in a psychiatric hospital with methamphetamine psychosis, and a shattered elbow in a cast. I learned incredible criminal skills far beyond my college education. At the time, I was very proud of my new skillset.

I've betrayed my spiritual, moral, and ethical boundaries, and my beautiful, wounded husband was my mentor and partner in crime. He was a bright, shiny, brilliant man with a trauma story of his own, but we didn't have that language or understanding then. He could have been saved too. We roamed the streets of Philadelphia to feed our addictions and our less-than-legal lifestyle.

We thought we were evil, bad, and defective. What I discovered is that, under the influence of any addiction, we are capable of anything. We must later pay the price for the moral injury we experience, and the moral injury we cause.

Tommy never got to hear the message that saved my life: "We are not bad people trying to get good; we are wounded people trying to heal."

On March 25, 1973, after a night of using multiple drugs and alcohol with my husband, I came to and with horror discovered my husband was dead next to me. There had been many overdoses that year, but never in my wildest imagination did I consider death would come so close to our lives. So many more would follow that path to death by overdose and suicide throughout my life. My children were eighteen months, three years, and four years old when Tommy, their daddy, died. The story the family told for thirty years was that he died of a cerebral hemorrhage, but the truth is Tommy died of an overdose. The family kept that secret because of shame, of course, and to protect the beloved son and grandchildren.

I know that my children and I experienced years of post-traumatic stress disorder (PTSD), beginning in utero. Each of us has worked separately and together on our healing process. It took a lot of painful but truly healing work to process through the layers of trauma, loss, grief, guilt, shame, and remorse. It's an ongoing process as long as we continue to experience life at its fullest, because life continues to bring grief and loss as well as joy and triumph.

In my wildest dreams—and I have many wild and amazing dreams for my life—I never would have expected to find recovery at forty-two, complete my master's degree at age fifty, become licensed as a therapist at fifty-two, start a treatment center at fifty-seven, sell the treatment center at sixty-seven, and found another treatment center at seventy-one. I have always wanted to be a writer and here I am, at seventy-one—finally a published writer. I've always been a late bloomer. I never expected to be a leading voice for trauma treatment or trauma resolution, or the many aspects of the intertwining of trauma and addiction, trauma and mental health, and trauma and behaviors. I am a therapist, a teacher, a writer, and a thought leader. I stand on stages all over the world and openly share my experience, strength, and hope. I'm an expert at helping to heal wounded souls of trauma, and I could never have imagined a greater life's purpose than to make a living making amends for my past.

I am sought after for my expertise and no one is more baffled or stunned than I am. My little girl sometimes comes out and questions whether I deserve to be in this place, but I have learned to shush that voice that says, *Who do you think you are?* We all have those voices and must learn to shush them.

I've worked within the criminal justice system, with pregnant and addicted women, the homeless, veterans, European royalty, cinema and theater royalty, and wealthy CEOs and their families. This I know: these individuals are wounded little boys and girls looking for love, connection, and to unravel and understand their story. Each of those wounded children wants to rewrite and claim their rewritten story. Most of them manage to embrace their rewritten story, but for others the trauma story has become so much a part of their identity that it becomes truly an existential struggle. We just have to continue the unraveling.

Please, please remember this: behaviors always, always, always make sense when you unravel the trauma story. Most behaviors germinate as survival mechanisms. We do a huge injustice when we point our finger and make judgment about behaviors rather than recognizing the innate goodness of most human beings.

Today I know that the pain and horror of my life are also the miracles and gifts of my life. As we walk through this work together,

I hope you'll unravel your story to understand the behaviors and the pain so you can rewrite your story. In *The Trauma Heart* I'll give you a blueprint that can lead to your rewritten story. There's a place of sadness in my heart for those who don't hear this message or receive the gift of a triumphant rewritten story, which can take the broken shards of our hearts and fill the broken places with gold.

The person we judge the most is ourself. Let's work to change those messages so we can understand the shining, glittering miracle that we are.

INTRODUCTION

I n 1996 it became very clear to me that chronic relapse in alcohol and substance abuse had a more profound cause than just the substances themselves. I looked at the core issues, the family system, and the trauma events that impacted addicts. Often sober people were angry and dry drunks. Often addicts picked up other behaviors, sober from substances but in sex or relationship addiction, self-harming, eating disorders, gambling, gaming, pornography, or a multitude of other behaviors. Or they had many years in recovery but were ready to commit suicide. That was my impetus to start a program that addressed trauma along with addiction. As you read *The Trauma Heart* you'll understand how excellent visceral, cellular, trauma treatment can break the cycle of chronic relapse in all addictions, and mood disorders and behavior.

I speak at and attend many conferences and often attend the presentations of my colleagues. However, I have absolutely become a groupie of Dr. Gabor Maté. For years I trumpeted our belief that trauma work needed to be done along with addiction work, and that 90 percent of addicts and many other people have trauma. It was hard to make that case with hard-core addiction professionals who

1

had focused solely on the addiction and perhaps a dual diagnosis. I walked into Dr. Maté's presentation one fateful day and, for the first time, heard a professional assert with grace and compassion that trauma is *core,* and relapse is to be expected if the trauma is not resolved. I went to every presentation of Dr. Maté's that day and have read his work. What also impressed me was that he had been doing his own trauma work, and as a result he recognized in utero and intergenerational trauma, that addiction was a disease of broken or dysfunctional relationships, and that building relationships and healthy attachment assisted in the healing process.

I felt so joyful for our industry that we were being validated by such a prestigious yet humble man. He worked in the trenches in Canada with street addicts, many plagued with HIV/AIDS, hepatitis, and a myriad of health issues. Dr. Maté's belief in compassionate care and the healing process, his ability to identify with addicts with his own behaviors, his recognition that addiction is so much more than substances, and his understanding of the role of neurotransmitters in trauma and addiction are vital to understanding and healing this brain disease.

Others in our industry believe as I do, including pioneers whom I respect and admire such as Dr. Patrick Carnes, Judith L. Herman MD, Dr. Peter A. Levine, and Bessel van der Kolk, MD, but no one has given the message as passionately and as in sync with what I know.

Trauma can be identified and healed no matter what your survival/coping behaviors are, if you are willing to do the very deep work and to do it in tandem: trauma and addiction, trauma and behaviors, trauma and mood disorders. I believe these are interdependent.

When I was in treatment in August 1987 my counselor told our group, "Look to the right of you, and look to the left of you, only one of you will make it." The odds were not good. That didn't engender a lot of hope! Out of a community of fifty, only three of us were clean and sober after a year. I was one of the fortunate committed threesome, and we stayed connected. So I paid attention. I was always self-willed, too bright for my own good, but this disease brought me to my knees over and over again until finally I could no longer get high. My tolerance was so monumental, I could only maintain so I would not get sick. The ghosts of my past would come. My children—sixteen, eighteen, and nineteen—had given up hope. My mother had raised my youngest, my middle daughter left the house for her own journey, and my son was in and out. One time he returned home to this scene: I had broken a mirror and was holding a sharp edge to my wrist. I threatened that if he didn't help me to get some alcohol or drugs, I would kill myself. With great disgust he said, "Go ahead," and walked out the door. *That* was my bottom. I called my sister and begged for another trip to detox. With her children on board she stopped and got me a fifth of VO that I drank on the way. I was already in withdrawal.

I called myself the "Detox Queen of the Western World," a self-effacing remark that just dripped with the poison of guilt, shame, and remorse. I had been to detox many times over the years and Camden detox did not want to see my face again. One of the mental health techs scoffed at me and said I was never going to get sober, I was one of those, "constitutionally incapable" of finding recovery. I was devastated, but deep down I agreed with her that I was a hopeless case. I was in detox six times in six weeks that summer when my sister came "just one more time."

This was a different, new detox. The staff were kind and compassionate, and I was a wreck. I had such shame, guilt, and remorse. I truly believed I was a horrendous person because of the things that were done to me and the things I had been capable of in my addiction. Those things haunted me and frightened me.

One of the staff gave me a book, *Adult Children of Alcoholics* by Janet G. Woititz. In the beginning of the book is a "Laundry List" of signs and symptoms. I read it over and over and fell apart. I wailed and snotted and cried for a very long time.

Some of the characteristics of an adult child of alcoholics are:

1) We become isolated and afraid of people and authority figures.
2) We become approval seekers and lose our identity in the process. I always described myself as a chameleon, for example, "Tell me who you want me to be."
3) We are frightened by angry people and any personal criticism.
4) We have an overdeveloped sense of responsibility and it is easier for us to be concerned with others rather than ourselves; this enables us not to look too closely at our own faults.
5) We have "stuffed" our feelings from our traumatic childhood and have lost the ability to feel or express our feelings because it hurts so much (denial).

At ten years old, I found a dead man at a construction site near our home. He had fallen asleep or was drunk, and had frozen to death. It was in the newspaper but no one ever talked to me about the horror and terror I felt, and I never talked about it. These "secrets" are very common in the families of trauma survivors, and are part of addiction and coping behaviors. There were many traumatic events that I just didn't talk about; instead, I medicated the feelings and the pain. The secrets I held kept me sick and wounded. The list went on and

I was stunned to think it wasn't just that I was a bad seed or black sheep; maybe it was more than that. This Laundry List is not just for alcoholics. Dysfunction and trauma in any family system can produce these characteristics.

The staff was trying to convince me to go to treatment after detox and I resisted. After all, I'd been to treatment and it "didn't work." That evening they showed a video, *Soft Is the Heart of a Child*. The film was about an alcoholic father, out of control and angry, the mother very co-dependent and focused on him, and three children. The youngest was a little girl, terrified and hiding. The middle boy was angry, distant, and acting out. The oldest boy was trying to care for and protect his siblings, an adult before his time.

When the lights went on, tears were streaming down my face. In that film, I saw myself as the little adult-child whose job was to hold the family together; my acting-out sister; and my two other sisters needing my protection. At the same time, I saw the cycle extending to my own children; they were lost in the morass of my addiction and taking on the necessary roles. *It was time to break the generational cycle.* I went to my counselor, agreed to treatment, and began my very early trauma work.

For the very first time in my life I followed directions and did everything I was told. I was very broken, could no longer read at any length, stumbled a lot, and could not make a decision to save my soul. I had to call my sponsor and ask very simple questions like blue shoes or red, shower or bath, and what am I feeling? Oh, *that's* what anger feels like; *that's* what sadness feels like! I had no idea about emotions because they had been driven down so deep for so long.

The good news is that, after eighteen months, I regained all of my cognitive functioning, my memory, my physical well-being, was able to make decisions, and I was finally very connected to my emotions. My relationships were healthier and deeper.

Healing my "trauma heart" has been the greatest gift and I continue that work today with my own therapist because as long as I live, life brings challenges. I face them in the here and now and if I don't, I pay the price of deeper pain. I hope this book brings you the gift of hope.

I believe in the healing properties of love, compassion, witnessing, genuineness, and, most of all, hope.

As you move forward through *The Trauma Heart*, I think you will identify and find answers. I believe you will experience hope and great possibilities for healing, living the life you choose, and, most of all, dreaming big.

Before we get to the story of a young man named Zac, I want to introduce a poem by the Persian poet Rumi called "The Guest House." The Guest House is the name of my newly opened treatment center in Ocala, Florida. Like the poem, trauma treatment ultimately invites "the guest" to be aware of it all. Be aware of everything that surrounds the trauma, makes up the trauma, makes up you, and then invite it all in so that you may embrace it. We *must* invite in all of the elements of our life, and yes, that means inviting in the pain, breathing in all that is presented, feeling and experiencing life to its fullest. Through reading this book you'll come to realize what I mean. Welcome!

"The Guest House"

This being human is a guest house.
Every morning a new arrival.

A joy, a depression, a meanness,
some momentary awareness comes
as an unexpected visitor.

Welcome and entertain them all!
Even if they are a crowd of sorrows,
who violently sweep your house
empty of its furniture,
still, treat each guest honorably.
He may be clearing you out
for some new delight.

The dark thought, the shame, the malice.
meet them at the door laughing and invite them in

Be grateful for whatever comes
because each has been sent
as a guide from beyond.

—Rumi

♛

In the trauma/addictions arena, we use the word "trigger" to describe what may happen viscerally, sensorially, and cellularly to a person when something creates an emotional response that can often be uncomfortable or even cause memories, flashbacks or a physical response. So this is a trigger warning!

The stories in this book are about some of the deepest and painful traumas. The stories are about the triumph and victory over trauma that has immobilized and kept our storytellers prisoners in many ways.

In order to get to the rewriting of our story, however, we must tell the story.

You, the reader, may be triggered because of your own history. We invite you to use the Reflections after each chapter to describe and release the emotions that may come up for you. Also, go to page 127 and use the "healthy soothing" behaviors recommended and continue to journal your experiences.

There are resources available for you, and at the end of the book you will find websites for appropriate therapists in your area, and a way to contact The Guest House for additional resources.

I invite you to read the story below. It's about Zac, a delightful, strong, bright, and handsome young man, often with a beautiful bright smile on his face. Zac is a staff member at The Guest House Ocala, and he earned that position the hard way—through life experiences and running from, stumbling through, and doing battle with his own trauma story. Zac's body bears the evidence of his battle. Self-harming behaviors have left physical scars. Trauma has also left emotional scars.

Zac had been in multiple treatments, but inevitably the memories and flashbacks would overwhelm his ability to bear the emotional pain, and his body would bear the brunt as he sought relief.

ZAC'S STORY:
SCARS THAT HEAL

My name is Zac. I am an alcoholic, a drug addict, a love and sex addict. Most noticeably, as the photos on the following pages show, I am a cutter. I self-harm. I do these things to escape life, to escape the pain that I have lived with for so long. My story begins when I was around eight years old. This was when I started being sexually molested. I didn't know what was right or wrong, I just learned that this is how I was desirable. Sometime later, when the molestation stopped, I no longer felt loved and desired. I hated this feeling and didn't know how to cope. I'm not sure where I learned the action but I started to cut myself up on my shoulders. I didn't do it often, or deep. The feeling gave me relief from my pain of no longer feeling desired, an outside pain to hide the inside one.

As time went on, I started drinking and having sex at a young age. To me I felt I had to have as much sex as possible to prove I was a man. At the time, I didn't realize I was also using sex to run from my feelings. I always needed to feel desired, loved, validated. Women did that for me, only I could never  have a healthy relationship and cheated on all my girlfriends. I needed everyone to want me, because my molester no longer did. Alcohol did the same for me. When I drank I felt warm inside, like

I belonged and was needed. It helped me relax and be part of the group with other people; only I could never control my drinking. Once I started, I could not stop. I would drink until I could no longer feel, no longer remember what I had done while intoxicated.

I somehow managed to graduate high school, always just doing enough to pass my classes. I was a football star and I loved the feeling of being on the field, with a thousand people watching me, wanting me to tackle the opposing team. I've always been a calm, nonaggressive person, but when I put that helmet on, I knew I could actually hurt someone and get away with it. I loved when I could make someone bleed, and even more so I loved when I made myself bleed. When I hit so hard, and played so strongly I got hurt. I felt tough and manly, all the while getting some release from my pain inside. I started community college after high school, though I was usually too drunk to remember what was discussed in class. My molester went to college, so I didn't want to. I went to make my parents happy. By this time, I didn't even want to live. I had made some minor suicide attempts before this point, and was now just passing time until I died. I didn't care what happened to me, as long as it could just be over.

I started playing rugby, and soon after found myself playing in Australia, far away from my parents, my dog, and my few friends who still put up with my drunkenness. I was an outsider, but all eyes were on me. Wherever I went in town people recognized me as the American. I felt desired, but not enough so to keep me from drinking, and now it was an almost everyday occurrence. I remember on my twentieth birthday I finally admitted I had a drinking problem and called my mom long-distance and cried and cried to her for a while. I didn't want to drink any longer, but a few days later I was, and as always, I couldn't stop. When I got back to the States I spiraled into an even bigger depression; it was almost like I picked up right where I left off. Not caring anymore, just waiting to die. I had no direction, and felt I had no purpose.

My father is a marine biologist and travels the world saving coral reefs. He started taking me on trips with him, showing me how good life can be, how everything on the planet had a purpose, even the smallest of creatures. I love the ocean, and my father, but they were not enough to lessen my pain. At the age of twenty-one I started doing pills, then quickly turned to heroin. Alcohol was no longer even a thought for me. Heroin numbed my pain like never before.

My life soon turned into what one would expect from a heroin junkie: stealing, lying, cheating. I was arrested a couple times, and started my run with treatment centers. After my first treatment, I stayed sober for just a month or two, quickly reverting back to the drugs to run from my pain. I had yet to tell anyone what had happened to me as a boy, and didn't understand how much this affected me. When I went to my third rehab I found myself back in South Florida, near where I was born. I did really well in treatment, and actually, for the first time in almost twelve years, told someone about the molestation. They wanted to send me off to another facility. I said no, that I didn't want that, it didn't affect me. I got kicked out of that facility for having sex with a woman, and was sent to their partner facility in that town. I graduated there and soon was living at a halfway house. I started working and life was going well for about eight months. Then again, I relapsed and was soon living out of my truck, using public restrooms, and showering on the beach to stay clean. I remember my mom driving the three hours to where I was to chase me and try to help me. She got me a hotel room and into another halfway house. I was kicked out only a few days later. After some time, I called her, willing to go into yet another treatment facility for help. Only this time, it was one where I would have to talk about what happened as a boy.

I arrived at Judy's treatment facility in Central Florida and started working on trauma. I did therapy about being molested,

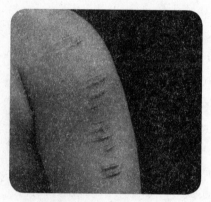

and about my drug and alcohol usage. I was willing to live without those two crutches, only I wasn't willing to live without women. I still hadn't realized my need to be desired. I fell in love with a girl at the rehab and soon got wrapped up in everything that I shouldn't have. I again attempted suicide, and was readmitted into treatment. I was still unwilling to let go of the girl, but I cheated on her in treatment. I didn't take things seriously and was honestly just staying there because I promised my parents I would. I planned on leaving and killing myself. This is exactly what I did; I ran away and attempted to take my own life. Luckily, I failed at my attempt and decided I needed to try something different.

During this time, my father was in a place called Saipan. It's a small island about 800 miles from Japan. It was the location of a major World War II battle; several thousand Japanese soldiers and civilians committed suicide there to avoid capture when Allied Forces took control. I called my father to once again ask for his help. He told me how he had been in Saipan, that all over the island there are signs for Suicide Cliff, the place where those thousands went and jumped to their deaths. He told me he was plagued with thoughts of losing a son, that maybe I will never find peace. He was willing to do anything to help me, to give me a life of happiness. He made me promise to go back, and not to leave until the therapists said I should.

So this is what I did. I went back and took things more seriously. I started doing what I was suggested to do, and work on assignments to heal myself. I took away the drugs, the alcohol, and now the women. I started cutting again; I took razors to my chest, to my arms, to my leg, even my face. I wanted the world to see how ugly I felt inside, how full of pain I was. Only now I couldn't get away with the little cuts I had done when younger; I needed bigger, deeper cuts to get the release I craved. As with all that I do, I started cutting addictively. I couldn't stop, nor did I really want to. I needed the feeling of my skin opening up at my hand, to watch the blood pour out and drip on the floor. I needed to feel the punishment for my actions, for not being good enough for my abuser. At one point I was sent to the psychiatric ward for observation because they were worried I was going to kill myself. Only they didn't understand I was doing this because I was trying to learn not to want to kill myself.

My therapist then, Tom Pecca, threatened to quit if they did not allow me back. I came back and did the work. I tried my hardest to show I was serious and to get better. I learned all sorts of techniques to not cut, healthier outlets to get through the pain I had inside. He finally told me I was ready to go and I was terrified. I still had open wounds from my cutting and didn't know how to even live in the real world. He told me I knew what to do, and had the tools to continue on a healthy path, but it was up to me to continue to do the work and keep healing myself.

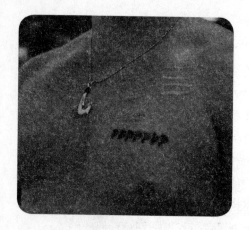

Two weeks after leaving
treatment, I found myself
on a plane with my father
heading to Saipan. I had
the ocean, my dad, and a
purpose for now. I didn't
cut the entire time I was
there and started to feel
better about life. I believe
it was around two weeks
into our stay there when my dad took me up Suicide Cliff. During
the drive, he told me how he had come up here and prayed for me,
hoping that I would find peace. He told me he had accepted the
fact that I might not live longer than him. He told me how there has
been nothing worse in his life than the fear of my death. We got to
the top and out of the car. We walked over to the edge of the cliff
and I leaned over the railing, looking down to where so many had
perished. I began thinking of how much pain I had caused him and
my mother. How much I've done to them that no parent should ever
have to go through.

He told me to turn around from the edge of the cliff and look.
We could see the whole island from there. The resorts on the beach
and the people in the water, the coral reef under the crystal-clear
water, and even the shipwreck under the surface from the battle.
The trees blowing in the wind and the birds flying around; it was
beautiful. My father then told me he felt that if some of the Japanese that had marched up there to die had only turned around and
seen the beauty of the island, of life, that perhaps they wouldn't
have jumped. He told me that I had focused on the negative, and if

I could just turn around and focus on the positive, on the beauty of life, that everything would be okay. I remember the next morning I woke up, and thought to myself, "What a good day to be alive." I used to wake up and think the opposite.

This is the beginning of my story, and I don't mean everything you just read. I mean that last thought. I don't know what my future holds, but I know great things are in store. Today it has been over eighteen months since I cut myself, even longer since I've had drugs or alcohol in my body. I even work with Tom Pecca these days, and get to help others just like me heal their trauma. Today I know that I am enough, that I am loved and desired, and that I don't have to hurt myself or others to get relief from the things that bring me pain. I am a miracle.

Suicide/Banzai Cliff

Today Zac is clean and sober, and a walking, breathing example of hope and resilience in the face of what feels like unbearable pain. Now Zac's purpose is to help folks who read this book to know that surviving is just a step or two away from seeing your pain as a gift, as is described in the poem, "The Guest House."

Beginning Thoughts

"At my core I am a unique and glorious being of infinite worth and potential. I am valued and loved beyond my comprehension."

—Author unknown

We are not bad people trying to get good; we are wounded people trying to heal. The majority of people addicted to substances or process addictions such as sex/relationship, eating disorders, self-harming behaviors, gambling, pornography, money disorders, and variations of these, are trauma survivors. Relapse is inevitable without trauma resolution. Many don't identify as trauma survivors until they are helped to look at their history: personal, family, intergenerational, and in utero. That is the *"Aha"* moment when puzzle pieces fall together and the behaviors make sense. Behaviors always make sense when you unravel the story.

For almost thirty years I've worked with clients and families who are in such great pain around addictions and behaviors gone amok, believing their loved one must be bad, wrong, defective. The "identified" client believes that to their core, when in reality the whole family is embroiled in their individual survival coping mechanisms. The identified client is often the red flag that the family needs healing. These families come from every walk of life and they/we relate to their struggle and their desire to heal that little boy and girl inside.

BEHAVIORS ALWAYS MAKE SENSE WHEN YOU UNRAVEL THE STORY.

Trauma creates the need for soothing/coping behaviors, and those behaviors are what initially help us to survive until they turn against the individual as addictions.

Travel into *The Trauma Heart* with me and explore the many ways that life's events impact each member of the family. *The Trauma Heart* offers the essence of trauma and addictions treatment through the stories, art, and assignments of former clients and the staff who worked with them to reveal a snapshot of their pain and healing. Then together we can change this trauma world we live in, one person, one family, at a time. In this book:

→ You'll explore the meaning of trauma, addictions, behaviors, and identify and relate to your own history.

→ You'll be given the opportunity to understand what we mean by, "We are not bad people trying to get good; we are wounded people trying to heal," and, "Behaviors always make sense when you unravel the story."

→ And finally, you'll walk through the process of trauma/addictions treatment through very personal stories, art, and assignments from clients *and* the clinicians who have done their own trauma resolution. You'll be offered reflective sketches, and personal assignments you can do if you choose to explore your own history.

Walk through the pain and experience the joy, the courage, and the transformation of these warriors.

REFLECTIVE SKETCHES

❧❧❧

1) Why did you buy *The Trauma Heart*?

_____

_____

2) What do you need from *The Trauma Heart*?

_____

_____

3) What emotions did you feel buying *The Trauma Heart*?

_____

_____

4) Are you ready to look more deeply into your story?

_____

_____

5) What would be the best possible result that could come from reading this book?

_____

_____

6) Please make an intention to have the best possible result. Your energy will invite healing.

_____

_____

7) Please journal your thoughts, feelings, and complete the reflective sketches.

_____

_____

CHAPTER
1

SECRET
KEEPERS

*"Anything will give up its secrets
if you love it enough."*

—George Washington Carver

❦

T rauma *is* a big word! I invite you to join me on a journey to explore what trauma is, how it manifests in individuals, and what makes excellent trauma treatment. Learn about trauma from the trenches as I draw from personal and professional experiences working with some of the most courageous and resilient clients and families, who have struggled with addictions, mental health and behavioral issues, and life in general due to a history of trauma or painful life events. Families who seek help for the "identified problem child" of the family are often shocked and amazed to discover that the whole family experiences the signs and symptoms of intergenerational trauma. Although trauma has reared its ugly head in this generation, in this branch of the family, it has been impacting everyone in a myriad of ways.

Sad, painful trauma stories are the beginning of a much bigger story that allows us to share our triumph, compassion, and joy, and by doing so, *create a life of purpose.* This journey of triumph takes time, and the love, empathy, and talent of clinicians and staff who reach outside of the box to create a healing environment for clients and their families.

I want to emphasize that although we will be talking about addiction and trauma, we'll also discuss the ways that trauma impacts mental health issues such as mood disorders, depression, anxiety, attention deficit hyperactivity disorder (ADD/ADHD), obsessive compulsive disorder (OCD), hoarding, compulsive shopping, addiction to social media, gaming, pornography, and many other behavioral issues.

This is about trauma, the life events that impact us in a negative way, and what we believe about ourselves and our place in the world as a result. Let's be clear that positive events also impact our vision of ourselves and our place in the world. We'll see how all of those events mold who we have become, and how we can re-mold the who, what, and why of the spirit we choose to be.

My goal is to present a picture of Trauma with a capital T (major trauma), layers of trauma, and trauma (usually a single incident or less emotionally intrusive trauma). More importantly, what are the signs that trauma may be an issue in your life, your family's life, the life of someone you love, or someone you know? Trauma responses affect every aspect of our lives: social, workplace, school, and relationships. These triggered responses are often misread by others, and misdiagnosed by well-meaning caregivers and professionals. I hope everyone who reads these pages understands that when you unravel the trauma story you understand the addiction or behavioral story, and then you can create the recovery story.

WHEN YOU UNRAVEL THE TRAUMA STORY YOU UNDERSTAND THE ADDICTION OR BEHAVIORAL STORY, AND THEN YOU CAN CREATE THE RECOVERY STORY.

You Have the Power

My fear is that you will see the word addiction and assume it doesn't apply. That is often a reaction that emanates from fear, embarrassment, denial, and other emotional responses.

Please move beyond that because we are talking about *behaviors*, i.e., coping skills that are created by our trauma story in order to survive. We are talking about the essence of you. And you *have the power* to change or enhance that story.

I'm honored to share with you stories of people I've worked with. I believe that you'll relate over and over again to these amazing, courageous people; you may even see your story written in these pages. I'll present to you extraordinary clinicians and other passionate people who are part of a team committed to the journey of survivors. This process may become transformative for you or someone in your life, or perhaps your relationship, your family, or your community.

If you are looking for answers for someone else, I invite you to also keep your heart open to looking inward. Every human being is impacted by the events and story of their life, each little piece makes us who we are today: the good, the bad, and the ugly.

Please hear me when I say there is no good or bad, no right or wrong. We withhold judgment while we unravel the story. Remember, we're not bad people trying to get good; we are wounded people trying to heal.

Many people that we've worked with for over twenty-five years have contributed to this book. They bring the hearts and souls of alumni, their families, and the staff that served them by walking in partnership on their journey. I want to celebrate and lift up these folks who go so deeply to their core to change their lives and the lives of everyone they touch. Once you have entered the journey just by being, you carry the message; your life is the message. We can change the world, synergistically: one person, one family, one neighborhood, one city, one state, one country, and one world.

I hope you will laugh and cry, applaud and denounce, join the fight for a more authentic life, and then celebrate with me the possibilities.

TRAUMA:
A PORTRAIT

I want to share a story about an angry young man in his early thirties, extremely bright and educated, with a history of chronic relapse, legal problems, alienation from family and friends, and extreme loneliness. His drugs of choice included meth, cocaine, and Adderall—which had been prescribed to him when he was seven years old. We were titrating the Adderall (that is, lowering the dose over time); he was not happy. I asked him what was going on at seven years old that he had to see a physician who prescribed Adderall.

"I was angry, acting out, couldn't focus, and was hyper. My parents didn't know what to do."

This man/boy had been to treatment five times but no one had ever asked the really important questions. This young man's history from seven years onward becomes a map for the astute and well-trained, compassionate, intuitive, insightful, well-trained trauma therapist. The map describes bullying, broken or nonexistent relationships, family discord, self-hatred, employment difficulties, domestic violence, and jail.

We've heard this story over and over again with minor variations. The variations may be the gender of the client, life circumstances and other things, but the essence is there. Many of the wounded come to us sharing for the first time their trauma events simply because the questions have never been asked: "What happened to you at seven years old?"

We asked that question. For the first time, at thirty, he answered.

"I was sexually abused at seven by a camp counselor and I never told anyone." He was shocked that we asked the question and more shocked that the puzzle pieces were falling into place. He had PTSD, not ADHD. Of course he was angry, acting out, out of control! He was seven and he wasn't safe or protected. He held the secret because he had been threatened. He was hypervigilant, untrusting, unable to focus, and filled with fear for the next onslaught. Meanwhile his family was terrified that they were not able to soothe his hyperactivity.

They didn't know his secret, nor did they ask, "Sweetheart, what's going on? What happened to change my sweet boy?"

The counselors, the teachers, the powers that be, all told the family that their child's brain wiring was defective, not understanding that his soul had been wounded and he was responding from the visceral, sensory, cellular depths of his being.

Yes, the neurochemistry is affected and changed, but the soul wound must also be healed.

The variations of this story may be age, gender, ethnicity, or socioeconomic standing, but the vital variations are the events that create the trauma responses:

→ Bullying.

→ Physical and medical trauma.

→ Holding a secret for a parent or family member, such as substance addiction or infidelity, or the pain of a sibling's secret.

The soul of a child may begin to be tarnished very early in life and the fallout can last a lifetime.

As clinicians we can provide a safe, soothing, and healing environment for our clients to begin to unravel their trauma story. Our most important role as clinicians/healers is to hold space and witness while we provide an environment of trust and safety, that is rich in experiential, visceral, sensory, and cellular modalities. Also it's vital that trauma therapists continue to do their own healing work, that is, "Practice what we preach."

As a trauma survivor, have you received witnessing, safety, trust with warm, compassionate, and talented clinicians? If not, please make that part of your trauma resolution. Demand it! Don't settle for less. Your life, your recovery, and your soul depend on this healing process. Unresolved or unexplored trauma is the number-one cause of relapse in all addictions and coping behaviors.

UNRESOLVED OR UNEXPLORED TRAUMA IS THE NUMBER-ONE CAUSE OF RELAPSE IN ALL ADDICTIONS AND COPING BEHAVIORS.

My journey to understanding trauma and PTSD came twenty-five years ago while working with two populations: male addicts who were frequent visitors to the criminal justice system, and women who were residents of an excellent long-term women's program. The similarities were chronic relapse, relationship issues, hopelessness, despair, and trauma histories that had not been explored or identified, and certainly had not been healed. This is what invariably triggered relapse and additional trauma events. In the early 1990s, the signs and symptoms of PTSD were very evident but not well understood. I envision the world in big pictures, and I've found that I can put pieces together from this way of seeing the connections. I saw the connection between the pain of our history and the need for relief and soothing, and it made sense to me that addiction treatment alone would never be enough. The statistics in our field were dismal, with multiple treatment episodes the norm, not the exception. There were others who saw the world as I did and they became my teachers. So we looked at our clients for similarities. Many of these folks had been sober or abstinent for periods of time, but memories, flashbacks, and being uncomfortable in their own skin had sent them back to substance or process addictions, or other unhealthy behaviors.

**I BELIEVE THAT WHEN TRAUMA
OR PTSD CREATES THE IMPETUS FOR SUCH
DESPAIR, THERE ARE ONLY THREE CHOICES:
RELAPSE, "GOING CRAZY," OR SUICIDE.
RELAPSE IS THE HEALTHIEST CHOICE
AND I BELIEVE THIS IS WHERE CHRONIC RELAPSE
OCCURS. THERE IS A FOURTH CHOICE—
TRAUMA RESOLUTION, A PAINFUL BUT
AMAZING JOURNEY OF HEALING.**

Last year I read a post on Facebook from someone who finds joy
and motivation in the writings of Joel Osteen: "He [God] is called the
'Great I Am,' not the 'Great I Was,' or the 'Great I Will Be.'" God is
always in the present. I'm not espousing a religion or faith; I'm inviting the possibility that we can take heed of this message. So much of
our lives and the lives of our clients are spent in preparation for the
"perfect" future:

➡ When I find the time
➡ When I'm not depressed
➡ When I lose weight
➡ When I have the right job, situation, home, spouse . . .

When everything is perfect, then I will be "the great I am." Then I
will have my life. But so many of the moments of our lives have been
given to pain, sorrow, hurt, sadness, fear, and regret. We turn around
and it is a year later, or five years later, or twenty years later, and life
is speeding by and moments have eluded us. So when will we do the
deep work to heal? Now is a good time!

What Is Trauma?

With this in mind, let's begin first with several of the most
renowned trauma specialists' own definitions of trauma. Dr.
Gabor Maté, physician and author of *In the Realm of Hungry Ghosts*,
looked at the epidemic of various addictions in our society and wrote:

> If people who become severe addicts, as shown by all the studies,
> were for the most part abused children then we realize that the war
> on drugs is actually waged against people that were abused from the

moment they were born or from an early age on. In other words, we are punishing people for having been abused. That's the first point. The second point is that the research clearly shows that the biggest driver of addictive relapse and addictive behavior is actually stress.

I have great respect for Dr. Maté. He spent years serving addicts and HIV patients who had incredible stories of abuse. Not only is he a physician, he's a clinician and researcher who has done his own emotional healing and continues in that vein.

For the last twenty years we have recognized this phenomenon of trauma, stress, and relapse. In treatment we expect those things to happen; those are juicy therapeutic opportunities for insight and healing.

An enormous percentage of our population has experienced abuse in all its many forms, including the abuse of abandonment and neglect, as well as other traumatic events, such as: growing up in a dysfunctional family, long-term family illnesses, disabilities in the family, deaths, suicides, financial deprivation or privilege, divorce, multiple marriages, multiple moves, adoption; the list goes on and on.

Dr. Maté speaks of stress as the biggest cause of relapse, however, let's expand those relapses to include *all* types of addictive behaviors as well as relapses into mood disorders, anxiety, or depression. These relapses become a place of comfortable discomfort. The goal is relief, release, soothing, numbing.

Relapse becomes the sanest option because the alternative is insanity or suicide. I know that sounds counterintuitive, but there is a kind of relief in relapse. The true alternative is to unravel the trauma story.

Dr. Judith Herman has embraced the idea of addictions as coping mechanisms and states:

Psychological trauma is an affliction of the powerless. At the moment of trauma, the victim is rendered helpless by overwhelming force. When the force is that of nature, we speak of disasters. When the force is that of other human beings, we speak of atrocities. Traumatic events overwhelm the ordinary systems of care that give people a sense of control, connection, and meaning. . . . Traumatic events are extraordinary, not because they occur rarely, but rather because they overwhelm the ordinary adaptations to life. . . . They confront human beings with the extremities of helplessness and terror, and evoke the responses of the catastrophe.

And whether the trauma is a puppy kissing your face when you are three years old and it's perceived as an attack and you fear death, or someone holds a gun to your head and you fear death, the body, the emotions, the senses respond in the same way. And that's why it's imperative to honor your feelings and your body's responses, no matter what the event. It's not the event, but how the residue of the event drives your life today—body, mind, and spirit.

We can find ourselves still operating in the world today driven by early trauma, the messages the trauma created, and the visceral, sensory, cellular memory that remains.

It's also important for us to honor the feelings, the responses, and the perspective and the experiences of the people in our lives, to ask loving, compassionate questions, and give loving, compassionate, honoring responses. To create a safe environment to support one another. To create a safe environment to share family history, family secrets.

Everyone's perspectives are different even when they've experienced the same events, and everyone's resilience level is different depending on their life's experiences.

Bessel van der Kolk, MD, the author of *The Body Keeps the Score: Mind, Brain, and Body in the Healing of Trauma*, tells us, "Trauma is not the story of something that happened back then—it's the current imprint of that pain, horror, and fear living inside people."

Author and recovery pioneer Pia Mellody states in her book *Facing Codependence*, "Abuse is anything less than nurturing. When we suffer from childhood trauma, nurturing is not a part of our life experience. We become accustomed to criticism, neglect, and poor or unrealistic limits. Self-worth is held hostage by serving the demands of others, hoping that in doing so we can forget our past. But the past haunts us in our dreams and memories, relentless in its chase. To cope, we develop habits that promote self-destruction. These habits become addictions or distractions, helping us avoid feeling reality."

Believing abandonment and trauma are at the core of addictions, Dr. Patrick Carnes, a leading specialist in sex and love addiction, emphasizes how trauma affects the brain and how people are affected by trauma over time in eight ways. He calls these ways trauma reaction, trauma arousal, trauma blocking, trauma splitting, trauma abstinence, trauma shame, trauma repetition, and trauma bonds. As Dr. Carnes writes in *The Betrayal Bond*:

There are two essential factors in creating and understanding traumatic experiences: they are how far our systems are stretched and for how long. Some events happen only once or just a few times, but the impact is so great that trauma occurs. Trauma by accumulation sneaks up on its victims. They become acclimatized. Traumas that are horrendous and long lasting are the worst. Emotional scars can be so severe that generations descended from those surviving will react in ways that still reflect the original trauma. No amount of normalcy makes it safe. Patterns and attitudes evolve far beyond the individual and are incorporated into family and society.

According to psychologist and author of *Waking the Tiger*, Dr. Peter A. Levine, "Chronically traumatized individuals generally show no change or even a decrease in heart rate. These sufferers tend to be plagued with dissociative symptoms, including frequent spaciness, unreality, depersonalization, and various somatic and health complaints. Somatic symptoms include gastrointestinal problems, migraines, some forms of asthma, persistent pain, chronic fatigue, and general disengagement from life."

A clinical explanation of trauma and post-traumatic stress disorder was outlined in 2013 by the American Psychiatric Association, when they revised the PTSD diagnostic criteria in the fifth edition of its *Diagnostic and Statistical Manual of Mental Disorders (DSM-5)*. The *DSM-5* introduced a preschool subtype of PTSD for children aged six and younger. Also, diagnostic criteria for PTSD includes a history of exposure to a traumatic event that meets specific stipulations and symptoms from each of four "symptom clusters": intrusion, avoidance, negative alterations in cognition and mood, and alterations in arousal and reactivity. The sixth criterion concerns duration of symptoms; the seventh assesses functioning; and the eighth criterion clarifies symptoms as not attributable to a substance or co-occurring medical condition.

Definition

I'm going to share with you a very simple definition of trauma, knowing that for some people *trauma* is a huge and frightening word. Very simply, "Trauma is any life event or series of life events or ongoing life events that create a negative impact on your life that changes or distorts your vision of yourself and your place in the world."

Some of those events or situations might include:

- ➡ Abandonment and neglect (most common and devastating)
- ➡ Emotional, physical, spiritual, and sexual abuse
- ➡ Accidents, fires, natural disasters, random acts of violence, financial concerns; events that can involve too much, too little, or sudden loss
- ➡ Terrorism, constant and repetitive viewing of terror events on TV and social media.
- ➡ Divorce, adoption, bullying, domestic violence, multiple moves, death, or loss of pets
- ➡ Childhood medical or mental health issues
- ➡ Medical or mental health issues of adults or people close to you.
- ➡ Death or suicide of family members
- ➡ Grief issues
- ➡ Veterans, war, or having a loved one experience war or combat
- ➡ Intergenerational trauma
- ➡ In utero trauma

This list is extensive but by no means exhaustive; you may have a few events to add to the list.

Be thoughtful about what you have read in our list. If so moved, make your list. No emotion attached and no judgments. Just make the list. You may feel emotion so just *breathe through* the emotion and allow yourself to make the list. You may be making the list for someone else. Please know that this is just a blueprint, a beginning.

If your list has more than two or three events, chances are you have experienced PTSD at some time. This means that layers of trauma have impacted your vision of yourself and your place in the world. Consider carefully if you or any of your loved ones experienced any of these events or situations whether it was at a low level or greater level of intensity or duration. Trauma is trauma and cannot be measured or defined by another individual's experience. Your trauma is your trauma and it is imperative that you own what has affected you so deeply. Don't disparage your experience by saying, "Oh, it wasn't so bad, so many others have such terrible trauma; mine is nothing." Wrong! If it makes you more comfortable, describe these experiences as life events.

It's important to understand that all life events impact the way we see ourselves and our place in the world. This is true on so many levels. Those extremely positive, nurturing, or life-enhancing events provide the path for resilience, and oftentimes so do traumatic events.

After trauma, some people become more resilient, more committed to their lives, and more driven to overcome the path that brought them there. We call this the "blessings of trauma." The triumph of the spirit is the nature of the spirit for most trauma survivors. We just have to help survivors take the risk to have another perception. When we can see the power of triumphing over our past we can do or be anything because we survived. And when we can work with the whole family the successes are multiplied exponentially to present and succeeding generations. So just as Zac on Suicide/Banzai Cliff in Saipan was able to turn around and see the beauty of life surrounding him, the story is rewritten. It's a good day to live!

Everyone has a story. I've been privileged and honored to be a witness for the healing of some of the most courageous spirits in the universe. The stories, the lives of these extraordinary survivors are often difficult to hear, and many can't or won't hear them. So I want to share the experience of being invited on this journey with the survivors, their families, their perpetrators, and also the healers.

It takes a very special person to be invited along; trust is a gift that is given very slowly. Often our survivors begin to tell their story only to hear:

➡ "That's not true."
➡ "Didn't happen."
➡ "*Shhh*! Don't tell; not yet, not me, I'm not prepared to hear this."
➡ "Don't do this work until you are five years sober."

They may also hear threats of harm or worse, and see the horror in the eyes of the listeners that says they can't bear hearing the story, or the subtle flinch in the face or body that says, "I'm not supposed to hear this." The truth is few are prepared and so the story stays an untold secret and the survivor bears the pain alone. But they can't stay sober or abstinent in their addictions because those are the behaviors that saved them from the pain early on. All they ask, all they need, is for someone to witness, someone to shed the tears and demand, "How could someone do this to another?" and in doing so, validate the horror that the survivor has carried. To say, "How miraculous that you survived all that happened to you!" and validate their commitment to healing.

To witness is to begin. Slowly, so slowly the witness will be tested. "Can you bear to hear this? How about this? No, you haven't deserted me yet. Wait, this is worse, can you bear this and stand with me?"

Often when the secrets are finally told, the pieces to a puzzle fall into place. Many times the acknowledgement of the secrets is followed by a huge cleansing breath—it finally makes sense. The body relaxes and changes. After sharing long-held secrets there is very often a physical transformation, the face seems younger, we walk taller, voices become stronger, eyes brighter, breathing more relaxed, and smiles and laughter more spontaneous. I have seen these changes many, many times over the years. Other clients remark on the changes. People who have come to trauma work with childlike voices come into their mature adult voices as they learn to speak and stand up for themselves, no longer stuck in that childhood event or events.

However, too often the level of loss and despair in living in this pain trumps the secrets—yes, secrets. Many, many people have kept secrets from very early childhood and yes, secrets keep us sick. Secrets are kept for many reasons:

➡ We don't air the family's dirty laundry.
➡ It would only hurt them to know.
➡ It can't be true, don't ever say it again.
➡ If you tell I will hurt you or your family.
➡ They won't believe you, they will blame you.
➡ It's your fault anyway.

I suspect that many of you are surprised at the events that are considered trauma, however, pay attention to the memories that have been evoked for you while reading these pages. The people who set out on this journey are afraid, yes, but courageously they move one step at a time toward freedom from pain.

"Secret keepers" are often children who may be abused or bullied, or who carry a secret for a parent like infidelity, substance abuse, or pornography; they somehow feel responsible so shame and guilt preclude them from telling their secrets. Children are very intuitive and can feel the energy in the home and their surroundings. They know when there is tension, anger or rage, sexual energy, or sadness. When they ask, "What's wrong?" adults often say "Nothing, everything is fine." This is why children begin to believe they can't trust their feelings or trust that their caretakers will tell the truth. Have you been holding a secret for a parent or for the family? Have you been held hostage by the secret?

As a relatively new therapist in a small women's program, I was having some personal family pain. A client asked me what was wrong and I responded, "Everything's fine." I was pulled aside by a wonderful veteran therapist who chastised, "Don't ever do that again. You're reinforcing an old family message that says they can't trust their own intuition and senses." And she was so correct.

I went back to that client and said, "I have some family pain, I'm sad but I will be okay, I just need to honor being sad." And that was a corrective moment in our relationship, therapist to client. Telling the truth can be that way for any relationship. That correction or amends takes the relationship to a more intimate and trusting level, and honors the "gut" of the other person.

When I relayed this story in one of my intensives (an intensive is five days of intense trauma work in a group setting), one of the women, Stacy, spoke up and said she so resonated with this. She conveyed that when she was young her family never talked about negative feelings or what was wrong, however, she knew things were wrong when she was growing up but felt so confused and alone because she thought she was the only one who felt that way. Because her parents didn't have age-appropriate conversations with her when she asked what was wrong, Stacy stopped asking. She took it upon herself to figure out if something was wrong, to take in the atmospherics of a room, and then conform to those atmospherics. If her mom was depressed she remained quiet; if her mom was angry and giving her the silent treatment, she tried to be so good so that her mom would talk to her again. Stacy learned to say "Everything's fine," and "Nothing is wrong" from her upbringing. When she had a daughter she was the same way with her because she didn't know any different. What this did to both Stacy and to her daughter is silence them when they were feeling sad, angry, scared, overwhelmed, or alone. This meant they had to bear those feelings alone and couldn't ask for help.

Stacy and her daughter have done tremendous work through my programs and now have tools to talk about their feelings, whether they are happy or sad, and they've learned to honor those feelings. Kenzie, Stacy's daughter, wrote the poem that follows. Kenzie was raped when she was eight years old by the father of her stepmother. She held this secret for a long, long time for fear it would tear her family apart and she would lose the tenuous relationship she had with her father. Then her father abandoned Kenzie. When the pain of the sexual abuse, the secret-keeping, and the abandonment became too much, Kenzie started cutting and later used drugs to numb the pain she didn't want to feel.

Kenzie's Poem

what's it gunna take
when ya gunna break?
you know i'll be your demise
i can see it in your eyes
you won't make it out alive
you can't get enough of me
the death of you i'll be

just when you think you got this
i remind you, you don't got shit
you're weak, i own your soul
i haven't even begun to take my toll
give up, stop trying so hard
you never make it very far
maybe to step 3 or 4
then you're knocking at my door
you're a worthless junkie, nothing more
a prostitute, a dirty whore
i'll beat you up, break you down
leave you 6ft underground
forever alone, except for me
through good & bad i'm all you need
family & friends only get in the way
they hate when I come out to play
"i'm done. i'm gunna stay clean this time."
the same story of lies
a few weeks go by . . .
relapse
stick a needle in your arm,
cross your heart,
hope you die
flatline
was it an accidental overdose or suicide?
every morning waking up sick
clogged my work, i need a new rig
go to the pharmacy down the street
let me get a 10-pack, 31-gauge, 100cc
a bag of dope, a couple rocks

loading up another shot
a broken heart, a jaded soul
homeless, street kid, sleeping in the cold
"you party girl?" "you wanna work?"
his hands are going up my shirt
"get off me! stop!" i beg & plead
i have no voice. they're silent screams
he drops me off like it was nothing
i climb into my heroin laced coffin
the pain i endure mostly self-inflicted
anything for dope, i can't resist it
i never thought i'd end up like this
turning tricks for one more hit
25-year-old female found dead, just another statistic
rest in peace, no. rest in shit
dancing with death. a drawn-out suicide
empty, soulless, dead behind the eyes
jails, institution & death. i pray for the latter
bruised, broken, beaten, battered
i'm worthless, useless. if i'm gone it won't matter
i don't fear death. what i'm scared of is living
barely getting by. day to day. simply existing
the world i live in is hell on earth
miss misunderstood. a beautiful disaster. drowning in hurt
a lost cause. too far gone. terminally unique
everybody wants to help. can't they see there no saving
went from smoking blunts to doing drugs iv
track marks. sunken face, infected with hep C
dirty needles. bent spoons with scorch marks
tourniquets. blood. the depiction of a broken heart
not even a mother's tears can stop this madness

loved ones feel the wrath & are engulfed in sadness
consumed with pain, my soul physically aches
i wish i could start over. a new life. a clean slate
i can't do it anymore, this isn't me
heroin and i aren't meant to be
i surrender. white flag. i wanna break free
so you go to your meetings & start reading your book
i pop into your head. a simple thought was all it took
"just one more" you said. instantly hooked
little did you know it would be your last
a blink of an eye it was over that fast
as i rush through your veins i whisper "where have you
been?"
i missed you
remember me?
your best friend
heroin

This young woman is now sober and living a full, healthy life. Her mother was in the room when she read her poem. I later asked her what was happening to her during the reading. She said that it was the first time she understood that her daughter did not choose to live this way and that, by hearing this poem, she was able to drop the negative feelings she had toward her daughter. Her mother saw that Kenzie was mortally wounded and just fighting to stay alive.

Grownups often struggle with telling children what's going on in the family. My experience is that most children come to treatment many years later, sharing how they knew about domestic violence, kept secrets of infidelity, thought they were responsible for divorce because it was never discussed openly, knew that there was pornography in the house and had found it on the computer, that addiction was in the home and hidden in secret.

There are so many other scenarios of secret keeping. I remember being told, "Don't tell Daddy or grandparents" just so there would be no conflict. So I did the same thing in my life for a long time just to avoid conflict.

Please remember, we teach other people how to treat us by what we accept, and we teach our children how to be men and women by how we behave in relationships and what we accept. We accept behaviors or behave in ways that we would never want for our children, but they learn from our actions not our words. They learn what it means to be a man or woman from our behaviors.

Secrets keep us sick and, more importantly, we can't have integrity, or be authentically ourselves if we are holding secrets. As we move along, you'll see the freedom that our clients have experienced by telling their truth, and changing their path with healthier choices.

Someone asked me once, "What's the message that drives you?" I ask this question of people all the time in my work. I help people to find that answer in order to help them change the direction of their lives by finding the "lie" in the message they've been given that brought them to their current situation.

I've often said that my message was, "You will never be good enough," which is a message or driving force for many people. However, after reflection, I realized that no, the real message was:

"You will never be good enough," followed by "Who do you think you are?"

That was the real message, because I always tried to be "good enough," and when I succeeded, which I often did, the real message was, "Who do you think you are?!"

Now, logically, I understand my mother was raised that way with that same message. Seeing her at ninety, I can see how much of her life and dreams she gave up or diminished in service to that message—a message delivered over generations by well-meaning, fearful people.

My father would tell me, "You can do anything you want, even things that boys can do that girls are not allowed to." This was the 1950–1960s. We were four sisters. I was the oldest and he offered me that gift of confidence and hope. However, he only embraced that message for himself in his dreams. Though he had plenty of dreams, he was unable to translate them into his living, breathing life, and it showed in his actions.

So, maybe because of that, when I succeeded my father's message became, "Who do you think you are?" My parents further reproached me with, "How dare you reach for the stars!" That came from a place of love *and* fear; if you settle for less, you may not be hurt so deeply. It was watching my mother and father fall so far from their potential that was confusing. They lived in fear of their darkness and in their own way tried to protect me from my "light."

Those memories make me sad because so many of us have operated in life as if someone was standing over us with that shaming, pointing finger: "Shame on you!" And our shininess begins to tarnish.

Mixed Messages

Those incongruent messages have played tug of war with my spirit for many years, and the events of my life continued to support the push-pull of the messages. I know I'm not alone in this place. These are typical push-pull messages you may have grown up with:

victim ⟷ victor	spectacular ⟷ embarrassing
brilliant ⟷ impaired	graceful ⟷ clumsy
caretaker ⟷ selfish	mature ⟷ immature
plain ⟷ ordinary	good ⟷ bad
beautiful ⟷ ugly	

Growing up hearing these conflicting messages is enough to make any child confused and unsettled. What is the truth, and whom do I trust to tell me the truth? Well, I hope that as we move along together on this journey that we can become a community for each other, a tribe of healing.

When I was little, my refuge was a rock on the banks of Cooper River near my house in Camden, New Jersey. I had big dreams but life and circumstances took me down a different, much harder path. I was a child of the sixties: sex, drugs, and rock and roll, the Vietnam War, civil rights, rebellion in the streets, feminism, bra burning, and Woodstock.

I was a young woman of great promise; an intelligent, active student with an excellent work ethic, funny, popular, with big dreams. However, a series of events and an innate feeling of being "less than" created the impetus that set me on a very different and painful course.

My primary purpose through the sixties, seventies, and eighties was my addiction. It consumed me. My husband was my partner in crime, dying of the disease of addiction at the age of thirty-three. I was a widow at twenty-seven, left to raise our three children. Still, I continued to use. I just could not beat it and because of my addiction, my children suffered. Still, I could not stop.

I used for another fifteen years and then after many, many consequences (spiritual, physical, emotional, and financial) and many, many detox experiences and two treatment visits, the miracle happened for me and my children. I was gifted with sobriety on August 4, 1987 and the pink cloud quickly enveloped me. (A pink cloud is a feeling that everything is great, happy. Some recovering addicts feel this during their first part of recovery.) Of course, after twenty-five years of drinking and drugging on a daily basis, the pink cloud probably had a lot to do with my brain and body being free of damaging chemicals for the first time in many years. I just felt so good! Every day got better and every moment became precious. Over the years I've paid attention to all the ways that life follows in divine order if I stay out of the way.

Sobriety found me at just the right time. My life has been incredible since then; not easy, not perfect, but incredible. And I have finally shared all the secrets that I held for so many years.

This story is not so much about me as it is the miracles that happen as a result of recovery. It's about the amazing people that have been put in my life, who have shaped my soul, and helped to give me a life of purpose after living a life of destruction.

To give back, I volunteered to answer the phone for other drunks who needed an ear or some direction. There was karma in answering the phone because under the influence and in blackout, I used to call at all hours of the day and night, crying out for help. In my addiction, the next day I would not remember speaking to those patient people. I volunteered to drive one of those white vans to meetings for a women's treatment center. I started a meeting at a women's prison and really began to understand that my past had a purpose, because I had something special to share with those women: my experience, strength, and hope certainly, along with the fact that I also had been at a really low bottom; a mother who had been hurtful to her children, and a widow who had been a battered wife. The most amazing thing is that my story gave hope because if I could find recovery, these women recognized that they could, too. Telling my story and my secrets gives people freedom to tell their own. My secrets no longer keep me prisoner or define me. I have a new, honest vision of myself, as I hope you will. No one can ever again hurt me with my truth.

I realized at some point during my recovery that not only did I need the Twelve Steps, but I had to heal my lifetime of emotional traumas. I went back to school and started working in the addiction field. I earned my BA from Rutgers University while still in my addiction and made the Dean's List—imagine that! I always had a handbag filled with a variety of addictive substances. I often wonder what I could have done had I been clean and sober. In recovery, I completed my master's in mental health counseling summa cum laude from New York Institute of Technology, became licensed as a mental health therapist, certified as an addictions professional in Florida and internationally, certified as a sex addiction therapist, trained in hypnosis, eye movement desensitization and reprocessing (EMDR), and became a specialist for healing trauma and PTSD.

In 1997, I started trauma work, asking each of my clients the same question, "What do you need?" I discovered most folks who chronically relapse are struggling with other issues, and usually those issues have to do with emotional traumas and PTSD. I realized that it was imperative to have trauma resolution to maintain healthy, long-term recovery. Too many dry drunks never get to do that work and have a miserable recovery life. Too many folks with multiple years of sobriety commit suicide because they have not addressed the trauma work. Too many folks resort to other addictions to fill the empty hole that trauma creates.

Those other addictions (eating disorders, sex and love addiction, gambling, and self-harm such as cutting or burning) can be as lethal as drugs and alcohol. We are looking for "relief" from what feels like unending emotional pain and suffering.

I have more than two decades of experience working in residential and outpatient settings. In 2003, I took my specialized training and distinctive insights on treating trauma and addiction to a forest—literally—and created a treatment center. Focused on trauma and a new wellness model that included a ninety-day treatment program (in contrast to normal twenty-eight or thirty-day programs) and many healing modalities, this model has grown to become one of the foremost in treating trauma/PTSD and addiction. We also have a brilliant team. Unfortunately, in the twenty-eight day model, clients are barely coming out of the fog. Extended treatment is preferable to multiple twenty-eight day treatments with chronic relapse. Extended treatment is more cost effective and trauma can heal.

We founded our treatment center to begin where many other treatment modalities end. Rebuilding emotional trust and regaining one's resiliency takes time, encouragement, and vigilant therapeutic support. My treatment philosophy and practice has been to establish a protected environment and safe milieu to allow the clients to explore the intensity of their fear and the strength of their resources. Specifically focused on trauma resolution, my perception of healing comes from the client being able to re-establish a profound trust between the clinician and the healing process.

Thanks to hard work, and a series of extraordinary events, the healing place we created in a forest has been successful for ten years. From clinicians to kitchen and maintenance staff to house managers, we taught the team how to love and nurture our clients, and sometimes lovingly kick their asses. Our clients worked so hard, they went into the black hole and with our help came out the other side, into the light and their rewritten story.

After ten years of running this treatment center, I was ready to begin work on my next project: Spirit2Spirit. We now teach a course for clinicians on how to work with trauma survivors where they can earn a certified trauma therapist (CTT) certificate.

The Heart of Trauma, *a painting created by one of our clients.*

The heart of trauma as beautifully portrayed as a painted black-and-red heart is the healing work of an incredibly talented young lady who has overcome enormous trauma and become a shining star, a woman of substance and purpose. Her story is riveting: she awoke one morning and found her fiancé overdosed in her bed. She was unaware of his heroin addiction; it was a secret. The enormity of this secret-keeping overwhelmed her ability to cope in the here and now. Her recourse was overwhelming depression and dissociation.

For about a year and a half her substance use became unmanageable, and she cut or burned herself every day. Distraught and in pain, she went into treatment, where she continued to self-harm. Ultimately, she joined us at our treatment center. The behaviors continued even as she bonded with peers and staff, doing some deep work. When confronted with the possibility of having to discharge to a higher level of care, this very gutsy lady decided that she would fight for her bed, and paint in black and red rather than self-harm. And paint she did! Dozens of paintings, all emblematic of a specific feeling that drove the desire to self-harm. She painted her way through trauma resolution. It is vital to understand that self-harming behaviors are not a prelude to suicide but an attempt to "feel" or "numb" emotions. In addition the brain releases *neurotransmitters* which create an addictive cycle to self-harm, so soothing behaviors can become addictive.

This was a decision to heal and to enter into the painful emotions and allow the grief process to proceed. Today, ten years later, this courageous woman is sober and free of all self-harming behaviors and process addictions. (A process addiction is an addiction to food, gambling, sex, working out—addiction to the process. They are powerful coping mechanisms that help trauma survivors to dissociate from trauma pain.) She sponsors other women and recently married a remarkable young man. She never expected that she would trust her heart again, yet life is good and became truly blessed for this very special couple when they were gifted with a beautiful baby girl.

The symbol of the heart of trauma is significant because we enter into the pain and experience it to completion in order to heal our heart, mind, body, and spirit.

This brave young woman painted through the pain and darkness to the bright life-affirming painting that followed it. The "Heart of Trauma" painting, along with the cutting paintings, and then the "Puzzle Heart" are elegant depictions of the journey of trauma resolution; telling the trauma story, feeling the trauma story, and having the puzzle pieces begin to re-write the healing, recovery story.

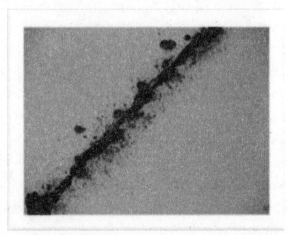

At the time I had twenty therapists who, in one way or another, interacted with all of our clients—a real team. And so our young miss painted twenty trauma hearts on canvas for each therapist. In addition, she created a memorial to her fiancé on our Memorial Trail, in a very cleansing and self-forgiving honoring ceremony.

In the first two to three years post treatment, she had a couple of self-harming episodes. When those occurred she called and reported, without shame, what triggered the event, what she felt, and what she did to acknowledge the feelings and accept them.

In this book, we'll look at all the variables of trauma events and patterns, the correlations between addictions and coping behaviors, and a myriad of current issues related to working with trauma. Together we'll explore multiple areas, and identify important skillsets and cutting-edge information vital to trauma survivors and clinicians working with them. Reflective questions at the end of each chapter are provided as an opportunity to see where you or a loved one fits into this wellness model.

REFLECTIVE SKETCHES

1) Do you have secrets that you're keeping?

   _____

2) Are they your secrets or someone else's?

   _____

3) Why are you keeping these secrets?

   _____

   _____

   _____

4) How is keeping this secret impacting your life and your vision of
   yourself?

   _____

   _____

   _____

5) What are the emotions around this secret: shame, guilt, remorse,
   confusion, sadness, pain, or something else?

   _____

   _____

   _____

6) What is the "payoff" for keeping the secret?

   _____

   _____

7) Imagine the best/worst things that can come out of keeping the secret.

   _____

_____

_____

_____

8) What is the best/worst thing that can come out of telling the secret?

_____

_____

_____

_____

9) Write the secret down in a letter and mail it to yourself. How did you feel when you received it and opened it?

_____

_____

_____

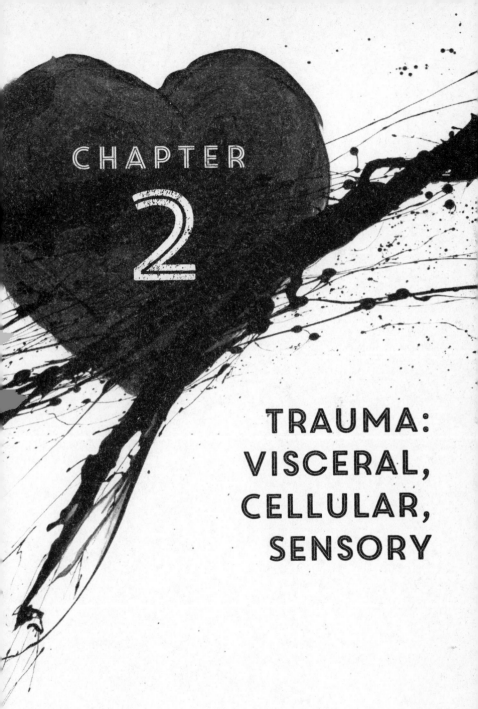

CHAPTER

2

TRAUMA:
VISCERAL,
CELLULAR,
SENSORY

> *"An abnormal reaction to an abnormal*
> *situation is normal behavior."*
>
> —Viktor Frankl

❧

Trauma is visceral, sensory, and cellular. It's a soul wound that impacts the very core of who we are, what we believe about the world and our place in it. We experience trauma with all of our senses: taste, touch, smell, sound, sight, and our sixth sense, intuition.

We weep and wail, cry, tears streaming, chest heaving, gut wrenching, brain exploding overwhelmed with visual images, sounds and smells, our whole being in turmoil. That may be the extreme of a trauma response, however, our body, mind and spirit, the whole of how we experience and respond to the world, can also appear rather benign if you don't know or ask *What is happening to me now?*

The website *www.medicine.net* defines viscera as "the internal organs of the body, specifically those within the chest (heart or lungs) or abdomen (as the liver, pancreas, or intestines). The *American Heritage Science Dictionary,* describes the sensory cortex as the somatic, sensory, auditory, visual, and olfactory regions of the cerebral cortex. And finally, according to Luis Diaz in "Cellular Memory Release," on the website *www.cellularmemory.org.* "cellular memory is a complete blueprint of your history, your existence. It is an energetic expression of you as a holistic being." Cellular memory release is a process of releasing toxic body memories.

To understand trauma responses we must understand that we are holistic beings experiencing our lives with every cell of our body, mind, and spirit. Trauma healing cannot happen by "talking through it." Trauma healing happens by "feeling" through it, i.e., completing the flight, flight, freeze, acquiesce cycle.

So *What is happening to me now?*" is a vital question because unless we clear or detox our whole viscera and cellular memory of the trauma effects, we won't resolve our pain. We'll continue to respond to loud, angry voices; banging doors; certain smells or tastes or texture; and we'll continue to re-experience the trauma in our relationships. Then we continue in soothing survival behaviors that no longer protect us.

Our body records everything that ever transpires in our life; the smell, the taste, the sound, the feel, and the sixth sense that intuits and translates the events for our mind and memory. So consider the impact and response to the following:

→ Smell of garlic on the breath or cigarettes on clothes
→ Sweet aroma of a favorite meal
→ Sound of angry voices, slamming doors
→ Gentle cooing of a mother's voice
→ Jingling of change in the pocket of a critical, punishing parent
→ Sight of a little girl wearing red tights
→ Sound of footsteps as they come to deliver punishment or abuse
→ Sound of a door opening as an abuser slips into the room again
→ Loving touch of someone who comforted you in times of sadness or terror
→ Taste of food that was forced on you
→ Taste of food that was offered with love and caring
→ Sight, smells, and sounds of a hospital or doctor's office

- Smell of wood smoke
- Noise of a car backfiring/gunfire
- Feelings a church, temple, or synagogue evokes if there was humiliation, shame, or abuse, or comfort and love.

This list is endless. Each person who carries trauma has their own experiences that remind them of the time they were traumatized or the time they were comforted.

When Grief Came Knocking

Here is a seemingly simple assignment: at the top of a blank page in your journal write:

"When Grief Came Knocking." This is an assignment I often use in group therapy sessions.

Now sit quietly and breathe. Contemplate that sentence and then begin to write. There is no right or wrong, good or bad. Just write what comes to you; the format doesn't matter. A wonderful and extremely talented therapist, Cheryl Bailey, introduced me to this assignment. Seems simple enough, almost benign. Hundreds of clients have presented this assignment and there are never two with the same somatic responses. I've seen this technique, for instance, release a thirty-year-old memory of being held hostage. The client screamed, "I'm alive! I'm alive!" That memory was held in her body, and truly held her hostage but now she was free.

I watched Ben, a stockbroker, read his grief assignment. It appeared that he had no emotional connection to the work, however, when you looked more closely with trauma-trained eyes, you could see that Ben's clothes were drenched in cold sweat. He was shivering (though he was not aware of it); his eyes were dilated, and his breathing moved only to his throat. Ben's emotional experience was enormous. A peer put her hand on Ben's and, with that loving touch, he finally let go and sobbed and wailed, falling to his knees.

That began a process of trauma healing that astounded everyone who knew him. Friends had thought Ben was "a little bit Asperger's." The reality was that from his early childhood Ben did not feel safe showing emotion in a family that was numb and without connection to each other. Being emotionally numb was great for a stockbroker, but it impeded every personal, emotional relationship that he'd had, except with his son Chris.

After the exercise there was an immediate change in his affect and his perceptions; suddenly, his body and emotions began to be in sync. Ben had lost Chris to suicide. Ben had adopted Chris, and he felt safe with him and was protective of him. He was able to guide and love this young man in a way his biological family could not, and this was one of the only relationships in which Ben had allowed himself to experience a real emotional connection. Chris's suicide was devastating on so many levels, from survivor's guilt, to pain and remorse for not "doing enough" to save Chris. Because he believed he was responsible and was filled with shame, Ben had a moral injury. Although Ben repeatedly spoke of the suicide, until this assignment, Ben's heart and spirit were locked down. Although he was racked with pain, his body had been numb, holding all of the pain in his viscera, his cellular memory. He was able to recite the traumatic events of his life like a shopping list because he was numb. But when he became aware that his body was tightly holding on to the grief and he allowed himself to "feel" it, he was able to grieve and place his son's memory in his heart.

Another woman in the group, Rose, had lost her sixteen-year-old son due to a medical issue. When she read her grief assignment, her whole body heaved with sobs as she re-experienced the loss of her son, finally being able to give voice to the overpowering body memory. Every cell of her being held the pain, and finally putting voice to the loss and allowing the body to discharge the existential grief was tremendously healing.

Rose was a Latina and had a wonderful, expressive personality. She was very in touch with her feelings, but was unable to just grieve and find a place in her spirit to let go of the deepest pain. This also meant she was unable to be available for her other children. Two sides of the same coin: grief!

We speak about the insides and the outsides not matching. Many of us have not truly been connected to our body or to our emotions; we've been numb most of our lives. Our goal is to become congruent, when our body, mind, and spirit are truly one. So our spiritual commitment can be to integrate those parts of us that have the various elements of who we are—into one being.

As you experience and celebrate survivors and their rewritten stories, you may find a path and hope to rewrite your own trauma story. Remember, our behaviors *always make sense* when we unravel our trauma story!

Sometimes the layers of traumatic events become confused, overlaid in time and memory, and create a subtle misinterpretation or perception of those events. Time frames may be confused, events rolled together, places intertwined, and those are the overlays of memory.

However, our perception of the events of our life are exactly how we operate in the world, how we make choices, decisions, create behaviors—solely based on our perceptions. That is our truth. Interestingly, that means there are many truths.

I often say, "No right or wrong, no good or bad, just what was." And what is or was is our perception within the framework of the non-negotiable facts. If there are four family members experiencing an event, there will be four different perceptions of the event. Each perception will be the truth for that individual; that was the way that person experienced the event. This means that from that moment until the perception is changed, we can only operate from that belief.

Healing trauma is an exercise in unraveling. It's a mystery and we must gather all of the data. It's also like a puzzle, finding the pieces and slowly building the final, completed picture. The "*Aha!*" moment comes when that final fact or puzzle piece is assembled, and all of the behaviors, feelings, memories, and flashbacks fit into place, and make sense. Making sense of the pain and behaviors associated with the trauma events gives us a sense of relief when we finally understand, "We are not bad people trying to get good; we are wounded people trying to heal." Many trauma survivors feel a depth of guilt and shame about what happened, as though they were responsible or caused it to happen. Those feelings can finally be relieved with the last puzzle piece.

You may relate to my experience. As a child, I felt strangely socially confused. I felt introverted *and* extroverted. I could easily spend time with friends and neighbors and family, and seem very social and extroverted with lots of friends from a myriad of different backgrounds. In the fifties and sixties I was very much a bright and cosmopolitan child/adolescent/young adult. I could fit in anywhere and be a chameleon. But what looked okay on the outside was not a reflection of what was going on inside. I spent a good bit of my life, even up to today, trying to figure out what was the secret that everyone else seemed to know about; just exactly how to be and feel.

That's my place of introversion, where I have to fill my spirit with the drama of books, movies, theater, and music, without the interplay of people. This essentially means I need my alone time, too, in order to replenish and to sit back and marinate with my emotions and sort out what I'm truly feeling—what's mine and what's yours. My saving grace is that I can adapt if I can figure out what is expected of me. Movies, music, books, and theater became my teachers.

I was a voracious reader. My mother would stand over me and yell, "Judy, Judy, *Judy!*" I was so immersed in my world of books and films that I was truly dissociated from my surroundings. Movies, especially old classic movies, were a wonderland for me. They taught me how to behave and feel and speak and dress and so much more. I studied the characters' faces; I studied their expression of emotion. I observed everything in any new surroundings, proper etiquette, which knife and fork to use. Through voracious reading and watching movies I created my bucket list; what I wanted to do, where I wanted to go visit, whom I wanted as friends. I had a huge and wonderfully rich fantasy world—much of which has been achieved.

One day when I was visiting London for a conference, several friends and I decided to take the Chunnel over to Paris for the afternoon. I was giddy with these experiences: seeing Buckingham Palace, changing of the guard, going to Parliament for a meeting to discuss addiction, and then an afternoon in Paris, standing in front of the Eiffel Tower, and feeling *déjà vu*, as though I had been there before. My dissociation with books, movies, music, and theater have given me a rich and juicy agenda to fulfill while I am on this Earth.

When I was young, I always wanted to write and did much writing until my addiction intruded. Interestingly enough, I remember quite clearly thinking I needed to *experience more of life* to be a truly talented writer like Hemingway. I thought to myself, *How can I write about what I haven't experienced? I haven't been to jail, or done drugs,* and a myriad of other insane thoughts. Well, I managed to experience a whole lot of life that has awed, amazed, and horrified me.

I waitressed a good bit of my life, and I'm really good with people because I'm selfish. I want to know everything about you and to remember your story and what makes you special. It's selfish, because knowing you makes my life richer. Being in jobs of service helped me to be a really good therapist because I love people and I celebrate our ability to not just survive but to flourish in the seemingly worst of circumstances. Of all the things that make me a great therapist, though, perhaps the most important is that I have "walked in your shoes." Our history, our story, can be the greatest blessing of our life. I would not exchange anything that has come into my life because at my core my life and spirit have been enriched by the good, the bad, and the ugly. I would like to bring you into just a bit of my dissociative world of movies. Films can bring us to a safe place to experience our own emotions through someone else's story. Get the popcorn, pull up a comfortable chair, and just allow yourself to breathe and *be*.

In 2014, I gave myself the gift of watching almost the entire list of Academy-Award nominated movies. And I had the most extraordinary revelation. Every one of those beautifully made, emotionally driven movies was about trauma in the lives of ordinary and extraordinary people. The effects of these stories impacted generations and their messages—pain, sorrow, and triumph—were universal, which is why we are so drawn to movies, theater, music, and art. Those gifts of the visceral, sensory, and cellular reach to the centers of our soul.

Dallas Buyers Club brought me back to the horror of the AIDS epidemic in its earliest days. Desperation and despair walked with bigotry and hatred and the LBGTQ community suffered immensely as death and dying ensued. Many, many of my friends and their families continue to experience the pain generations later. As the LGBTQ community continues to fight hatred and bigotry, we can re-experience and remember through this masterpiece of a film. We can celebrate the ability of young men and women coming out of the shadows with less fear. And in 2016, with the long-fought-for approval of same sex marriage, and our armed services and government being integrated with the LBGTQ community, the raging battle of the moment is bathroom rights for transgender folks.

Lee Daniels' The Butler, 12 Years a Slave, and *Mandela* provided that same emotional catharsis for the victims of slavery, segregation, apartheid, and hatred. Through the intergenerational trauma created through more than five generations we can have clarity and find a safe place to revisit the reality of what is inflicted by humans on each other, and by natural disasters. One of the raging battles recently is the proliferation of young black men being killed by other black men and the police; the rise of black lives matter and blue lives matter. In each case the landscape of violence creates impulsive and deadly trauma reactions, hatred, bigotry, and the inability to recognize the underlying intergenerational trauma reactions.

When we consider even the most benign or loving experiences in our life, every experience we have in a lifetime is imprinted on our senses, on our spirit, and on our soul. Trauma events have a huge and lasting impression on the viscera, as do the joyful, life-affirming events.

Understanding the signs and symptoms of PTSD is understanding this concept. Trauma survivors experience flashbacks, dreams and nightmares, disturbed sleep, dissociation, body memory, somatic issues, and a diminished sense of self, low self-esteem, despair, hopelessness, and a myriad of other sensory symptoms.

The movie *Philomena* is a riveting example of how those flash-backs and memories remain in our viscera for decades. The title character attempts to find her illegitimate son who was torn from her and sold for adoption by the Catholic Church. The long-held secret affected Philomena's relationships with her daughter and husband, and impacted her vision of herself. She had lived in trauma shame for decades. In her search for her son came trauma resolution, even so many decades later.

Healing trauma must be visceral, sensory, and cellular, and must heal the soul. In treatment, we must create a safe place to utilize experiential, sensory, and somatic modalities which are incredibly effective in processing trauma resolution. Trauma healing is a process of *pendulation:* going into the trauma story, experiencing some of it, coming out and building more resources, going back in deeper each time and then building more resources.

I was also riveted by the Academy Awards as *Spotlight* was awarded Best Picture. *Spotlight* told the story of the *Boston Globe's* extraordinary work exposing the depth and breadth of the clergy abuse in Boston all the way up through the hierarchy of the Catholic Church. Over the years we've worked with multiple archdioceses as well as every other denomination and faith to help the healing of survivors of clergy abuse. After the movie was released and after the Academy Awards ceremony, many survivors picked up the phone and came out of the shadows to seek help. Clergy abuse engenders in many the feeling of betrayal by God. This heightens the difficulty in the healing process until the individual can make peace with these thoughts.

I also watched *Room*, an incredible story of a young woman kidnapped and held as a sexual hostage for seven years in a shed that she called "Room." She had a beautiful boy who is five as the story opens.

Their life in Room, their relationship for those five years after his birth in captivity, is total dependence on each other with no connection to the outside world and constant fear and abuse from the kidnapper. The story of their escape and their struggles with PTSD and relationship to the world is nothing short of genius, and is a stunning and inspiring tribute to survival of the spirit. Movies create a unique opportunity for us to experience our emotions, pain, and joy from a safe distance and yet, at such a visceral level that renewal can happen.

My favorite thing to do with my grandchildren is to watch animated films. *Happy Feet* is the story of bullying, betrayal by your tribe, triumph over differences, and transformation. What a safe place for children and adults alike to relate and recognize the differences and similarities! *Kung Fu Panda* is a story of adoption and building a tribe, fitting in, and survival. *Up* is about attachment and relationships, and love's healing properties. As my grandchildren are growing older, we have added *Harry Potter, The Avengers* and *Guardians of the Galaxy*. As a therapist I ask them, "How is this like your life?" and I'm astounded at the honest answers; honest because it's a safe venue. These kids teach me more than I could ever teach them. There are so many other movies that move us and help us relate to our own lives. Watching movies together is a safe way to check in with people you love and care for.

By utilizing cinema therapy and other experiential, sensory modalities, the trauma survivor is provided a safe distance to process a very cellular experience that can help to bring them catharsis and resolution. What movies, music, plays, or books create catharsis for you?

One of our therapists, when he finds himself shutting down from the depth of the trauma stories, goes to his office, puts the Do Not Disturb sign out and watches *Steel Magnolias*, which taps into a deep well of emotions in his spirit. He cries and snots and embraces his emotions again; then he's renewed for the next wounded clients who come into his life.

Experiential therapies create the environment for this process. For instance, psychodrama becomes a safe vehicle for engaging in observation of a trauma event. Amazing healing happens in this process. Peter Levine's model of somatic experience is a modality that we use as well as hypnosis, dialectical behavior therapy (DBT, which assists survivors raise their level of emotional and cognitive regulation and control of emotional stability), EMDR, art and music therapy, grief work, equine, and adventure therapy. All of these modalities should be available; there are many ways into the spirit.

Of absolute importance in trauma work is for clinicians to recognize that substance and process addictions and self-harming behaviors are coping mechanisms that are often created by trauma events. Our staff at my first treatment center were trained in all of these modalities. We also had several certified sex addiction therapists, and eating disorder therapists. Everyone is trained in trauma and addictions, and each clinician and ancillary staff are encouraged and provided opportunities to do their own healing work. I believe we cannot ask clients to do what we haven't done. I advocate for all clinical professionals to be highly trained in trauma treatment. Chances are, most clients you work with have experienced trauma events and protect themselves with coping behaviors that no longer serve them.

Here is a gift from a very talented and special heart-centered grief therapist.

CHERYL'S STORY:
CONTINUING TO DO MY OWN WORK
AS I LEARN AND GROW AS A THERAPIST

My professional career began in the back wards of a state hospital before deinstitutionalization took place. Over the years I worked in community mental health, emergency services, and then thirteen years with hospice. There I discovered that I had a passion for working with people who were grieving, especially those who were experiencing traumatic losses.

I came to work with Judy Crane in 2008, not without some trepidation about working in a residential treatment center. Working with addictions was new for me although I got sober in AA and had thirty years of sobriety under my belt, as well as years of working on my own issues. However, when I was in graduate school in the 1970s, PTSD was a relatively new concept and we were not taught about how to treat trauma. It was a steep and challenging learning curve for me as I began reading about concepts and research that were new to me such as trauma bonds, trauma reenactment, how trauma is stored in the body, and the many experiential treatment modalities used at Judy's treatment center. I began reading Patrick Carnes' The Betrayal Bond, Peter Levine's Waking the Tiger, Bessel van der Kolk's work, and other similar material.

At that time, several therapists, myself included, stayed in cabins on the property during our work week. As I read and absorbed this new knowledge, I was stunned to find the pieces of the puzzle of my own life beginning to fit together and make sense at long last. I vividly remember many nights sitting on the porch of my cabin rocking and sobbing as I finally grasped why I had done the things I had, and understood the emotional pain I had experienced for so much of my own life. My emotional life began to make sense to me for the first time. This was a priceless gift for me, but it also gave me invaluable insight into the pain, trauma manifestations, and resulting addictions of the clients I was working with. Never had I encountered a treatment center where the clinical staff were allowed, even encouraged, to be "real" with clients. I began to see how what I had been through in my own life was something I could transform and use in my work with others. I came to love the power of the group in healing. Most importantly, I experienced how integral compassion is in the healing process.

How many times did we hear Judy say, "We will love you until you can love yourself" to our clients? And we did.

I continued to do my own work as I was learning and growing as a therapist. It is my absolute belief that we cannot take our clients any further than we ourselves have been and are willing to go. We have to be able to sit with and bear witness to the shock and pain from the often-horrific experiences people have endured as we help them realize they have survived, and find a way to release the effects still held in their bodies.

As part of the training to learn Somatic Experiencing I volunteered to be the client in a demonstration of working with inescapable assault. As I recounted some of my experience to the instructor, I trembled and shook violently. When my body finally stopped shaking, I opened my eyes and the instructor asked me what was happening. What came out of my mouth was a startled, "I'm alive!"

"Yes," he replied. "You are alive. Say it again louder."

I said it again and again realizing that there had been a part of me that did not know until that moment that I had truly survived. I had expected to die that day over thirty years ago. This and other powerful experiences showed me how cellular trauma is and why we must include the body as part of therapy. The other critical thing I learned was the importance of educating clients on how trauma affects the brain and body. Shame is often part of the aftermath of trauma and thus the more knowledge we can give about how this works, the easier clients can begin to let go of it.

I am grateful for my experience working with Judy. It has not only made me a much more effective therapist, but it has been instrumental in my own healing journey.

What follows are three extraordinary collages of Cheryl's journey. This brilliant work was done in her limbic brain, the part of the brain that feels, experiences, and translates our trauma experiences.

For much of life I had no real idea of who I was. I distinctly remember walking around my various apartments and living spaces studying the pictures on the walls, the furniture, and objects on them, trying to see them through the eyes of others in order to see who I would appear to be. With people, I was whoever they wanted me to be. In other words, like a chameleon I would change myself to blend or fit in.

When I was younger I would joke that I couldn't have a party and invite all my friends at the same time because I wouldn't know how to act. I didn't understand why this was and I didn't do it intention- ally. I really didn't have much sense of myself as a solid person and I certainly didn't think anyone would want to be around me if I was myself—whoever that was!

The Chameleon

The collage is pretty obvious, but there is an image in the center of a figure walking away from a mask on the ground. This symbolizes me finally coming into myself. This was a direct result of the work I did while in the forest.

My Addictions

"My Addictions" collage is a general snapshot of my years lost to various substance and process addictions. There is an actual photo of me at age eighteen in there on a road trip to New York where the drinking age was then eighteen. I was primarily a whiskey drinker, nicotine addict, and pot smoker, although I dabbled in whatever was available. I had my first blackout at seventeen. During those years, I struggled with depression and ever-growing shame. I sought relief any way and anywhere I could. It led me into some very dark and scary places.

Rising from the Ashes

"Rising from the Ashes" is about getting sober and finding a program of recovery. I was waking up out of a dark and despairing landscape. I had been to the depths of hellish emotional pain and at times wanted to end my life.

Here is a journal entry from 1978, six months before I stopped drinking (now thirty-nine years sober):

> I am in my office. This day will never end. I am sick—hungover. My body is poisoned, my brained soaked. How much longer can I go on this way? I have to admit I am an alcoholic. I have lost control over my drinking. I'm ashamed and embarrassed about my behavior last night. I don't even know how I got up and made it to work. The hangover didn't even hit me bad until lunchtime. Now I feel dizzy, nauseous, and shaky. I really hurt. Beyond the second drink I have no control—cannot stop, not until I get sick. I had a quasi blackout last night. The last two hours are vague and patchy. I can remember glimpses of what I did. I remember hanging on the toilet trying to be sick. I passed out the second I hit the bed. Don't remember setting alarms, undressing, don't remember the ride home—thank God I wasn't driving—surely would have killed myself or somebody else. I did this two Fridays ago also. And I've been starting drinking earlier in the evening every night. No matter how much I promise myself not to, every night I drink. This is it: rock bottom. I've missed one day of work from drinking last March. I've known I had a problem for years but guess I haven't really admitted the full extent. This is it. I have to stop now. I feel that this is going to be the toughest battle of my entire life. Somehow, I have to muster the strength to do this.

As much as I wanted to stop drinking, I was fearful of living without being numbed out. Recovery was like the proverbial phoenix rising from the ashes. I was blessed to find an amazing group of women with whom I could identify and who were smiling and enjoying life without alcohol and other drugs. Thirty-eight years later I can still remember the hell I lived in but now it seems like another

*lifetime—or a very bad nightmare from which I finally awoke. Six
months after I stopped drinking, I quit smoking cigarettes. I got into
therapy and onto a spiritual path. I now feel grateful for every step
on this amazing journey.*

Isn't this the therapist you want for yourself and your family? A
clinician who is genuine, authentic, and continues to grow as a clinician and as a trauma survivor, who will not ask you to do what she
hasn't done herself. A person who will be available, hold space and
witness for you, (just being there for someone in their trauma without judgment or putting their own experience on it, and witnessing
without trying to fix it) who will walk through the fire with you, and
never give up on you or your loved ones.

A Rubik's Cube, a labyrinth, a jigsaw puzzle: trauma resolution is
very much like trying to solve a jumble of puzzles. Working with the
human condition is like trying solve all of those puzzles.

Our behaviors always make perfect sense when we unravel our
story. Each piece of the puzzle that we discover adds to the story
and ultimately allows us to understand ourselves and others. We can
become congruent like the Rubik's Cube, matching in color on all six
surfaces. We find the center of our spirit just as we walk a maze to the
center, a place of peace.

The most exciting part, however, is putting together that big jigsaw
puzzle. Remember laying out all of the pieces with the excitement of
making the picture whole? Maybe a puzzle of a simple block pattern
or a more challenging Statue of Liberty. Some lay out the outline,
others try to start with linking pieces that are most obvious and gathering them together. There is no right or wrong way to complete the

picture. There is no good or bad, just the chance to understand the whole. The truly skillful trauma therapist has a multitude of modalities and interventions in their tool bag for exactly this reason.

The truly skilled therapist continues to explore and heal their own wounds, and maintain resources and supervision for themselves. Trauma therapy is not for the faint of heart and everyone has a story.

I think to discover the *who* and *why* along with the *what* and *how* of our life is a journey that takes courage, resilience, compassion, desire to change, desire to understand, and willingness to stop the pain, despair, confusion, and sadness. The most difficult part of this path is that you often must experience those events again, sometimes in great intensity. You can't take this journey for anyone else but you, and you must be clear about your reasons for taking the first step. There will be surprises and disappointment and angry spaces as well as despair for a time, but there will also be relief, understanding, excitement, joy, and resolution. And perhaps peace, and perhaps an exciting path of discovery. With each piece of the puzzle our behavior makes sense.

You may also discover that you can't or won't do it alone. Many of you have been trying for a long time to understand the void, chaos, or insanity, or any of the myriad of places you have gone with your pain. People need relief from fear, numbness, and pain so when we find something that will soothe us it becomes a lifeline.

Those of us who are genetically predisposed to addiction will find relief with drugs, alcohol, sex, food, shopping, gambling, and many other destructive behaviors. Why? Because at the time of fear/ trauma we believed we were going to die, even though logically as adults we know better. For children from conception to early childhood through adolescence, fearful and traumatic experiences can be a very different experience. Truth be told we are fighting for our life, our survival. Whatever will soothe the fear or terror of the moment becomes our lifeline.

For many of us, mood disorders, depression, anxiety, or other mental health behaviors become a comfortable place after a time. At first trauma takes us there, but if we continue to experience the ongoing trauma reactions these behaviors become the place of uncomfortable comfort that we know. They become a kind of solace.

The story of Hannah is a powerful example of intergenerational trauma. She found the puzzle pieces falling into place through the experiential process of writing poems about pain and triumph. The poems eloquently explain how the behaviors make sense when you understand the trauma story. I have worked with six members of Hannah's family. One by one, they've begun healing the loss of a son and brother, the ravages of addiction and divorce, and have come together creating a family of hope and joy. The grandbabies will have a space of safety and love and nurturing to grow. It's a joy to watch the healing.

This is a family of trauma, addiction, grief, pain, and triumph. As a result of the intense work each member of this family did on their trauma, the family is more intimate, communicates with each other, has healed old wounds, and three of the grown children now have babies of their own. The intergenerational cycle of secrets, addiction, and trauma is broken. The new parents are in loving, open, honest relationships, and are amazing parents. Therein lies the triumph.

HANNAH'S STORY
THE HEALING VOICE OF FAMILY

If you know my family's story, I feel like it explains mine. I was just a bossy little girl trying to cope with a chaotic life I didn't understand, and take care of my little brother when others failed us. I was so angry at everybody for so long and internalized everything because I wasn't allowed to be the one to break. I had to be the good student, the perfect daughter, the exceptional homemaker, the chauffeur, etc. and always knew it wasn't fair. Once I left the nest and had no one to take care of but myself, I realized how inept I was at taking care of someone like me. Substance abuse and self-harm seemed like appropriate coping mechanisms, so I participated and became everything I was embarrassed to show my friends all those years.

After a couple years of failed college classes I decided to leave Ocala and try to make a brand-new life. After two more years of dragging around baggage, substance abuse, self-harm, and an abusive relationship, I finally started working with a therapist. She was a great help along with people who actually loved me and didn't just say they did. I finally got to become the strong competent woman I strived to be.

Now here I am with my first baby on the way, a great job, a loving man, and a wonderful family who has my back no matter what!

There once was a lovely couple married in 1983, two beautiful, generous loving spirits; let's call them Matt and Suzanne. They are blessed with three perfect, beautiful, bright and shining lights; let's call them Ryan (born in 1984), Mark (born in 1985), and Paul (born in 1987). The dilemma was that this lovely couple had a "drinking problem," which created havoc. Life was tumultuous and divorce was inevitable.

Alcoholism and addiction is surely in our DNA, but the debate on nature versus nurture continues. However, alcoholism and addiction have been considered a disease by the American Medical Association (AMA) since 1956. These are the facts, but the emotional and spiritual destruction created is more powerful than any of the "facts" of alcoholism. And the facts could not save this family from despair.

Ryan, Mark, and Paul were three, five, and six years old when this painful divorce took place. Ultimately Suzanne remarries and has two more children, David and Hannah, and a few years later divorces again. This family is rife with grief and loss around the divorces. The children have their own individual ways of reacting and coping, and in varying degrees and in multiple forms the children find solace, relief, soothing and numbing, or dissociating from the layers of trauma. The parents also continue in their alcoholism until, one by one, they find twelve-step recovery and separately begin to slowly, very slowly, heal some of their wounds.

That's important because the "disease" of addiction and the trauma monster was not through with them yet. What followed was chapter after chapter of events and consequences that once again tore the family's spirit apart.

The youngest son's girlfriend was murdered in 2006 and Paul saw it happen and was powerless to intervene. All three boys were in and out of jail for various drug-related activity. And then in 2010 Paul and his current girlfriend were murdered in a horrible, highly publicized shooting. At the time, Mark was in jail, and Suzanne and Matt in recovery. Matt keeps the family together and ultimately he and Suzanne take to their sofas for years, each in their own home, as despair sets in.

However, this family is blessed. Mom and Dad in their individual recovery through their despair, Mark finds real recovery in jail, Ryan follows. Both of those boys marry sensitive, loving women who are in recovery and both couples have the most warm and loving children.

So Mom, the three oldest boys and their wives, all individually come to treatment for their trauma and find some peace and resolution, and find real joy in their life. Mom gets off the sofa and finds purpose in her life working with wounded trauma survivors, helping them heal. Actually, Mom, her two oldest sons and her daughter-in-laws all find a real purpose in life working with wounded people, helping them to heal.

Healing is different for everyone. However finding and having a purpose for your life is an imperative and these members of the family found a purpose and a solution for their pain by helping someone else who suffers into the light.

David flies under the radar, joins the armed services, and travels abroad to guns and war. We all have our ways of coping in the world. David's return home was a glorious celebration of life.

Hannah finds her own way along this journey, and she is the family member who helps to tell this story. What follows are the heart-wrenching, healing words she wrote which were instrumental in her healing process.

Learning How to Breathe

Learning how to breathe,

I never thought it would be this hard. My lungs are dry,
My lips are cracked,
My throat aches with the screams I never allowed myself.

My ribcage betrays me as I try and suck in the warm air that
is supposed to give life to my frail organs.
Even my tongue,

a muscle I always deemed sharp and strong,
lays flat and unmoving in my arid mouth;

afraid to orate the fear of attaining knowledge
so easily bestowed on others.
How is it that I, a grown woman,
have yet to know the feeling of taking a breath not saturated with rage.

My body has been on fire for so long, starved of oxygen,
that there is nothing I fear more than losing that pain.
That pain has kept me alive.
But what a life I have lived. No more.
I brace myself,

white knuckled in this unfamiliar place, and I breathe.
I breathe and cry like shards of glass are ripping apart my insides.
I breathe my first real breath of change.
I breathe through this new pain.

The embarrassment of such a crutch
That used to make me hurt so much
Makes me feel so ostracized
Like there's no truth behind my eyes "I'm fine" I'd say like nothing new
And always smile right on cue

Pull down my dress to hide away
The bloody mess I'd made that day

Each little cut so harshly placed
My leg, my arm, my chest, my waist
Couldn't speak the violent pain
I fought with every day in vain

Why did I maim my tender skin
As if that white-hot ache within
Would cool and heal by sharpened knife
And give my dying heart new life

Blood had become a form of tears I never cried over the years
My cherished marks were only mine a secret behind every line

I hid this so no one would know
Made sure my scars would never show
For who would love this damaged soul
With a body that's much less than whole

I beg my mind for mercy still
And struggle with a waning will
Just for today I'll love myself
And put my knife back on its shelf

I crave the sting like a lover's touch
A familiar friend I miss so much
But bright red lines are fading white
The longer I put up the fight

Skin will heal and scars will fade
As I pay for the mess I've made
—Every demon I'll outrun
Just by trying means I've won

Getting Off the Sofa

A nd then there was one . . . This family came together and begged Dad (Matt) to go to an intensive to heal the enormous grief and loss that continued to numb every part of his being. It was clear the family struggled to move on into their own light and joy, for fear of leaving him to die of grief on his sofa. And Matt made a decision to try to move on and allowed himself to take a leap of faith that there might be life after all the death and loss.

Dad came to the intensive where a group of eight other trauma survivors had gathered to do their own healing. The question I always ask at the beginning of our intensives is, "What would you like to happen or be different at the end of this week?" Dad said to his group, "I want to get off the sofa and back to my life."

The group process is so very powerful. The group asked Dad to burn the sofa to short circuit the isolation and immobilization. Several members of his group and most of the members of his family, including grandchildren and myself, joined him on the beach to bear witness to his process of letting go of grief, sadness, and despair. It was magnificent! Dad marinated with this for a few weeks and gradually moved back to his life. Now please understand that this beautiful intervention is not recommended for everyone. This was a unique and grace-filled intervention. I invite you to look for those moments when making just one change, one shift in behaviors can change the whole direction of life and provide healing. This family has come together in such an extraordinary process of individual and family healing. They can speak freely about their pain and celebrate each other.

Most medical schools and universities that train therapists do not provide training in alcoholism, addictions, mental health, or trauma. That's truly unfortunate because our patients and clients are often not served well as a result of practitioners not knowing what we don't know.

However, there are many professionals who are highly qualified as a result of on-the-job training and personal experience. Dr. Doug, as we call this special man, is one of those extraordinary people. Dr. Doug had his own struggle with addiction and a traumatic life. That is his power! He "knows what he knows," has lived and breathed the life of being humbled and brought to his knees by addiction, and consequently raised himself up into a spiritual life of recovery. He has walked the walk and lives in integrity and compassion.

The gift of having a doctor like Doug on board is that clients and staff trust and believe in him. Dr. Doug spends endless hours being a great doctor but even more time as a model of health and healing. He practices what he preaches. He has my utmost love and respect for the lives he has saved and enriched. *Namaste,* Doc!

DR. DOUG'S STORY:
HE KNOWS WHAT HE KNOWS

I *"Sufentanilled"* my way out of an almost half-million-dollar-a-year career as an anesthesiologist on a cardiac surgical team in late 1998. I got four months of solid treatment and a decent foundation in twelve-step recovery at Talbott Recovery Center (TRC), although looking back, nothing too deep regarding grief and loss or traumatic experiences that I had encountered in my life.

Back home I slowly woke up to the fact that although TRC cleared me to return to anesthesia, the universe had other plans. After sixteen months of grappling with returning to the OR and working on my recovery, Dr. Ken Thompson and Dr. Mark Gold offered this phoenix a suitable pile of ashes from which to rise: a slot in the addiction medicine fellowship at the University of Florida. Again some solid training, but looking back, something was missing. I was fortunate to be offered the medical directorship at a community-based addiction treatment facility and poured everything I had into helping people heal from this life-destroying disease. But a few years into my addiction medicine career I was beginning to flame out. "Why aren't people getting better?" I'd whine, forgetting, as Lois pointed out to Bill W. decades earlier, "at least the work seems to be keeping you sober."

About that time, several things happened: I juiced up my self-care program immensely when my bride catalyzed my discovery of hot yoga; and I met an Irish-Canadian fellow (Murray Kelly) who introduced me to the concept that all therapy is basically grief work; that we experience transgenerational brokenness, delivered in the form of a vast array of traumas, and we operate in a wounded state stemming from our disconnection from ourselves and from the larger family of mankind. Medicating this condition with alcohol, drugs, and—perhaps most insidiously of all—tobacco, now became perfectly understandable, and it opened me to the fact that given the depth of treatment we were offering to patients, it was no wonder that our recovery rates were what they were.

And then the call came—Judy Crane wanted me to take a look at her treatment center. I may have been primed for this career move, but I still had a lot to learn. I remember a family-week group that I sat in on shortly after I arrived, where all the patients were introducing themselves and saying why they came to seek treatment with Judy. I heard much that was familiar, "I'm addicted to this," "I'm addicted to that," but then also a few adding "self-harm, sex addiction, gambling" or, even more jarring to my ears, stating that they were in treatment solely "for trauma."

What Judy slowly showed me was that the traumas we experience are the core drivers of our pain, of our dis-ease with life, and that it bubbled up as addiction to substances, but also addiction to processes that the brain finds rewarding or at least numbing (sex, overeating, gambling, video gaming, et al.). There can seemingly even be addiction to mood states and things classified as behavioral disorders. Judy showed me that, unless you understand the trauma that is foundational to the pain that drives all those behaviors, your chance of changing them is frustratingly small indeed. I love that Judy reframed for me the highly shaming diagnosis of "borderline"* as so often being unresolved trauma in disguise.

What working in the house that Judy built has done for me has deepened the clarity that I have in seeing that we're all connected, we're all really the same. I've still got a ways to go but I'm sure that it's made me a better son, a better brother, a better husband, a better father, a better coworker, and a better doctor. It taught me what Fred Rogers (of Mister Rogers' Neighborhood) had learned: that there isn't anyone you couldn't learn to love if you just knew their story.

---

* Note from Judy: Borderline personality disorder has shamed clients for years with the prognosis of never being able to heal when, in fact, this and all of the personality behaviors are weapons to give protection and relief to the wounded. The signs and symptoms of personality behaviors can be recognized as the armor that a survivor dons for protection, which also interferes with the ability to be in healthy relationships. When the armor becomes so entrenched that a therapist can't find a way in, then the behavior becomes a personality disorder.

I invite clinicians to compare the signs and symptoms of trauma and PTSD with personality disorders and contrast and compare. Which came first? If it was trauma, then we may have the opportunity to help our clients heal, if we are willing to do loving battle with the armor.

REFLECTION SKETCHES

❧

1) Think of the sights, smells, tastes, sounds, and sixth sense that you
   can recall that represent your life events. It might be the smell of the
   kitchen when your mother baked chocolate-chip cookies; the smell
   of boiled vegetables while visiting your grandmother's nursing home;
   the smell of mothballs at your favorite childhood caretaker's garage
   apartment. It might be the sound of a truck on the highway on a
   quiet summer night; the sound of a voice raised in anger. It might be
   the sight of a little girl in red tights. You get the idea.

   _____

   _____

   _____

   _____

   _____

   _____

2) Where do you feel these "senses" in your body? What memories
   come to the surface? What are you feeling?

   _____

   _____

   _____

   _____

   _____

3) Close your eyes and imagine your safe place, where you felt
   protected. It could be the ocean, deep in the woods, your
   grandmother's kitchen, your grandfather's garden, or even a Bruce
   Springsteen concert. Notice the feeling in your body; notice your
   breathing. Journal about these.

_____

_____

_____

_____

_____

4) Think of the movies that you relate to, that represent your life or
   events in your life. Write a movie screenplay of your life or an event
   in your life. Choose the actors to play the significant people in your
   life and yourself. What movies heal you? What movies make you
   anxious? Explore through journaling why this is.

_____

_____

_____

_____

_____

CHAPTER

3

MORAL INJURY: THE SOUL WOUND

"Forces beyond your control can take away everything you possess except one thing, your freedom to choose how you will respond to the situation."

— Viktor E Frankl

❦

Over the years I've tried to explain and describe what a *soul wound* is. I can only get close to its essence through movies, music, theater, art, and other sensory, ephemeral explanations.

Recently, however, my soul has been brutalized and bloodied by reports in the media on wars and terror attacks, natural disasters, and painful visions of the world in trauma.

My vision of the soul wound is in the terrified or empty eyes of the children who are experiencing the horrors of the world. Those children who bear the outward wounds and filth of a world that allows babies to be harmed in even the tiniest of ways, let alone to bear the burden war—the insanity of others—on their tiny shoulders.

The eyes of the children speak to me of the wounding of a soul. When we are abandoned, neglected, abused, or experience any of the myriad of traumas I've described, imagine or envision the eyes of the children. No matter how old we are when grief comes knocking, it is that wounded child who steps up and receives another layer of pain. The soul wound is found in the eyes, experienced in the heart, and throughout the viscera. The soul wound is sometimes quiet and hidden, silenced, and sometimes it screams and screeches and appears bloodied, begging to be acknowledged.

The soul wound is inflicted by betrayal and shame, fear and diminishment. It is a wound so deep that sometimes we don't even know it is there.

Our Deepest Fear

Our deepest fear is not that we are inadequate. Our deepest
fear is that we are powerful beyond measure. It is our light,
not our darkness that most frightens us. We ask ourselves,
'Who am I to be brilliant, gorgeous, talented fabulous?'
Actually, who are you not to be? You are a child of God.
Your playing small does not serve the world. There is nothing
enlightened about shrinking so that other people won't feel
insecure around you. We are all meant to shine, as children do.
We were born to make manifest the glory of God that is within
us. It's not just in some of us; it's in everyone. And as we let our
own light shine, we unconsciously give other people permission
to do the same. As we are liberated from our own fear,
our presence automatically liberates others.

—Marianne Williamson, *A Return to Love*

Marianne Williamson is a visionary, a healer, and a talented teacher with profound depth of character. She has taken her history and turned it into a life-changing, world-changing opportunity for others. Nelson Mandela used this brilliant and insightful "deepest fear" quote as part of his inauguration speech. Like-minded and kindred spirits intuitively grasp the truth of this inspiring message.

Research surrounding PTSD and trauma has indicated that traumatic events impact the very essence of a person's vision of the world and their place in it. Early childhood trauma affects the attachment process and can create a lifetime of relationship difficulties, which can begin in utero and be intergenerational. This leaves many trauma survivors searching for a place to belong; attempting to find a tribe, and to find meaning for their lives, often the military, as first responders, in the church or religious organizations, and often even in gangs.

Traumatic events can impinge on the spiritual, moral, ethical boundaries, and limits of a victim's soul. This is *moral* injury, whether imposed by another's behavior, the code of the tribe, or their own step outside of their moral beliefs. This damage to a person's vision of themselves becomes far more damaging than the original traumatic assault.

When my husband overdosed and died, I embraced my responsibility that I didn't save him, that it was my fault that he died. I swam in the deep and muddy waters of shame, remorse, regret, and deep, deep sorrow, believing I was beyond evil and there was no redemption for me. I lived in my addiction for another fifteen years, never sharing with another soul the nature of my wrongs and the deeply held guilt. Fifteen years later, when I read my life story to my group of seven men and our counselor—my confession and all of the actions and behaviors, the pain and brutality throughout my life—I read it like a shopping list, with no emotion. I could always give "the list."

I finished and looked up to see tears rolling down the faces of those men. They were crying for me when I could not, would not, cry for myself. They heard my confession and absolved me of my sins. I will be forever grateful for those tears. *That* is the power of the group. Now I can hold sacred space for others and allow tears to flow. That was the beginning of my own trauma work and the healing path of my family.

Traumatic events often create the impetus for coping/survival behaviors and mechanisms such as substance abuse, process addictions, and presumed mental health disorders such as depression, anxiety, OCD, ADHD and bipolar disorder, to name a few. Many of these diagnoses can be traced back to the original trauma event; they become exacerbated by ongoing layers of trauma. Add to this moral injury and it creates a therapeutic challenge for trauma resolution. A timeline created by a client illustrates very strongly the concept of moral injury.

BRADFORD'S STORY:
A BURST OF LIGHT

The following gorgeous work is a timeline created by a client who is also a wonderful therapist, who has experienced moral injury to his core. For years he hid the depth of his struggle even as he helped so many other wounded people as a talented therapist. This beautiful, sensitive, brilliant man has suffered with multiple sclerosis for a very long time, ultimately in a wheelchair with little hope of leaving the chair. This man came to the forest and continued to fight for his place in the world. And fight he did, moving from the chair to crutches to a cane.

The rapport that he developed with his trauma therapist was awe-inspiring. As they partnered in the healing process, he was challenged over and over again to deny and refute the guilt and shame that he carried as a survivor, to understand that there had been a moral injury perpetrated on him over and over again by a cruel and heinous man. The gorgeousness of his timeline belies enough the evil that others imposed on him. You will also see masks that he created later in the book. This is a man who walks today without crutches or a cane. It was stress hormones that made it possible for MS to ravage his body and, as he has found resolution in so many areas, his physical body is healing along with his mind and spirit.

On the pages that follow, Bradford describes the artistic representation of his journey, from trauma to healing.

Panel One

1) Timeline starts from a burst of light (my birth).
2) The three trees represent me and my siblings (older sibling born in July, me in November, and youngest in January. So, the three trees show each season.
3) The two guys in cowboy hats represent my first perpetrators (first two of five). Our parents were best friends, and all worked horses together. These two brothers were sixteen and eighteen, and I was five.
4) The Bud Light bottle represents the alcohol that the two brothers used to help "calm me down," or "get me more in the mood for it." Again, age five.

5) The arm reaching up out of the "river" of alcohol represents a sixteen-year-old girl who drowned less than 10 yards from me in the river, shortly after she took me to the shore for my own safety. I was five.

6) There is a coiled-up snake. I have the "Black Irish Luck," and have been bitten four times by poisonous snakes over the years. Copperhead at age four to five, cottonmouth at twelve, and two times by a timber rattlesnake at thirty-seven.

7) The bleeding hand . . . this is a toughie. When the two brothers initially started raping me, I screamed and fought back. Repeatedly they threatened me. If I didn't "play along" or "calm down," they were going to "Show me what real pain was." They told me that they would make sure "I never scratched, or fought back" again. So, after I scratched the oldest brother on his chest, they held me down and drove a nail through my hand into a board. They had stuffed my mouth with a sock (I think). I was in absolute shock, and quite honestly numb to the fact that they went ahead and continued raping me, while I was nailed to a board. Again, I was five.

(Note how the yellow river of beer/alcohol turns to a red river of blood. I primarily did this because the blood represented pain/shame/distrust that carried with me throughout my life.)

Panel Two

1) You can see in the upper left-hand corner a pill bottle. Somewhere around the age of seven, the two brothers had me take acid, "rush," cocaine (once, it didn't do very well with me at this age), a variety of pills, marijuana, and even "shrooms." (The mushrooms made me vomit. I didn't have to do it again.) The main pills that "worked" on me, for their purposes, were the pain pills and benzodiazepines. Of course, alcohol was always used on me and really became one of my closest friends. It helped numb me out and cope with it all. This all started between ages six and seven, and continued weekly, until they stopped the first years of the rapes when I was about twelve or thirteen.

2) Lower left-hand side represents my "Keeper of My Night Terrors," My mouth is covered because I was taught from the earliest years to keep *everything a secret*—no matter what. Lie, cheat, whatever, just never tell what you know.

3) The minister baptizing in the river represents my loss of all trust/belief in the institution of organized religion. In fact, the minister doesn't baptize these people; he drowns them. Their drawings represent how perverse the church leaders and hypocritical people are. I would rather believe in a flower; its beauty is real. Oh, did I happen to mention that the oldest of the two brothers became a minister (yet, he later rapes me for an additional six years from sixteen to twenty-two) and during my three-year break from the brothers, they told another eighteen-year-old in the Protestant church they attended, and he lured me out for a "fun night of mudding" in his huge, yellow, jacked-up pick-up truck, only he took me out to a dried-up lake and raped me. He went on to rape me for about a year. Later on, he was convicted of raping six local boys and given forty years in prison. I was number seven, but no one knew, because I lied to the cops when they asked. After all, I

was trained early on how to keep secrets. I was quiet, depressed, and drinking (secretly, of course). Then, things started to look up! I got a job—working at the local Catholic church. However, I had to quit after a month of working, because the priest had me and another boy do sexual favors for him. The other boy went on to "live" with this priest, because his home life was so chaotic and not a "good environment." I say all of this to explain why I have such distrust and hurt, when it comes to the institution of the church, or religious people (no matter what faith).

4) The bent license plate represents a car wreck that left me in a coma for quite some time. The recuperation period was almost a year. During that year, mainly because of my quiet disposition and obvious depression/anger that I had along with the physical problems, I was recommended to a psychiatrist. This psychiatrist saw me twice a month for over two years. He dove into a lot of my rapes, and any/all sexual areas of my life. He knew everything about me. Abruptly, his office called and said that I had been "Discharged from his care. If I needed further assistance, they could give me referral contacts." I thought that I had done something wrong. Less than a month later, he called my house and asked me if I would like to join him and other men, who would be working on his lake house. Said he knew I could use the extra money for school. I agreed and went. There were no other men. There was no work. He knew exactly what he was doing; he was my fifth and final perpetrator. These rapes went on for almost a year. Many years later, he had a stroke. His oldest son and daughter-in-law asked me to join them at the lake house. I had horrible reservations, but I went. They knew everything. In fact, they had seen everything. The psychiatrist had secretly video recorded *all* of his sexual exploits. I was only one of many, and many of those were his clients. We destroyed the tapes, and I dove deeper into my shame, blame, anger, drinking, and using. I'm saying all of this to point out: who the hell could I trust?

5) So, above in the painting, there is my grandmother who took me in at twelve. She and my grandfather took me in, because they said "There are only so many 'accidents' a child can have." They knew there was abuse, but had no idea how bad. My grandmother helped me see the beautiful things: flowers, nature, unconditional love. The skeleton on a horse (right-hand corner) represents Death. My grandfather died when I was twelve, crushing my world. He was the only positive male role model I had.

6) The bird hunting represents the fun activities that my grandmother helped me to find and enjoy, especially hunting and fishing. They were escapes from everything else, especially the bad.

7) The kangaroos represent my process addiction with sexual addiction. Between all of the rapes and trying to date, I have always maintained a very open relationship to the idea of being bisexual. Others may judge me for this, but they have not walked in my shoes. I had no choice to the traumas that I suffered. However, I have had choice in seeking trauma repetition in an effort to find that level of intensity. That has been a choice. My favorite phrase is "Labels are for clothes." I simply say, "Yes, I am sexual." My therapist once told me, "I believe that you would fuck a kangaroo if it came hopping across the

campus, if you could catch it!" My response was, "How fast is it hopping?" So, to this day, he always asks me how things are going with the kangaroos.

8) The two turtle doves represent one of the happiest points in my life, my marriage.

9) The butterfly represents the birth of our daughter. In the midst of five miscarriages, having our daughter was a huge blessing.

Panel Three

1) The pocket watch and chain, represent *time* and you will notice they cross over to each panel.

2) This panel is where I try to show in my timeline how things are starting to come together, get resolved, and simply look brighter.

3) The pig with wings on the launch pad represents the fact that someone said that I would get clean and sober, "When pigs fly!" Well, after thirty-nine years of using, I am now three-and-a-half years sober!

4) The two boys at the river represent my Inner Child and my Hero (this person has changed over the years . . . it might be Billy . . . and then the next month, it might be Mark. . . . And the list goes on. My Hero is now any positive male that I can find, respect, love and know that he will help my Inner Child recover from all of the men who have abused me in life). The Hero helps the Inner Child to let go of things/feelings/thoughts that have been haunting the Inner Child, such as "Ego, Hurt, Anger, Fear and Shame." As the Inner Child and Hero release these boats of trauma . . . the boats go down the river . . . and the blood turns back to normal . . . the blue-green river water and the boats are eaten by a Florida alligator!

5) Elton John singing and playing the piano, represent my mantra "How *wonderful life is* while you're in the *world!*" I was asked by my therapist to pick a theme or mantra that I would like to use as my own personal life/attitude goal. I became suicidal. In fact, had several attempts. I mean, why the fuck not? Look at this "fun life" that I had been put through. That was the way I thought. I believed that I deserved any and all bad that could ever come my way. I was damaged goods. I can't really say that I loved anyone else, not really. How could I? I fucking hated myself. Then, with many, many years of help, I know that *life is wonderful* as long as I'm in the *world!*

6) The rose garden and stone with *joy* on it represent my meditation garden, where I spend many hours doing meaningless things, and loving the fact that I am able to be present with myself. I am *beautifully* made, and I am *worthy*—just as I am today!

7) The Wilson volleyball by the garden represents how a lot of people say that they have all of these tons and tons of awesome friends (when the reality of their entourage of friends is *not* that loyal a group of friends at all). All I need is Wilson! Give me one or two good friends, and I am incredibly blessed. I have learned (by harsh lessons) that *not* everyone deserves my trust, friendship, or my time. I don't wish them ill; I just wish them to stay "over there!"

8) The boy meditating toward the "Sun of a Bright Future," represents me finding these new enjoyments of life . . . at the middle of my life. I never painted. I never gardened. I never did meditation. Shit, I was too busy getting high and drunk, running from perpetrators and police! (All of this is to say I learned that I am never too old to find happiness, peace, and enjoyment.)

9) All of the items in the far right-hand side (the gnome, cat, jackass in a suit, and sign) were all ways that I was able to take a stressful situation at the time and make fun with them. The jackass represents the corporate part of the business world. You can put a suit on a jackass any day and call it COB (Chief Officer of the Barn)—he's still just a jackass in a suit!

10) The sign represents any and all roads where I've traveled, and really do not want to travel again. Lessons learned! "Dangerous Road! Watch for potholes, sinkholes, and assholes!"

11) Finally, above Elton John's piano, you see a man, facing the future, butt/ass naked, arms raised up in the air, saying, "Well future, here I am! Bring it!" And a key point worth noting: on this wise man's ass, which is facing the past, is a tattoo of a pair of lips! (Which is Beagan, but now I have the same tattoo! *Ha!*) Those pair of lips are letting the past know exactly how the new me feels about the past and how I am looking to a brighter day ahead!

A Spiritual Dilemma

Moral injury, the soul wound, creates a spiritual dilemma and as clinicians we must face this with a very full toolbox which includes healing and cleansing ceremonies. The shininess of our spirit begins to tarnish with each assault on our sense of self. Spirit becomes tarnished, dulled by deep pain, sorrow, and doubt about the essence of our goodness. Self-doubt and low self-esteem enter our spirit and cast a darkness that must be lifted to heal, then polished vigorously so we can once again share our shiny brilliance, and claim or reclaim the essence of who we authentically are.

The term *moral injury* is believed to have been first used during the Vietnam War by marine veteran and peace advocate Camillo Bica,

PhD, who wrote and spoke about moral injury experienced by soldiers as a result of their actions, or being powerless over the actions of others, that were outside their personal moral/spiritual boundaries.

As a result of Vietnam, PTSD and moral injury have been explored, researched, written and spoken about. This has led to an understanding of the impact on humans and humanity. We will discuss both, define both, and see where they come together and where they must be treated differently.

In an article appearing on the website of the National Center for PTSD entitled "Moral Injury in the Context of War" by Shira Maguen, PhD, and Brett Litz, PhD, moral injury was described this way:

> Like psychological trauma, moral injury is a construct that describes extreme and unprecedented life experience including the harmful aftermath of exposure to such events. Events are considered morally injurious if they "transgress deeply held moral beliefs and expectations." Thus the key precondition for moral injury is an act of transgression, which shatters moral and ethical expectations that are rooted in religious or spiritual beliefs, or culture-based, organizational, group-based rules about fairness, the value of life, and so forth.

In findings from The Moral Injury Project at Syracuse University, researchers Kent Drescher, David Foy, Caroline Kelly, Anna Leshner, Kerrie Schutz, and Brett Litz defined moral injury as "disruption in an individual's confidence about one's own or others' motivation or capacity to behave in a just and ethical manner."

Drs. Maguen and Litz determined that the aftermath of moral injury may result in "highly aversive and haunting states of inner conflict and turmoil including: shame, which stems from global

self-attribution 'I am an evil, terrible person; I am unforgiveable,'"
and guilt.

Other symptoms they report include anxiety about possible consequences, and anger about betrayal-based moral injuries. Typical
behaviors can include:

➡ Alienation/social instability caused by breakdown in standards
  and values
➡ Withdrawal and self-condemnation
➡ Self-harming (for example, suicidal ideation or attempts)
➡ Self-handicapping behaviors (for example, alcohol or drug use,
  self-sabotaging relationships, etc.)

Maguen and Litz go on to say moral injury has been posited to
result in re-experiencing, emotional numbing, and avoidance symptoms of PTSD. In addition to grave suffering, these manifestations
of moral injury may lead to under- or unemployment, and failed or
harmed relationships with loved ones and friends. PTSD and moral
injury overlap, but moral injury can stand alone. As an industry
we *must* begin to understand the healing process for moral injury
(whether standing alone or in concert with PTSD), and the very serious consequences of not addressing it and finding resolution.

Almost all of the research is based on the experience of combat
veterans, but I would like to offer my experience with moral injury
in survivors of trauma. We have a long and deep and healing history
working with veterans, and that has led to my conclusion that moral
injury impacts many trauma survivors, usually those with the deepest shame and guilt; often those who cannot see or believe in their
innate goodness; typically those with a higher moral, ethical, and
spiritual code that they believe to their core that they have broken

and dishonored, and thus are beyond redemption. What are those horrendous acts that they believe they have committed?

1) Heading the list is childhood sexual abuse, the moral injury experienced by the child. Very young children have a sense of right and wrong, and good and bad. Although they are the victims, and the injury has been perpetrated upon the child, children nevertheless embrace the concept of their "wrongness," their own evil. The child may not even have the words but the assault is embraced as their fault. Too often the perpetrator reinforces that belief with statements such as these:

> It's your fault, you made me do it.
>
> You have bad blood.
>
> You wanted it.
>
> If you don't come with me, I'll take your sister, brother.
>
> I'll kill your family.
>
> No one will believe you; they know you're bad.

A child embraces that guilt and shame and believes they have sinned, and they are haunted by sorrow, believing they are not worthy.

2) Abortion. Many years later clients come to us who have had abortions and are in such pain, believing they can never be forgiven.

Often when a woman is sharing her painful story, the men in the group will break down and talk about the abortions they insisted on, not supporting the mother, or not being told about the pregnancy/their child until after the abortion. Sharing that pain, shame, and guilt can be cathartic, especially when we add a cleansing ceremony.

3) Other events that create moral injury are injuring or killing another human being, or being unable to save someone.

4) Giving up a child or being forced to give up a child.

5) Often adoptees embrace the deep primal wound of being given up.

6) Starting someone else on drugs. Witnessing an overdose or suicide.

7) Infidelity or keeping the secret of infidelity for a parent.

8) Survivor's guilt for surviving when others did not.

These are all moral, spiritual dilemmas and there are others that can be added to the list. Moral injury creates a deep sadness and sorrow, a belief that one can never be forgiven.

Overdoses and suicides have grown at an alarming rate. I believe trauma survivors who attempt or commit suicide often are in this very deep, dark place of inability to forgive themselves, and they also believe that their God could never forgive them. Moral injury was originally defined as a result of veterans' experiences. I propose that just as the military helped us to see the universality of PTSD, so can we see that moral injury spans all sectors of trauma. As clinicians I would pray that we look more closely at that spiritual belief that drives our clients to despair—the soul wound. We can create an opportunity for a state of confession and self-forgiveness, for cleansing, healing, ceremony, and for forgiveness.

Addicts who enter a twelve-step program are asked to do the "steps." Step Four invites us to write a searching and fearless moral inventory; Step Five asks us to admit to God, ourselves, and another human being the exact nature of our wrongs. For many this is the beginning of the "sunlight of the spirit" entering our lives. But many others are terrified of this step and never get there, continuing to be mired in guilt and shame. It's just the beginning of the journey of trauma resolution.

As trauma therapists, we provide slow and steady intensive treatment, building rapport and trust, remaining without judgement, and being present as a witness in a safe and loving space. In that space, survivors may begin to heal.

That moral injury that so many experience is *never* spoken until finally someone asks the questions: What are the things that you believe you can never be forgiven? What does that mean about your place in the world, your vision of yourself? The answers to these questions may change the course of someone's life.

David Wood has written an incisive and compelling series in the Huffington Post titled "A Warrior's Moral Dilemma." It speaks to the reality of the overwhelming numbers of our troops who experience not only PTSD but moral injury, and the toll that this takes on veterans and their families.

I invite you to see trauma survivors, particularly those with layers upon layers of trauma complicated with moral injury, as the warriors that they are. Their stories and their work will provide a vivid picture of the courage it takes to walk through the morass of complicated grief and fear. Many, if not most, of our combat veterans become members of this tribe.

I would also suggest that the families of trauma survivors experience their own level of PTSD as they attempt to understand the changes in mood and behaviors in their loved one. Often they see the behaviors in moral terms—good or bad, right or wrong—when in fact they are survival, soothing behaviors. As we work with trauma we *must* include the family. There are so many puzzle pieces that begin to fit together when we explore generational and intergenerational histories, and examine traumatic events that may be two to three generations back; yet they continue to impact families in the present.

For instance, I would like to see a survey or research project identifying the number of veterans of Iraq/Afghanistan whose parent was in Vietnam, grandparents or relatives who may have been in World War II, and the impact that had on their lives as children and adolescents, their emotional connection with those family members, the messages they received. I've found a pattern of trauma reenactment among the vets I've worked with. Granted, that's a relatively small number but I wonder . . . If we were to do a large study I believe it would be eye-opening. I believe that this is an international/universal phenomenon.

David Wood writes, "It is what experts are coming to identify as moral injury; the pain that results from damage to a person's moral foundation. In contrast to Post-Traumatic Stress Disorder, which springs from fear, moral injury is a violation of what each of us considers right or wrong."

Wood continues: The diagnosis of PTSD has been defined and officially endorsed since 1980 by the mental health community, and those suffering from it have earned broad public sympathy and understanding. Moral injury is not officially recognized by the Defense Department."

Wood continues, "It is not fear but exposure that causes moral injury—an experience or set of experiences that can provoke mild or intense grief, shame and guilt. The symptoms are similar to PTSD: depression and anxiety, difficulty paying attention, an unwillingness to trust anyone except fellow combat veterans. (A trauma bond is created.) But the morally injured feel sorrow and regret, too. Theirs are impact wounds caused by the collision of the ethical beliefs they carried to war and the ugly realities of conflict." (The drive to survive.)

In 2014, David Wood wrote that "the definition of Post-Traumatic Stress Disorder doesn't cover all the symptoms of moral injury, the lasting wounds to the soul caused by participation in morally ambiguous combat events." The diagram Wood created identifies the symptoms of each, and those that overlap.

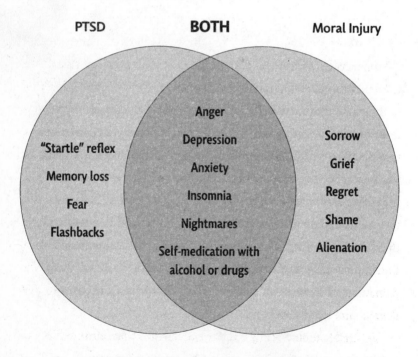

I would also add that PTSD in the military still carries an enormous stigma, which is often why so many do not seek treatment.

If they do, sometimes they avoid the VA for fear of stigma on their record or reputation.

So for all of our warriors—military, refugees, or victims of sexual abuse, abandonment and neglect, medical issues, domestic violence, natural disasters, and the multitude of other traumatic events—our role is to recognize the differences between PTSD and moral injury, and the areas where they overlap, to create the appropriate healing modalities and experience. This is illustrated in Wood's diagram on the previous page.

Warriors All

Some may criticize that my proposition demeans the experience of veterans, however, those warriors relate at a very intimate level to the pain, sorrow, remorse, and horrendous, terrifying, and de-humanizing stories of their peers. In intense trauma treatment groups, they share the experience of body memories, flashbacks, and hyper-vigilance: sitting close to a door with back against the wall anticipating the next assault, vivid nightmares, endless sleepless nights, and night terrors. Whether veteran or traumatized child who's now an adult, they are disabled by these experiences, unable to form trusting relationships, forced to create other coping/survival skills to numb the pain, often suicidal or in suicidal ideation, and both convinced that they are not worthy to be forgiven.

Vets relate to and recognize the universality and commonality of events, the emotional and visceral response to those events, and they share the courage and drive to survive and heal with other trauma clients. The group encourages and challenges one another to look at all the layers of their lives, including combat. A group process is a rich and vital part of trauma resolution. Just as veterans opened the world's eyes to PTSD, so now can they open our eyes to the depth of moral injury that consumes most wounded survivors.

The trauma-healing model we've embraced has been expanded and creates an additional layer of the healing process. We often speak of forgiving *yourself*, perhaps without fully understanding the depth of what that means. I invite survivors, families, clinicians, and recovering people everywhere to embrace our responsibility and awareness of moral injury and the part it plays in the lives of survivors.

As illustrated on David Wood's diagram, both PTSD and moral injury share the signs and symptoms of anger, depression, anxiety, insomnia, nightmares, and self-medication with alcohol and drugs. To these I would add all substance and process addictions such as sex and relationship addiction, gambling, eating disorders, self-harming behaviors, and any compulsive behaviors that flood the brain with soothing neurotransmitters. Also mood disorders, which often become the place of comfortable un-comfortability, are familiar friends for many trauma victims. I rarely see a person with just one survival/coping mechanism.

Wood indicates that PTSD symptoms also include a "startle" reflex, memory loss, fear, and flashbacks, and that moral injury includes sorrow, grief, regret, shame, and alienation. Without research to prove it, I believe through plenty of first-person anecdotal experience with clients, that there is much more of an overlap for PTSD beyond the visceral, cellular symptoms. I believe anger and rage often hide sadness or sorrow, and depression can be anger or remorse turned inward. Again, I have no proof, just years of observation. It's in the relationship that we build with clients that leads us to ask the deeper spiritual identity questions that may lead to forgiveness and redemption. After hearing their trauma stories, I'm astounded that they survived. I ask, "How did you survive all of that? Who were the people, animals, places, and things that helped to raise you up, help you to survive?" These are the same questions I would ask any warrior.

So what does moral injury and the healing from moral injury look and sound like? I offer you the work of several people who willingly offered their very personal and deep healing work, hoping to give at least one person hope, which would make it feel worthwhile.

The first work is done by Kate, a young woman who had been in multiple treatment centers and struggled greatly with substance abuse and self-harming behaviors. She was angry and acting out in destructive behaviors. As you view her art—poignant, visceral, haunting—and read her letters to her "Little Me," it becomes clear why her struggles have been so endless. I won't tell her story because she gives an emotional and incisive view of her path herself. This client worked hard to push people away, to be thrown away again, which is the reason a good trauma therapist fights for the time it takes to build trust with such a wounded person. It takes time and a lot of energy and engaging the community in building empathy and boundary setting. Discharge cannot be the first or second choice in most cases.

During treatment, clients are going to act out and this is what a good treatment center wants the client to do. This way, the therapist can work on the underlying issues causing the acting out. So, discharge for acting out in most cases is not the go-to recourse of a good treatment center.

KATE'S STORY:
DEAR LITTLE ME

Dear Little Me,

Hey there kiddo. *This letter is kind of hard to write . . . I'm so hard on myself, and at the moment feel a little silly. But I think you deserve to hear this. I want you to know that I'm proud of you. You endured so much crap and pain. You were so strong, stronger than I ever realized. Know that what those men did to you wasn't your fault. I know that you've questioned so many things. Did you turn him on? Did you actually want it? Was it your fault? No child, you did nothing to deserve those awful things. They were sick, nasty, twisted men and women. They made you believe it was your fault, so that way you wouldn't tell. Things were taken from you. You were robbed. You weren't left with a choice. They controlled you. You were just an innocent little girl, who up until the age of five knew nothing but Barbie dolls, Power Rangers, Barney, painting nails, playing in the dirt, jumping in the leaves, and being silly. Then someone took that innocence away. One after another they stripped it from you, causing you to grow up way too fast.*

You started drowning yourself in every activity you could: Girl Scouts, church activities, Lads to Leaders, piano, and the biggest thing: sports. Sports became your life, your escape. And you were good at them, especially softball and volleyball. You always had people there cheering you on, and teams were scared to go up against you. You practiced all the time to make sure you were good. It was a great release and distraction. Something you could control.

You also made good grades in school. I know you felt like you had to be perfect at things, but it is okay that you made mistakes every now and then. Nobody is perfect. I'm proud of you for the grades and succeeding at sports. But even if you didn't have those, I'd still be proud. I'm more proud of you for surviving, for doing whatever it took to live through all of that. You were brave. You were brave to take on as much as possible and lessen the load for others. You were brave to pull the trigger on yourself. I know you wish that you could've protected your sister more, but sweetie, there was no way; you couldn't. He controlled you, you didn't have a choice. I know you think there must've been some way, but there wasn't. You did your best. You kept her safe as long as you could; you saved her from the "worst" of it. Even if you had said "No," he would've just beaten you and still gotten to her . . . he always got what he wanted. So I'm proud of you for doing what you could. I'm not disappointed in you. I love you. I'm sorry that so many things happened to you, I really am. I'm sorry that nobody stepped in and protected you. That nobody saw through your shields. No kid should ever have to endure the things you went through. I wish you would've gotten more hugs and more I love you's. You could've used a few more.

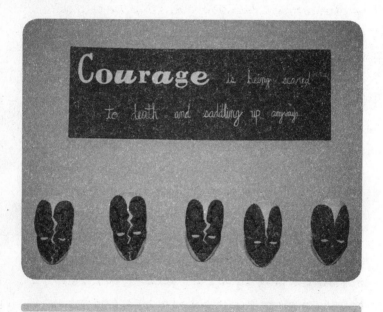

Here's another story written as part of a treatment assignment, graciously shared by Kylie.

KYLIE'S STORY:
AM I WORTHY?

Am I worthy? If so, why? When am I . . . all the time or sometimes? What am I worthy of? Was I more or less worthy in the past or present?

There are so many times when I don't feel worthy, of anything. The voices and the lies come back repeatedly telling me that I'm worthless, useless, damaged—not good enough. But then, when I pull myself out of that cycle and take a step back, I realize that all those words are lies. Nasty, filthy lies that put your self-esteem and self-worth in the toilet. I know deep down that I'm worthy. I'm worth more than silver or gold, or any dollar sign. I'm worthy of love and respect. I deserve to be treated right, with compassion, kindness, gentleness, and patience. I'm worth the encouragement. I'm worth people's time. Why? Well, first of all because I'm a human being just like everybody else . . . no greater, no less. Just like everybody.

I long for that intimate relationship with people. I long for closeness, acceptance, and love. I deserve to be seen as equal, not as somebody to be run over and trampled on. I feel worth people's time and them taking a chance on me because I truly do want to do better. I want to heal. I want to be healthy. I want to be free.

I'm working hard and trying my best. Things don't always click the first go-around, and I know sometimes I can be stubborn, but I eventually get it. I don't just goof off all the time. I'm not wasting the help. I listen intently and try to soak everything in. I'm worthy because I know deep down, I'm a good person. I'm compassionate, *empathetic, loving, caring, a good listener, trustworthy, honest, usually patient, encouraging, and hopeful. I want to be able to help people. I want to take what I've already learned, and am continuing to learn, and pay it forward. I want to help people be the best they can be and have a better life.*

I also think I'm worthy because I'm a child of God. I'm his daughter. No matter what happens on this Earth, I will always be his; he won't leave me and will always love me. He tells me I'm worth it. He sent his son to die for me, so I can be with him someday. He wants a relationship with me. The creator of all things, wants a relationship with me! I don't feel worth that, but because of that, I know I am. There's nothing greater than that.

Logically, I know that I've been worthy my whole life. But then my head gets in the way. I was worth everything before age five. From ages five to fourteen, I honestly don't know. There's a part of me that knows I was worthy and deserved better than how I was treated. But then the other part of me feels like I wasn't worth shit. But that time frame screws with my head a lot. And now I'm starting to feel worth it again. Feel worth time, intimacy, and love. I'm worthy.

We expect clients to act out in survival behaviors, especially in treatment. We have taken away their substances and invited them to go to the pain. Self-soothing is the rule of thumb, the rule of survival for trauma survivors. We expect clients to relapse in eating disorders, self-harm, sex and relationship addiction. The work is much more intense for staff but the payoff of recognizing how our people protect from the pain is a juicy therapeutic opportunity to prevent relapse by identifying *all* the behaviors that pop up. Rarely have I witnessed just substance abuse, or just sex addiction, or relationship addiction, or just eating disorders, or self-harm. We have many ways to protect ourselves from pain. In recovery I buy shoes, lots of shoes, and my neurotransmitters pop and ping in the same way; and I get relief from fear, loneliness, and insecurity.

I would venture that relationships and sex addiction, but more so relationships, are the number-one precursor to relapse because disordered attachment and inadequate socialization drives much of our trauma responses. The relationship between a baby and its caretaker determines the child's ability to attach to others in a healthy way. If a healthy, secure attachment is not created, then the attachment style is "disordered." Hence, clients reach out to other clients in attempt for connection. There's a saying among trauma residents: "Wounded people wound people," and so rarely do those "treatment romances" heal one another. But once again, a seasoned trauma therapist can create an opportunity to connect the original traumas with the drive for relationship, any relationship, and more often than not, a replica of the original wounding. If we discharged those folks they would go on to the next treatment center and repeat the pattern again and again.

Excellent trauma treatment is intense, exhausting, riveting, and rewarding beyond measure. But the commitment to do this work at the necessary level and the intimacy with trauma is often too intense for many programs. I applaud them for knowing what they do well and staying in integrity. Trauma work is a new level of commitment. A trauma program cannot be just one or two groups a week; it must be immersed in the milieu and it must contain visceral, cellular, sensory, body-centered, experiential modalities. The can include modalities such as psychodrama, Somatic Experiencing, art therapy, and music therapy, to name a few. The clinical staff needs to include experts in eating disorders, self-harm, sex and love addiction, and substance abuse. All should be cross-trained to understand each of those areas at a more granular level. That means everyone trained in trauma, Somatic Experience, and several in brain spotting and EMDR, psychodrama, and equine-assisted ceremonies of many cultures for cleansing (created by David Grand as an additional somatic therapy), lifting up, forgiveness, atonement, and the opportunity to find a spiritual path if possible for the individual.

Some more works from clients who have had soul wounds and moral injury follow.

Kylie's Poem

I am chained to a hate of some kind I lost myself that day

I lost all trust

It was all too much for my heart to take

Too much for my mind to forget

Will it ever erase?

I'm lonely inside

Even though you can't always tell I'm reaching out

For what . . . a hand, love, acceptance, and understanding

I'm trapped inside my own mind I've felt the strength of demons

If God made the day

Then the devil made this night

My depression grows deeper

Pulling me apart at the seams

Causing me to unravel and fall to my knees

Wondering desperately, how much worse can it be?

So I'm alone again

Another night of crying
A night of hiding
Is this ever going to end

I look in the mirror every day and see a girl
A girl who is staring back at me
I don't know who she is anymore
Cause she's not the girl I wanna be

I try to hide the pain
And carry on
Don't let anybody see
That I'm not what I'm pretending to be

I put on a smile
When I'm falling apart I say, "I'm okay"
When really pain fills my heart

This young lady was able to go to the darkness and share her trauma story with her group, participate in psychodrama, Somatic Experiencing, and other experiential, visceral, cellular, sensory therapeutic interventions that took her to the five- to fourteen-year-old little girl, feeling the pain, confusion, anger, and shame, and have a cathartic release. The work continues and her ability to identify the woundedness is enabling her to begin to find her worth and value. As you can see with the progression of her words, she is slowly rubbing the tarnished spirit and finding, slowly, her shininess. That doesn't mean that she is "cured"; it means, like most of us, she is on the path. And she offered us her favorite quote by Marcus Aurelius, "The best revenge is to be unlike him who performed the injury."

I often approach clients by asking, "How are you feeling?" The response is often, "I'm in the black dot." (See page 124.) I share how proud I am of their courage, that they are embracing the feelings of pain. Only then can we be free of the shadow of our traumatic experiences. Feeling brings us through the fight, flight, and freeze process to resolution. The trauma doesn't go away but it has less power, less of a charge, and doesn't have to rule our life and choices or behaviors.

TESSA'S STORY:
BLOODY DIAPERS

"Bloody diapers, goddamned bloody diapers. I was just a little girl, scared and angry all the time. My three brothers and my drunken father, but I was just a little girl, only three years old.

As a therapist, what am I supposed to do with that? Where am I supposed to go with that ugly story? I never told, never told, not until you. Please help me!"

Tears spilling down her face as she panted through the terror. Her raging, sad eyes matched the wild and crazy black, curly hair. Tessa let her anger show, always loud, obnoxious, and rude. She never held her tongue; worked at pushing people away. It all makes sense, of course. How else could she protect herself? A chronic relapser, a respected professional, in and out of treatment.

She tells me, "I'm not ready to do this work yet, but my little girl in my soul is demanding help. What can I do?" Tessa told me what she needed—her little girl not to be angry or frightened. The answer came to me.

"Tessa write a letter, tell little Tessa how much you love her, that you will protect her, and that she has a right to be angry. Tell her you are not ready yet; that you are preparing yourself to do the work, that you told the secret today for the first time. Soon, it will be soon."

Tessa wrote that letter right there in my office and she read it to her angry little girl who became willing to wait and give her peace. As she read the letter, tears streamed down my face.

Tessa asked: "Why are you crying?" I said, "Someone has to cry for that little girl," and we both let out a huge breath. That letter is still in my possession. That was a piece of trauma resolution!

The family never talked about this horrendous secret but Tessa was able to heal that pain. The events don't go away but they get less powerful and have less of a charge. Tessa took me to that dark place with her in the next year. She hadn't been able to stay sober until she told that awful, shameful secret.

Signs and Symptoms of Trauma

When we think of trauma and trauma reactivity, most people think it is a disorder of the mind. While this is partly true, the majority of the disorder is in the nervous system. At its core, trauma is an event or series of events that triggers our survival instinct. When this happens, we automatically respond in fight, flight, freeze, or acquiesce mode. When PTSD or PTSD reactivity occurs, our nervous system is reacting as if we are still in danger. We go in and out of survival reactions. These reactions are automatic and exist in the most primitive part of our brain; they exist to try to save our lives and we have little to no control over them. If our brain determines we are in danger, we simply react in whatever manner the brain decides gives us the best chance to survive in that instant.

The easiest way for most people to understand this is a traffic accident. Most of us have been in a car accident at some point in our lives and can relate to the experience that occurs in our bodies. There's usually a point as the accident occurs that everything starts to slow down, our senses are sharper for those few moments that feel much longer. This is the mind and nervous system reacting to enhance our perceptions and give us a better chance to react and survive. Those of us who have experienced this also know it's completely automatic and out of our control. At some point after the impact, or at the point of impact, our perceptions speed back up and we may shake, which is our body's attempt to throw off the shock to our nervous system.

What follows for many is that for the next day, few days or even longer, we are nervous in the car, we may flinch and react when someone gets what feels too close. If the accident was at a stoplight or on the freeway, we may be more anxious or reactive in those places. If we see a car similar to the one that was part of our accident, we may be more on guard or skittish. This is all trauma reactivity: our nervous system telling us we are in danger again, even though this may not be the reality. For most of us our reactivity passes, our nervous system normalizes, but if PTSD occurs then the reactivity remains or comes and goes. This survival reaction is meant to keep us alive. It's a drastic measure in an instant of danger or perceived danger that takes a tremendous toll on the body, nervous system, and psyche. When someone experiences this reactivity on a constant basis, it puts a horrible and stressful strain on our systems.

One way to think of it is like a balloon. You can fill the balloon with only so much air before it explodes. We have to let some of that air out, relieve some of that stress, so the balloon does not pop. In our bodies and nervous systems this is accomplished through soothing behaviors or activities. Some of these behaviors are healthier than others, but in the context of the balloon exploding, they all make sense in the moment. If our choice is to face what feels like an explosion inside of us or, say, use drugs to quell it, then in that moment the drugs are often a better choice. The problem lies when the effect of unhealthy coping mechanisms cause more damage than the physiological and psychological stressors that are reactions to perceived danger.

It's often difficult for family and friends and the rest of the world to see the behaviors of "addicts," behaviorally challenged, or people who struggle with mood disorders, as anything more than a moral issue. I've heard that discussion too often. What people don't understand, they may despair of, or look for someone/something to blame or label. So those who don't understand or know better may slot addictions and behaviors in a morality slot. They may also label people they don't "get" as black sheep, the bad seed, the sociopath, or borderline. We are not our behaviors, and to wag our finger in the face of a child and repeatedly call him or her the bad kid does not do justice to the child, or quell the need for the behavior.

To help families understand the cycle of relapse, we created the Black Dot to describe this phenomenon. It illustrates unresolved trauma, and feelings surrounding it.

As noted in the diagram on the following page, the blackness is the very center of the deepest pain. In trauma treatment we slowly walk into the pain that we have been avoiding with whatever survival behavior that seemed to work initially. As you absorb the trauma stories and the artwork, perhaps you will understand and feel the fear of entering the pain of the Black Dot; avoidance at all costs seems to be the answer. However, enter we must to heal and have the life we deserve.

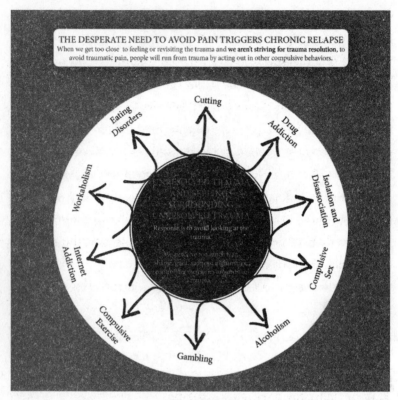

The Black Dot

We walk in slowly and feel some of the depth of feelings, but then we perceive too much fear, shame, guilt, sadness, nightmares, and more, plus controlling memories around the trauma. Most run from the pain which is the expected response, and most run to a soothing survival behavior to avoid the pain and it can be any of those behaviors surrounding the Black Dot. *That* is the relapse cycle: pain avoidance.

However, if we can partner with our client and their group and walk with them and support them in the center of the darkness most can and will walk into the pain, experience, truly experience what they have been avoiding, have sensory, cellular, visceral relief and discharge. This happens over a period of time with many and various tellings of the story, and culminates in rewriting their story. Perceptions shift and change, resilience and resources are built, and relapses in behaviors happen in treatment. Of course they do, and we should not discharge. Our clients are finding their way through the Black Dot, some kicking and screaming, some immersed in grief, because giving up their trauma identity can be a huge loss as well. Others charge in, ready to be rid of the chains that trauma has wrapped them in.

Please be aware that this is a long, exhaustive, and intense process. It can't be rushed and is difficult to do within a fifty-five-minute outpatient format; not impossible, but difficult. By sharing the diagram of the Black Dot, family and friends often are able to recognize the behaviors—not right or wrong, good or bad—but survival strategies.

Soothing Behaviors

Following is a list of some soothing behaviors broken up into common unhealthy and healthy categories. It should be noted that any behavior used to excess could become unhealthy. All these behaviors are used in some way to activate or calm the nervous system, whatever the nervous system needs, to create a sense of relief. Even though these unhealthy coping strategies all work on some level, they are not the best way to deal with our reactivity even though initially they are very powerful.

Unhealthy Soothing Behaviors

Substance use: alcohol, drugs, any mood-altering substance. This is a common soothing behavior for many trauma survivors, especially for younger ones, and the reason so many survivors are also addicts.

Food: another coping mechanism found easily and early in life that may express itself as binge eating, bulimia, or anorexia. Binge eating is eating to soothe from the intake of the food; anorexia creates a feeling of control by not eating; and bulimia is a combination of both, along with the body reaction of purging the food. This is in no way saying that this is all that exists within or explains these disorders, just the way and reasons in which they are sometimes initiated.

Self-harm: cutting, burning, scratching, head slamming, bloodletting, and any number of self-harming behaviors. This may seem counterintuitive, but self-harm is used for different reasons in a way that impacts the trauma survivor psychologically and physiologically. Sometimes it's used to calm the nervous system, and others harm themselves to excite the nervous system or "feel" something when they are numb.

Sex: sex can have both a physiological and psychological effect on us. This is often tied to sexual trauma, and, as with food, can be a bingeing or anorexic activity. Within the sexual realm are innumerable behaviors that are used to activate or numb, such as compulsive masturbation and viewing of pornography, prostitution and massage parlors, and the whole gamut of acting out sexually. Avoidance of sexual behaviors or sexuality can often be tied directly to trauma response, or used as a sense of control or avoidance.

Relationships: compulsive relationships or using another person to alter the way we feel. This is a very common coping mechanism for many people. Avoiding relationships can also be used as a form of control.

Work or achievement to excess: in an attempt to regulate our feelings of anxiety, we might focus our energy and attention on work or achievement. While this may seem healthy and is often admired or encouraged by others, in many instances this is done to the detriment of the rest of one's life.

Truly any activity or substance used in excess can be harmful, having a detrimental effect on our bodies and our lives. While they may provide short-term relief, they can create greater long-term damage. Soothing behaviors must be balanced and used in a healthy manner in concert with therapy. Some healthier choices may include the following.

Healthy Soothing Behaviors

Yoga

Healthy and balanced exercise

Meditation

Breathing techniques

Therapeutic writing

Therapeutic use of art

Activities in nature such as gardening, hiking, biking

Movies

Music

Driving in the car

Taking a bath

Prayer

Twelve-step fellowship

Hobbies

Religion or faith-based activities

When it comes to traumatic response, soothing behaviors can be as individual as the responses. What regulates one person may be triggering to another—this is particularly true with music and movie choices—so the idea is to find what works for you and add as many of these tools as you can to your toolbox. When the balloon is starting to fill, use the healthy soothing coping mechanisms to let air out. Learning to be responsible for self-soothing and self-regulation is essential to trauma resolution and leading a healthy productive life.

The definition of self-injury (SI), self-harm (SH), or deliberate self-harm (DSH) is deliberate infliction of tissue damage, or alteration to oneself without suicidal intent. Although the terms self-injury or self-harm have been used to refer to infliction of harm to the body's surface, the term self-harm may be used to include the harm inflicted on the body by those with eating disorders. Some scholars use more technical definitions related to specific aspects of this behavior. These acts may be aimed at relieving otherwise unbearable emotions, and/or sensations of unreality and numbness. Self-harm is listed in the *Diagnostic and Statistical Manual of Mental Disorders (DSM-IV-TR)* as a symptom of borderline personality disorder and depressive disorders. It's sometimes associated with mental illness; a history of trauma and abuse, including emotional abuse, sexual abuse, and eating disorders; or mental traits such as low self-esteem or perfectionism. A statistical analysis is difficult, as many self-injurers conceal their scars.

The relationship between self-harm and suicide is a complex one, as self-harming behavior may be potentially life-threatening, with or without suicidal intent. However, attributing self-harmers as suicidal is, in the majority of cases, inaccurate. Non-fatal self-harm is common in young people worldwide, and, due to this prevalence, the term *self-harm* is increasingly used to denote any non-fatal acts of deliberate self-harm, irrespective of the intention.

I want to offer hope and describe our clients as courageous when the most overriding drive they have is for "relief" in all its many forms, relief from the unceasing pain that so many experience in such a visceral, cellular, and sensory way, with the body, mind, and spirit on constant overload.

I want to move from the language of mental illness and addictive disease to a more honest language that defines those behaviors as imperative, useful, lifesaving, and spirit-redeeming.

I want to emphasize "behaviors" as the survival tools that they are, and that behaviors can change when we feel safe, trusting, and no longer in fear for our lives.

I want to invite our field to recognize that dual diagnosis is a myth; that unless we all become competent in all these areas—mental health, substance addictions, process addictions, and trauma—we will always be performing a disservice. These elements always overlap and support and define each other. As clinicians, our expertise has to grow and broaden.

Consider a poem that was written by one of my clients. This poem could have been written by hundreds of clients over the years. Olivia's poem has always touched my heart as it evokes the loss of innocence and safety, the soul wound, the moral injury that will always linger just below the surface. At thirteen, Olivia's innocence was ripped from her. As she continues to heal, she finds freedom and strength, a way to soar that can never be taken from her.

In the Moment

I'm flying with broken wings
I can't quite make it but I can fly a little
I'm flying with broken wings
It's going to take time for them to heal
But until then
I'm flying with broken wings
When they are healed, I can soar the skies
And no one can take that freedom away from me
But for now
I'm flying with broken wings

REFLECTIVE SKETCHES

1) As you read about PTSD and moral injury, what were the thoughts, questions, and feelings that came up for you?

_____

_____

_____

2) Identify any circumstances or events that you have taken responsibility for, felt guilty about, or felt shame for. Are you questioning the truth of that identity? Can you see that experience in anyone else in your life?

_____

_____

_____

3) What would you need to be forgiven? And who or what should provide absolution?

_____

_____

_____

4) We often have our own answers within. What is your inner voice telling you?

_____

_____

_____

5) Has your "shininess" been tarnished?

_____

_____

_____

6) Create three ways that you can begin to forgive yourself and begin to polish the brilliance and shininess that you were born with. It can be as simple as looking in the mirror and repeating positive affirmations, or finding pictures of yourself and recognizing that you were precious and just a little child who deserved more.

_____

_____

_____

7) If you have children or young relatives, can you see their beauty and brilliance? Would you allow anyone to hurt them by thoughts, words, or deeds? Can you begin to embrace the shiny child that you were before the trauma messages changed your vision?

_____

_____

_____

8) Choose just one change that you will make from today onward for yourself. Commit to that for one month, one day at a time.

_____

_____

_____

CHAPTER 4

LAYERS OF TRAUMA

> *"Your task is not to seek for love, but merely to seek and find all the barriers within yourself that you have built against it."*
>
> —Jalaluddin Rumi

❧

After reading the Preface, you might assume that there was no joy in our family, but that is so wrong. This often happens when folks are so immersed in their trauma story. It is vital, at an appropriate time in treatment, to identify the power of the positive in family dynamics that created resilience to survive traumatic events. I remember clearly there was love and joy mixed in with the pain. There were lovely family gatherings and wonderful, comforting food; my grandmother was "Apple Grandmom" because of her German apple cake, which my mother still makes today. I'm certain that any words and behaviors that my grandmother heaped on her daughters were the very words and behaviors that were heaped on her and her sisters and brothers when they were young. My grandfather was silent and stoic. Though he was never without a beer in his hand, I never saw him drunk. I tried everything I could to make him love me. I vividly remember bringing him my third-grade school photo. I was the oldest grandchild and he was proud of me. The photo was a typical school picture for a child my age. I was missing a tooth and my hair was sticking out.

His reaction took me completely by surprise. He said, "Why would I want that ugly picture?"

Of course, I was devastated. His hurtful words became embossed in my heart, which I further interpreted as meaning: "You are ugly, unlovable, defective!" And *that* is how we begin to define ourselves. My grandfather was joking; he didn't mean to hurt me. He would have been horrified to know that I added that to a long list that my "inner critic" was compiling against myself over and over again, just as my grandmother and grandfather did, as my mother and father did, as my aunt and uncle did, and all those people in my life who were repeating generations of self-demeaning mantras.

I believe that not one member of the generations of my family was malicious. Still, I believe that we repeat the behaviors and the scripts that were defined, refined, and passed down over decades. We don't realize that we carry these shadows of our past, but still we carry the fingerprint.

I can only imagine how horrifying it must have been for *all* of my family to see the addict I became, being arrested and on the TV news, my Uncle Joe (my Aunt Theresa's husband) coming to Philly to try and save me, my family bailing me out of jail repeatedly. My grandfather never saw me sober and I barely made it to the hospital to say good-bye. While in the hospital he was prescribed beer so as not to go into DTs. This was a case of the apple not falling far from the tree, except my grandfather functioned well his whole life, while my addiction progressed dramatically.

My father died one year before I found recovery, and I regret not being available for him as he was in such terrible pain from cancer. My insane life only added to his pain. However, I will always be grateful to my mother and father for raising my youngest daughter.

Please don't misunderstand; there were many fun times with the family coming together; the men watching the Eagles football team and the Phillies baseball team. My uncles and grandfather marched in the Mummers Parade on New Year's Day in Philadelphia. I remember fondly the drinking and laughing that went on, with the Mummers Parade being to Philadelphia what Mardi Gras is to New Orleans.

Growing up in North Camden, New Jersey, just across the bridge from Philly, I remember lots of get-togethers. My parents often had friends and neighbors over to play music. My father had a perfect ear and played piano, banjo, guitar, mandolin, and organ. The parties were loud and fun, filled with music and drinking and laughter. So there were plenty of wonderful gatherings and people enjoying life.

My mother and my aunt married at eighteen and quickly left the house where the energy in my grandparents' home was often painful. My aunt struggled with depression and low self-esteem. Like me, her most often-spoken words were "I'm sorry."

I'm certain that other family members experienced our family differently, but I felt the pain of being "less than," and I believe my mother and aunt did as well. I think it's time to do a more thorough emotional investigation of the generations of my family.

Layers of Trauma

In Utero Trauma

A growing body of research indicates that as babies in the womb we do feel, taste, learn, and have some level of consciousness. Author and obstetrician Christiane Northrup, MD, found that if a pregnant mother is experiencing high levels of fear or anxiety, she creates a "metabolic cascade." In such a state the expectant mother produces a substance called *cytokines* that impacts the mother and child's immune system. Chronic anxiety in an expectant mother can set a foundation for various trauma-based results such as prematurity, miscarriage, complications of birth, and death.

In utero trauma comes in many forms. When Momma has a difficult pregnancy, the baby is affected. If Momma is experiencing stress, sadness, pain, shame, anger, fear, depression, or anxiety, the baby is affected through shared brain chemistry, energy, and sensory stimuli.

If there is domestic violence, deprivation of nutrients, or substance abuse, the baby is affected. Imagine all of the possibilities! Traumatic events—the Holocaust, natural events such as tornadoes, hurricanes, flooding, and even car accidents—also affect the baby. Let's say that in most cases, if it happens to Momma, baby experiences it at some level. In other words, trauma begins in the womb. Momma's cortisol level increases with trauma reaction; now there is cortisol in the amniotic fluid, resulting in in utero trauma. Cortisol is released in response to stress. PTSD is a disorder of stress created by trauma.

On a positive note, providing music, reading to the baby in utero, physically rubbing the belly in a loving way, is also experienced by the baby, and baby recognizes Momma's voice after birth. So baby experiences the positive, and resilience also begins here in the womb.

Research is beginning to prove what therapists have intuitively and anecdotally suspected; that during pregnancy everything the mother experiences is experienced by the baby—emotionally, physically, and through brain and body chemistry as well as attachment development. Research continues to grow around the issue of emotional trauma in the womb, looking at the state of the expectant mother to answer the question, "Can a baby learn while he or she is in the womb?"

To answer this question drives us to ask more questions. In his blog "World of Psychology" on Psych Central, in an article entitled "Emotional Trauma in the Womb," Samuel Lopez De Victoria, PhD, poses some questions. What is the state of the expectant mother? Was she scared, detached, depressed, lonely, or resentful about her pregnancy? What impact does this have on a baby's mental health and well-being?

Research currently being pursued suggests that perhaps some of the emotions we experience in this life may well have come from before your physical birth. Those who experienced fetal life traumas may feel sudden, acute feelings of anger, fear, sadness, loneliness, hypervigilance, and co-dependent enablement, and often describe that they've "always" felt this way (angry, shame, depressed, anxious) and don't understand why.

Examples of Fetal Life Traumas

When my parents fell in love, my mother was eighteen, and my father twenty-eight and divorced. My parents ran away and Grandpop had my mother arrested and put in jail until they realized she was not a minor. I came along eleven months later. It hasn't even been a decade since I realized that, in the eyes of the Catholic Church, I was born out of wedlock. I can only imagine what my mother went through by defying her family and her faith in those times—1945. Her brothers and sister married and raised their children in the Catholic faith with the blessing of my grandparents. My mother was excommunicated by the church. Shame, shame!

We were the "black sheep" of our extended family. I always felt that, whether it was said or not, I don't know. But I can tell you I carried unexplained shame my whole life until I finally realized, with the help of a workshop partner, that I was my mother's shame. And I was the black sheep of my family. My mother and I talked about this recently. She said she never felt that way, but I know that she was courageous at a time when that had to be very difficult. We talked about how much alike we were. I certainly didn't believe that before; I never wanted to be anything like her. But with this new insight, I realized that she was a rebel, a risk taker, and a woman of her convictions. So much about who I am makes sense now. How much of her own life she gave up for us—her family—and how resentful she was sometimes when we "girls" were able to venture out into the world?

These experiences are not limited to the Catholic Church. Many faiths and many faithful experience shame and guilt for real or imagined sins, especially for children who are so impressionable and incorporate those feelings and experiences into the tapestry of their lives.

I speak all over the world and when I tell my mother's story I'm often deluged by audience members who want to share a similar story. They're asking for absolution or sharing their own healing process.

To confirm my mother's experience, I recently spoke to my eighty-two-year-old aunt/godmother. She confirmed the cruelty of my grandmother toward my mother, the judgement and humiliation, the impotence of my grandfather in the face of her judgement. And as good daughters, my mother and aunt took care of my grandmother until she died. My grandmother was sixteen years old when she married and I'm certain her history, which I don't know, created her anger, and her judgmental and critical nature.

I've been unraveling the mystery of my life for decades, the hurts and the glory, the soul wounds, and the gifts of a resilient spirit. Among many other things, I understand now why the opening sentence in the life story I wrote for my group in drug and alcohol rehab in 1987 was, "I'm pretty sure I was responsible for dropping the atomic bomb!" I guess you could say I carried a lot of shame and guilt as a child. I never could understand exactly what I had done that was so terrible; I just always felt filled with shame.

I'm the generation of the aftermath of World War II, the Cold War, "sex, drugs, and rock and roll," Elvis Presley, the Beatles, first McDonald's, the Mickey Mouse Club, Howdy Doody, and Roy Rogers. Black-and-white movies on TV created my vision of the world and the dreams for my place in it.

I am the child of air raid sirens, hiding in cloak rooms and under desks, bomb shelters, back alley abortions, and Vietnam and protest, segregation, integration, the sexual revolution, bra burning, women's rights, and campus upheavals. I was the first in my family for so many things, caught between moving into a class above my own, or rebelling and creating chaos and change, revolution—and craving both.

Early Childhood Trauma

Author Pia Mellody focuses on codependency issues. She wrote in *Facing Codependency*:

> When a person is unable to deal with traumatic events, he or she will often feel alone and struggle with recurring feelings of worry, fear, and worthlessness. Trauma sufferers often have difficulty in relationships and in dealing with emotional challenges, as well as low self-esteem due to the traumatic experience and feelings associated with the trauma. Trauma victims are haunted by memories that feel completely real and can cause the victims to become silent sufferers who believe that their lives are destined to repeat past events.

Experiences in a person's life can trigger a recurring experience of the original trauma, which makes healing from the original trauma an extremely important goal. Many trauma sufferers choose to deal with their feelings alone, instead of seeking appropriate professional treatment. These people may turn to substance abuse to dull the feelings associated with the trauma and the pain that comes with those feelings.

The deepest and most harmful of traumas is abandonment and neglect. The pervasive constant message is that an individual is not worthy of care and attention, that no one is really available or willing to care and nurture them.

So many children are lost emotionally and spiritually at the time when they most need care, not held, hugged, or celebrated; not applauded with kind and encouraging words, or given positive regard and encouragement. Who are these children in their adult form? At the core of trauma is the belief that your survival is at risk; at its deepest level being abandoned and/or neglected is life-threatening. Every infant instinctively knows they are dependent on the loving kindness of a caretaker.

Abandonment and neglect comes in many forms:

➡ The single parent who is doing the best they can raising "latch-key kids."

➡ The child who is daily given negative messages that they are less than, not good enough, fat, ugly, stupid, lazy, not worthy of the air they breathe.

➡ The child who experiences any kind of abuse or bullying. The parent might not even know but the child is unprotected and feels it at their core. What a huge and painful price we are paying today in the many shootings that are happening by lonely, bullied children who move into mental illness or addiction or both.

➡ The parents who are busy working, not emotionally available, or in their own abusive relationships or addictive behaviors. Children learn from parental behaviors.

➡ Children of affluence who have caretakers other than busy, unavailable parents.

➡ The adopted child—even when raised by wonderful, loving, adoptive parents—who carries the core message, "Something was wrong with me, I was thrown away."

The list of scenarios that create the energy of neglect and of abandonment is long and endless. Children are fearful that they can never be as "successful" as their parents, fearful that they have no talent or life skills because everything is "done" for them. They are often "saved" from consequences, deprived of important opportunities to develop life skills as a result, deprived of finding a life's purpose by loving, fearful parents who don't want their children to struggle, when in fact struggle is a visceral learning experience. The message received is often, "I must do these things for you because I don't believe you are capable." It's an enormous experience of deprivation, resulting in unhealthy egos.

We're not talking about "just" malicious abandonment and neglect. We're talking about unawareness, preoccupation, and an inability to recognize the human pain a child is experiencing but unable to verbalize. The inability to ask appropriate questions of children about their feelings, their pain, their joy, successes and failures. Many children *and* adults feel very alone.

When I ask folks to identify traumatic events in their life, abandonment and neglect seem the most harmful and pervasive. They set up a pattern of survival behaviors that make perfect sense when you unravel the trauma story. The overwhelming emotion that these folks experience is loneliness. I guarantee that if you look around in your social circle and you are mindful, you'll recognize these folks. The greatest gift you can give them is kind and loving words, inclusion, and an awareness and recognition of the wounded child within. My clients overwhelmingly report the most important part of their healing was the constant love, compassion, care, and validation of the goodness and worth of their spirit, and that neither I nor my staff ever gave up on them, no matter what.

Caroline asked to share a few words left unspoken with light and love for her sister that I treated for trauma and addiction twenty years ago.

My Beautiful Sister

I remember those beautiful big brown eyes and curly locks of love
I remember your innocence, I remember your will to love.
I've known you from the day you were born—I've known you ever still
Though even only 22 months apart . . . I know your heart, I know your will.

For you see, I remember where it all began . . .
When you began to act and began to react . . .
then you thought you had a plan.

I watched you grow . . . I began to watch you use.
You thought it was cool, but it was never really you.

Just a little bit more, let me try something new . . . I know what I'm doing . . .
I don't wanna use.

You struggled, you worked it, you used and abused.
We were left on the wayside . . . wondering and confused.

Forgive me my family I will make it right someday, but
for now I am embarrassed and very ashamed.

Years we waited . . . feeling her pain . . . Never stopped loving her . . .
Feeling our pain.

Somehow we knew her soul and her will was
stronger than the strongest pill.

Stronger than the next injection . . . Stronger than the next rejection.

She lived it. She owns it.
She makes no excuses

She found her will. She found her way

We are all very blessed. She is with us today.

This next story from an alumnus of ours, Roger, is difficult to read
and may well put you off, but please take a deep breath and continue
reading even if you find it disturbing. It portrays how intergenerational trauma can affect someone deeply, at many levels. Remember our mantra: behavior always makes sense when we unravel the
trauma story. If we allow ourselves to be present and witness without
judgment, trauma survivors can heal because they judge themselves
more harshly than anyone else can.

ROGER'S STORY:
LAYERS OF TRAUMA

For the first two years of elementary school I was a very poor student. I then realized that my mother liked me to do well in school. I transformed myself into a good student. I would make good grades and she would be proud of me for a few days. Then the emotional atmosphere would go back to normal—cold, angry, and vacuous. This lead to my behavioral trait that all love is fleeting and must be earned.

I am a physician. I had touched two female patients in a sexually inappropriate way. My state board referred me for treatment in lieu of canning me. I didn't like treatment, but I did tell the truth when asked. I trusted the process, but not any of those who were supposed to help me along the way. It seemed each therapist, psychologist, psychiatrist, and social worker delighted in watching my career slip through my fingers. The loss of my career was 100 percent my doing, but they didn't have to enjoy it so much.

At one of the treatment facilities, I told them about my trauma history. At age three I approached my mother who would beat me with a belt until I dissociated. This happened until I didn't want to be loved anymore. It required about twenty beatings. Many years later, Mother confirmed my memory after having denied it all and calling me crazy for fifteen years. Then her father orally or anally raped me repeatedly when I was three to six years old. Mother tried to get me to have sex with her until I was fourteen; at that time I requested she not return to my bed. There were numerous verbal insults. I was frequently told how I was stupid, ugly, and unlovable. It was a strange way to grow up if you think about it.

So, I was diagnosed with PTSD and referred to a treatment center in the forest where the pamphlet said, "Clients learn how to give and receive love." I wanted my medical license back. You can keep your love to yourself.

I arrived and tried to fit in. There were about fifty clients, men and women. We lived four or five to a cabin on fifty acres of land adjacent to a national forest. There were bear, deer, red-tailed foxes, and opossums. We were in the middle of nowhere.

I told a few jokes. I was trying to be friendly. I will repeat one little joke that I told, no big deal. "Did you hear about the woman who went fishing with five men? She came back with a red snapper." This joke, along with a few others, went over poorly.

There was more. Everybody at the treatment center created by Judy Crane has a trauma history. This would certainly apply to all the clients, but also most of the staff. People with a trauma history have a radar for danger—scanning the environment for what might hurt them next time. That included the body builder who had been sexually abused by a Catholic priest as a child. That included a woman in my trauma group that had been raped by her stepfather. That included everybody. And all the radars got focused on me.

The clients perceived me as a danger. They went daily to the director and asked (begged) that I get thrown out. A rumor had started that I was a psychiatrist who sexually abused his patients. I was seen as a problem. I was a perpetrator. The other clients were merely victims. People like me caused the problems in the world and I needed to leave.

The director, Judy Crane, asked to see me. I went to her office. She told me what everybody was saying. She asked me what it *was like growing up in my family. I said I felt hated. And Judy said that I was recreating that dynamic in this community, recreating my trauma. She said I was going to change my ways or else leave. She feared for my safety. I didn't even know what I could do differently. She said no jokes—ever. She asked if I had ever been diagnosed with Asperger's syndrome. I said no. She said to learn to be socially appropriate and to respect people's boundaries. As an example, she said not to ask people about the self-mutilation scars. I agreed.*

Later that same day, we had a meeting with the entire campus: all the clients, all the staff (clinical, maintenance, kitchen, and housekeeping). I stood in the middle of the room. Each person asked me questions. I answered each person until they ran out of questions. I lied and said I had never sexually abused former clients. I told the truth about everything else. They were all satisfied that I wouldn't harm them.

That one day changed everything. I realized the little things I say and do have a huge effect on people. I also realized I could change those behaviors. I realized that a blank affect and a sarcastic sense of humor wasn't necessary to live in the world and that it drove people away. It was also a huge relief to tell Judy that I had grown up feeling hated and have her know exactly what that meant. She got it in a nanosecond.

After residential treatment, during our outpatient treatment, it was recommended that Roger take an acting "improv" (improvisation) class. It was a tremendously effective intervention and taught this doctor social skills and to use his sharp sense of humor with great success. I invite you to recognize the intergenerational trauma of sexual abuse and detached relationships.

You may have a negative reaction to us working so hard to keep this man in the community, however, most trauma survivors who have stepped over sexual boundaries have been victims at an early age, and can be salvaged and healed within the work of the community.

We indeed took a risk when we brought the community and staff together and let Roger tell his story. By hearing it, other clients were able to empathize and recognize that this man had been emotionally and socially shut down for most of his life. He was in survival mode. His willingness to answer questions and respond to clients who had been triggered by his poor jokes and behaviors also empowered those clients to share their discomfort—and to ask for what they needed from him in order to stay.

The community came together. There was no more scapegoating, and other clients realized that we would not give up on them either, that we would fight for their right to find trauma and addiction resolution.

Intergenerational Trauma

Here's an example of healing history messages: at fifty years old, I finally realized that I was a beautiful, bright, talented, and gifted woman. My granddaughter, at eight years old, asked me what took me so long? From the mouths of babes! She already knows about and loves herself. She shares with me that she is Delaney, "the whole package, she is all that!" We are changing the faulty perceptions of this younger generation in our family. Even though my grandchildren have all experienced multiple trauma events, we have been able to love and support them, and talk about their pain and sadness as well as their joys and triumphs.

A Granddaughter's Poem to Her Grandmother

She is the new dress at Macy's
She is the middle of my heart
She is my smile
She is the drumbeat of Africa, the waves in California
She is the glue that holds me together
She is the bridge that helps me cross the lake
She is the bed I sleep in every night
She is the Beatles on my record player
She is the water in my cup
She is the bookmark in my book
She is my Yadda

This poem was written as part of a class assignment by my then eleven-year-old granddaughter, Delaney Rose. She is now sixteen and gobbling up every moment of her life. I find this trait in my grandchildren as they grow and mature and I am *thrilled*.

I was widowed at twenty-seven by addiction. Recently, my nieces visited me at my home. We spent time remembering those early years of my marriage to their beloved uncle, and the early childhood of my children. We laughed and cried as we unraveled the history and put more puzzle pieces together. It was healing for my grown children because they were very young when their father died and had many unanswered questions. Many secrets were revealed. It was beautiful, spiritual, cathartic, and led to more questions and more answers. And we experienced, truly experienced, each other in those moments.

THE MORE WE PROCESS AND RESOLVE OUR PAIN "IN THE MOMENT," THE MORE WE CAN EXPERIENCE OUR LIFE IN THE PRESENT AND NOT BE PRISONERS TO OUR PAIN OR OUR PAST.

For years we avoided the pain, the sorrow, the sadness, the anger, and the grief. We've avoided life in all its fullness. We all experience traumatic events; life becomes richer when we give ourselves permission to experience all of the myriad human emotions in the moment, knowing that pain will pass. That we can cry and weep and wail with someone we trust, and we won't die, and the tears will come to an end. This is what we do for our clients, and each other. We witness and provide a safe and loving sanctuary for the work as we support, encourage, and listen without judgment. We don't have to have all the answers; we just have to be present.

When we can release pain and have resolution, life becomes juicier. Walking through fear is our challenge, and the challenge we give to our clients. We must give this same gift to ourselves and find our own healing. I have never, ever spoken to a group of clinicians that couldn't benefit from more healing in their life. We must be willing to do *everything* we ask our clients to do. Life gets juicier!

I know the research is clear about the impact of life events of any type on in utero development. Those same life events impact the succeeding generations. However, research is just that: the culmination of a gathering of facts and figures to prove a truth.

I operate from an anecdotal perspective, which means we know what heals our clients, and the proof of the outcomes are anecdotal stories. So as you read these many stories of pain and suffering followed by outcomes which provide present-day evidence of life well-lived as a result of ongoing trauma resolution, you may have reason to be hopeful that your family can grow and change too.

When I'm with my grandchildren and can have the full effect of who they are, what they believe, how they feel, and how they operate in the world, I come away with a big smile on my face. As a family we've patiently (sometimes quickly, sometimes slowly), lovingly, in most cases with good intentions, attempted to create a healthy environment to shift the old, damaging dynamics of our family.

We can break the cycles that have kept our families hostage to our trauma history. Remember, we often don't even know what we don't know that has created a destructive pattern. I'm grateful that I've had to investigate my family history more thoroughly. We *can* change intergenerational patterns, Eugenie's story illustrates.

EUGENIE'S STORY:
ENOUGH!

Enough! When my employer approached us about the trauma cer-tification and training, I arrogantly thought I knew everything there was to know about dealing with trauma. After all, I was a qualified professional. I expected to walk into the course and pick up a few good techniques to add to my tool box.

Little did I know that I was not there to learn about "theory" but how to practice in a model that truly spoke to my spirit. The big surprise: experiential learning! The message: do your own work so you are clear once and for all what is yours and what the patient's is. Again I thought, This will be fine, I'll only share about XYZ. My protective mechanisms were in place so I could continue to pro-ject an image to the world that I am the "strong one" who handles "everything." Yet God blessed me with an amazing opportunity to get vulnerable and release my shame.

I had been in therapy as a teenager to cope with betrayal I experienced from my father's infidelity and the fact that my mother bravely put her foot down and made a decision to relocate from our hometown and follow through with divorce for our collective sanity. This was a ten-year struggle. We were a well-respected family in our community and the shame of my father's dishonesty, constant cheating, and empty promises were painful to live with. I assumed the role as the "rock" and peacekeeper trying to have close rela-tionships with both parents. This was complicated. In this process, I also became my father's emotional caretaker and rescuer during his depression, and bore the brunt of his manipulation, blackmail, and numerous threats and attempts to end his life. I was hooked in a cycle of guilt that was crippling me. I feared setting boundaries "in case" he took his life. I have now accepted that "in case" is no longer my problem.

I became a mother blessed with the boldest ray of light that is my daughter. Becoming a parent changed me; it provided perspective on the true meaning of responsibility. As a parent, I am responsible for my daughter's well-being; she is not responsible for mine. Things started to shift in my relationship with my father, and he took strain [got stressed out] because I was no longer mothering him. I started to distance myself from his chaos and pour energy into myself and bonding with my daughter.

Then came the trauma course. My father was on one of his downward spirals, providing threats and ultimatums. I just couldn't carry him anymore. Judy got me to stand up to him and say "enough" and the relief that came with that permission to let go was astounding! I followed through with this and put down firm boundaries with my father, handing back the responsibility I had carried for many years. Thank you, Judy, for giving me the courage to do this.

I felt very strongly as a mother that I would not allow my daughter to be exposed to any form of instability. If my father could not commit to change and be there for her whole-heartedly, then I was not willing to put her at risk. I want to prevent the cycle from repeating itself. She has many people in her life who adore her and to whom she is positively attached. My father, sadly, is too wrapped up in his own narcissism and victimhood to change. While I will always love and pray for him to be restored to sanity and healing, I can't have him involved in my daughter's life. I realize that he, too, has his own trauma story that he's reenacting, and I feel for him.

His relationship with his father was very abusive and damaging. Unfortunately, he resists therapy and is not open to addressing his issues. We haven't spoken in nearly a year. He hasn't attempted to apologize or make amends.

My journey now is about focusing on my needs and having people in my life respond to those with genuine love and care. I'm grateful for my mother, an angel and a one-of-a-kind parent who is my constant support, and my sister, who has always weathered the storms with me. She is my greatest protector and has walked this difficult journey with me. They both encouraged me for years to do this and were so proud of me for putting down this boundary.

Since the trauma course and my regained sense of self, I live in clarity and light. The dark times now bring lessons to me without fear. I no longer feel guilty and I live with integrity.

Professionally, it has opened many doors for me in terms of how I work with patients: I empathize with their struggles to change and connect to them spiritually. As a therapist I'm not scripted. I don't have magical powers; just my instinct, skills, and intuition that guide me. Being a mother has provided beautiful insight into the importance of attachment and how things can go wrong when that connection has not been formed. I offer this to my patients freely and go straight to the wound to provide a resolution. I'm not afraid of going there; I want to uncover what is hidden for ultimate healing to occur. Addicts have gaping wounds that they fill with harmful acts to themselves, abusing their body, mind, and spirit. To provide closure and prevent relapse, it's vital that they do work on their trauma. This will sustain their recovery and make sense of what has left them lost for a long time.

One of the most common statements by family members and clients is, "My life was wonderful and perfect; there is no trauma or causes. There's no reason for my despair, addiction, unhappy life, out-of-control behaviors, dysfunctional relationships, self-harming behaviors, low self-esteem, anger, anxiety . . . (fill in the blank)." And then we begin the story-telling process; usually stories from other group members that begin to awaken a sleeping tiger among the listeners. Clearly, when someone is recommended to see a therapist or go to treatment, there are signs and symptoms that are a red flag that someone needs help. Families report that their loved one is:

- angry
- depressed
- anxious
- shut down
- unmotivated
- slovenly
- unkempt
- hyperactive
- out-of-control
- isolated and alone

- acquiring new, strange friends
- shows signs of an eating disorder
- out all night
- failing in school
- changed eating, sleeping or social patterns
- been caught lying, cheating, stealing, using drugs, watching porn, self-harming, or dissociating

These reports all state that these are new behaviors for their loved ones.

The challenge is to not give a quick diagnosis, or to immediately medicate the signs and symptoms. The challenge is to recognize that the behaviors make sense when you understand the story, and that very often is a trauma story. Too many clients come to treatment with a long list of diagnoses and a suitcase of prescribed medications, often in conflict with other medications.

When asked to introduce themselves, these clients reel off a statement similar to this: "Hi, I'm Katie, I'm bipolar, borderline personality disorder with ADHD, I'm a cocaine and heroin addict with love addiction and self-harm." How very sad that her diagnosis and addictions have become her identity! We quickly invite these clients to let go of those familiar labels and begin with just being a trauma survivor, as we slowly sort out the reality of the labels and slowly identify the correct, if any, medications.

So, what stories are most prevalent? They are stories of inadequate and unhealthy attachment leading to difficulty in developing healthy relationships, and the ability to survive and thrive in social environments. This lack of or inadequate attachment may be the result of circumstances that their parents can't control, or by parents who are stuck in a generational cycle of unhealthy or inadequate attachment.

Another story line is neglect and abandonment where an individual's needs were not met consistently. This pattern is a core arena for low self-esteem and can set up a vulnerability to victimization or, for many, enormous resilience. Again, parents are often themselves stuck in a generational pattern of neglect and abandonment. These stories don't seem to be a big deal until you start outlining the layers of events that begin to weigh very heavily on a spirit.

Childhood and adolescent health issues loom large in explaining patterns of behaviors. Often, this is an arena for perceived abandonment and neglect, grief issues, loss of social engagement, and isolation. Behaviors associated with sexual abuse are often found in children with health issues because of physical intrusion, betrayal of the body, or strange adults in control of physical circumstances. Another scenario that explains the behaviors described is of course sexual abuse and rape. And so very often, those traumatic events have been kept secret.

Consider the following as I describe a "typical" trauma story. Born into a normal, middle-class family where both parents work, this child has a caretaker or begins daycare at three years old. The child's parents divorce when he is seven; child later discovers there was an affair. Mom is really angry for a very long time. She dates several men but never remarries, and she works a lot. At age eight the boy discovers porn on Dad's computer. It's a comforting and exciting experience because he's a lonely, latchkey kid. He has friends at school but is bullied by one big kid who terrifies him. He has no one to tell and no one notices anything because he does great in school. Around thirteen he begins to drink and smoke pot. He spends alternate weekends with Dad, but there is a new stepmom and other stepchildren. He's bullied by the oldest but never tells anyone, and he continues to drink and smoke pot in high school. He has a few girlfriends; one cheats on him with his best friend. The teen gets in lots of fights and is eventually kicked out of school. Then he's sent to a wilderness program for six months. He does well there, enters college, and starts to smoke just a little pot again. He has one girlfriend in college who gets pregnant. After she has an abortion, he feels terrified, sad, and guilty. He discovers it wasn't his baby. He begins skipping class, drinking and drugging, watching lots of porn and masturbating. Introduced to OxyContin, he gets hooked. He steals to get drugs, gets arrested for possession, and drops out of college. His life is out of control. He seeks treatment, again.

The behaviors make sense. Is he an addict? Probably, but also in jeopardy of chronic relapse unless we address his attachment issues, grief, loss of the perfect family, betrayal by Dad's affair, betrayal by girlfriends, bullying, and not being protected and cared for in the family system. We must also address his porn and masturbation issues which are intricately connected to all of the attachment, grief, and betrayal issues. And finally, this work must be done with the family in a thoughtful and sensitive way, without blame, and with everyone's "perceptions" of the events honored and heard. The family behaviors all make sense, too, when you understand how trauma stories intertwine. And intertwine they do. The very best work assists the whole family in the healing process.

Trauma in the Shadow of Our Ancestors

Everyone has a story. There is a personal story, a family story, a mythology, and a historical story that is often a mystery. There are answers awaiting us in our untold ancestral story.

I think most people have a story that their family tells about them. For example, when Maria was two years old she loved spaghetti so much she even poured it over her head—we have the picture to prove it! Chances are Maria tells that story but doesn't have a clear memory of the event, but it's part of family history. And it's shaped part of her vision of herself.

There are also the stories that shape us that we never hear, that are ephemeral and ghostly. For instance, what was my grandfather's history that made him so shut down and taciturn? I would see glimpses of his humor, love, and loyalty. I would see times when he seemed to connect to my uncles, but far too often I would see a silent brooding man. I craved his attention and approval but too often the responses were negative or nonexistant. Did his pain, anger, sadness, drinking, and ghostly history affect who I am? Of course it did! I created my own story about my grandfather to explain the absence of real connection. What I do know is that my great grandmother, his mother, was born in Ireland and came to the United States where she married my grandfather's father. He died when my grandfather was a small boy. They were Irish Catholic and raised in Philadelphia. With those few facts, I created a whole story to assuage my craving to understand the alcoholism in my family. I tried to understand why I felt so bad about myself when I was around him. Ancestry.com has proven that many of us crave the answers to "Who am I? What events created this person that I am, the people of my tribe?"

Recently I've had conversations with friends who are children and grandchildren of survivors of the Holocaust, World War II, Vietnam, survivors of the "troubles" in Ireland, the genocide of Native Americans and other indigenous people, the horror of the Bosnian war, the despair of the Middle Eastern refugees, apartheid, the Depression, and those who are children and grandchildren of sexual abuse survivors. They all shared that the mystery, to them, of the historical events—mysterious since the events were not discussed in the family—impacted their vision of themselves, as much as an overload of information impacted others. The answers of who we are, how we cope, personality traits, and continuing traumas are written in our history.

As clients begin to explore their intergenerational trauma, they discover patterns in their families that fill in the puzzle pieces: family history of war veterans who remain quiet and angry; multiple marriages the present generation was unaware of; and patterns of depression, suicides, or abuse, along with patterns of triumph and survival that help to make sense of present patterns and behaviors.

Historical Trauma

Intergenerational trauma and historical trauma are interwoven aspects of family trauma. Historical trauma refers to those large-scale, sweeping events that happen on a world stage. These events impact the core and makeup of not only various ethnic populations, but whole geographic areas. The intergenerational trauma that occurs as a result of ancestral events changes, challenges, and impacts succeeding generations often without their real knowledge or understanding. These are the "personal" stories in the midst of historical events.

I look to the men and women of my generation who experienced and lived throughVietnam, for example. We're now in the third and fourth generations of families impacted by the horror, courage, anger, sadness, and silence of a generation of soldiers who didn't receive the help they so needed and deserved. In the end, these soldiers coped as best they could. So often their families watched as they suffered in silence, depression, rage, addiction, and social isolation.

Children of these veterans suffered the same issues but without the war; the war was within their parents. Attachment issues and addictions are rampant in the generations that followed. These adult children often followed their parents into the military, looking for connection. The first real studies around PTSD occurred in the 1980s with Vietnam veterans. When we translate that symptomology, we see trauma elements in many more situations. That's why so many people spend a great deal of their life "coping," without understanding the what, why, or exactly whose trauma is impacting their behaviors.

As clinicians, we have the ability to redirect survivors to an under-standing of their strengths, and help them move toward purposeful living. But that takes time and the ability to help put the puzzle pieces together for intergenerational healing.

Everything, every event of our life, no matter how insignificant or momentous, affects the way envision ourselves, which in turn affects the way we live our lives and what we believe about ourselves. Even more significant to the whole, is what are the history, beliefs, and messages of the generations before us? What do we offer the gener-ations that follow us?

Epigenetics and Intergenerational Trauma

There's a dramatic difference in the way researchers and most therapists see the world and the people of the world. For very good ethical reasons, researchers generally do their magic with mice and correlate that to the lives of people. Well, I'm very excited about the study of epigenetics and its impact on the understanding of inter-generational trauma, particularly its impact on behaviors and coping skills of succeeding generations.

In 2013, Dan Hurley, a scientific journalist, published "Grandma's Experiences Leave a Mark on Your Genes" in *Discover* magazine. Hurley wrote with great simplicity and humor about the exciting research that describes what many therapists have recognized for years: "the apple doesn't fall far from the tree," "like father, like son," and "it's all Mama's fault!" The history of the proceeding generations often affects the present.

Hurley wrote, "The research indicates that changes occur in the DNA through methyl groups, which can be described as placehold-ers, attaching to each cell to select those genes necessary for those cell's proteins . . . Methyl codes reside beside but separate from the double helix DNA code, the field was dubbed epigenetics, from the prefix *epi* (Greek for over, outer, above)."

This is all Greek to me, but what I do understand is that these folks have discovered that traumatic events change DNA and that impacts the generations that follow.

Two researchers from McGill University, Michael Meaney, a neurobiologist, and Moshe Szyf, a molecular biologist and geneticist, joined their efforts to ask the question, "Can child neglect, drug abuse, or other severe stresses cause epigenetic changes to the DNA inside the neurons of a person's brain?"

Today this question is at the core of a new field, *behavioral* epigenetics, which is finding that traumatic experiences in our past, or in our recent ancestors' past, can leave molecular scars that adhere to our DNA. In this way, the experiences of our ancestors and our own lives are always with us as we "inherit" behavioral and psychological tendencies from experiences passed long ago—some known and remembered, others unknown. The interesting bottom line is behavioral epigenetics explains our behaviors' strengths as well as our weaknesses. Research continues on how epigenetic changes are impacted by maternal behaviors.

When I grew up with overwhelming shame and couldn't identify "my shame," it created an energy in how I viewed myself and my place in the world. What I now understand is that historical events in the lives of my great-grandparents, grandparents, and parents affected my DNA: the epigenetics of who I am. What happened to my mother and what she felt while I was in the womb affected who I became.

World events such as war, the potato famine, the Holocaust, apartheid, and so many more traumatic events affect the DNA and behaviors, changing the course of the lives of children born into families who survive trauma. That's why it is vital for us as clinicians to gather as much anecdotal history as possible, to assist trauma survivors to understand how generational trauma has impacted their lives. When we unravel the trauma story, we impact in a positive way the epigenetic makeup of our children and grandchildren. In treatment, I see that begin with families that work so hard to change the direction of their trauma story. Many of my most successful clients who struggled with attachment and relationships but found healing and purpose in their trauma stories are now having children. They've changed the attachment story to one about a healthy, nurturing relationship. They are now providing to the next generation the relationship they needed as children.

Epigenetics is exciting to me because it's proof that the story can be changed, that nature and nurture can synergistically change the direction of our very traumatic world environment. The healing of one individual can create healing for a whole family, and then a whole tribe, and so on.

A Tree of Life

Making a family tree is an assignment that has long been used in addiction treatment—to determine various addictions, co-dependency, and family traits of the addict. You know: hero child, mascot, scapegoat, co-dependent, comedian, parentified child, plumber. I made up the plumber role, but in my house that was an important skill to have, given that my father was a plumber and often left at least one part of the job undone or incomplete in our house. As it turns out, family trees are incredibly important to understand the width and breadth of intergenerational trauma.

In 2007, Peter A. Levine, Maggie Kline, and Merida Blanco conducted a study that resulted in tracing a five-generation account of the effects of violence on subsequent generations in South America that could be mapped onto the history of indigenous Australia. Their discussion on intergenerational transmission of trauma accounts for the breakdown of functional society over generations as follows:

First Generation: Conquered males were killed, imprisoned, enslaved, or in some manner deprived of their ability to care for their families.

Second Generation: Many men overused alcohol and/or drugs, resulting in loss of cultural identity and diminished self-worth. Various cultures dealt with this substance-use issue in different ways, including incarceration or confinement to the reservation, giving no support or treatment.

Third Generation: Increase in spousal abuse, domestic violence, and the breakdown of the family unit.

Fourth Generation: Trauma begins to be reenacted and directed at the spouse and child; signifying a serious challenge to the family unit and societal norms.

Fifth Generation: The cycle of violence is repeated and compounded, as trauma begets violence through increasingly severe violence and increasing societal distress.

If you consider their findings, I think you'll be able to see how this can be extrapolated to Native Americans and indigenous people everywhere. Also, given any historical trauma, how we could extrapolate behaviors. Consider the possibilities with children of the Depression and generations of soldiers and their families, and sexual abuse survivors, over the generations. Looking at my family tree, my father grew up extremely poor during the Depression. He was in a family of twelve children, who often went without food, and only six of his siblings lived to adulthood. My father-in-law grew up during the Depression as well, the only child of a single momma, an immigrant from Italy. The difference in the "money messages" and behaviors were extreme.

My father-in-law had an intense work ethic and saved everything. In the basement were #10 vegetable cans filled with buttons, nails, screws, safety pins, aluminum foil, etc. He saved everything, just in case. He and my mother-in-law had life and health insurance on everyone, just in case there was another financial disaster. My father's attitude was different in that he had a strong work ethic, but sometimes just "took off." It was very difficult for him to have a boss. He almost always worked for himself as a plumber. When he had a big payday, he'd celebrate and spend frivolously on the family. "Just in case" there was another financial disaster, he wanted us to at least experience abundance, even if it was fleeting. Our financial life was insecure: very good or very bad, never "just right."

I was the oldest child and had enormous shame about our poverty. I hated being dependent on anyone, and worked from the time I was eleven years old. I was the first in my family to do many things, including going to college and making sure all my children graduated from college with professional careers. I'm a dreamer—and I dream big. And I'm blessed that our intergenerational trauma, including addiction, has been interrupted. My in-laws were secretly secure, protecting the family but always "crying poor."

As my mother-in-law used to tell me, that's "family business."

The issues are never about money; they're about fear, insecurity, shame and guilt, grief and loss, and low self-esteem. Let's look at Alex's (a past client) family tree by starting with his story.

ALEX'S STORY:
A FAMILY TREE OF TRAUMA

Screaming until he's hoarse, raging, profanity, and threats. His face is red and blotchy, his eyes bulging. Twenty-seven years old and out of control, literally out of control. Exactly as he was at seven years old, being held down by five boys and beaten every day, and then one by one they molested him over and over almost every day for weeks. His whole stay at camp, despite hysterical calls to his parents who were used to his "spoiled brat" behaviors and thought this was more of the same. He never told the secret; the boys had threatened to tell everyone he liked it, that he was gay. If he told, they would kill him. To a seven-year-old boy, that is a real threat that his seven-year-old mind and body never forgot. The body remembers everything: the smells, the sounds, the taste, the touch, and the threats . . . and so much more. The body remembers! He'd make calls to his father who yelled back, "Just stop being a sissy boy. You're so worthless, why do I waste my money on such a stupid boy? I wish you hadn't been born." Those brutal messages from the people who love you are deadly to our psyche, even when they are said in frustration and anger—perhaps more so. Behaviors and choices always make sense if we understand the history and generational history, and the verbal and intuitive messages the child received, positive or negative.

For most folks, being on the receiving end of this raging behavior makes us turn and walk away, or otherwise choose not to engage. This is exactly what happens to Alex most of the time. He's extremely intelligent, well spoken, a good-looking "geek," with no social skills or ability to see outside himself. He does not have any empathy, or the ability to soothe himself. He loathes himself. Why wouldn't he? That's his experience of the world. The world loathes him, and he uses arrogance to cover that up, and to keep the pain away. "You will not hurt me again. I am smarter, richer, and I can cause you pain. Watch!"

And he does. Alex is clever. He sets peers up to do what he suggests and then becomes a tattletale to the authorities: "See what they've done? When will you punish them?"

Makes sense to me. No one believed him, protected him, or punished the perpetrators, so he does that symbolically to others and "reports" them, hoping for redemption. Is he cognitively aware of that? No, only after extensive treatment and it becomes one more piece of the puzzle.

The only relief he feels is when he uses alcohol and drugs, or is "stirring the pot" and creating chaos. Oh yes, and he feels relief when a girl likes him, and then she becomes his drug.

To understand how we got to today, to this moment, we have to understand the family history. Granddad Emile came to the U.S. from Germany as a nine-year-old on a ship by himself, with the equivalent of twenty dollars. He was met at the docks by a cousin who let him sleep on the floor in a corner of the kitchen. He went to work at a factory where they made women's dresses. That nine-year-old grew to live the American dream, going from there to owning his own small clothing factory. What it took for Granddad to get there was a desire to move out of poverty and "become" some-one. It said so on the statue in the harbor: "Give me your tired, your poor, your huddled masses yearning to breathe free." He believed and made it happen. He made it happen and that focus, courage, and single-minded drive also created a stoic, silent, hard, angry man. His anger and discipline was heaped on his wife and children, especially his son. They were steeped in the pride of their work and accomplishments but did not communicate, share intimacy, or tell secrets. You see, as a boy in his cousin's home, he was molested regularly by his older, bigger cousin. To escape, he needed to work hard and to hide money, and he did. He was told he would be killed if he told. Sound like a made-for-TV movie? I hear stories like this all the time, often from your grown children or you. So Granddad raised his children with anger, secrets, harsh discipline, an intense work ethic, and very little love, affection, or time. He worked all the time. Pride. He also raised his family to have pride, almost an arrogance at what they'd overcome. He should be proud but everything has extremes and this was a family of extremes. They yelled instead of talking, berating and criticizing in the name of love.

This isn't rocket science, so what comes next? Alex's father, Henry, is a hard-working, absent, angry, stoic, demanding man. He shows love through hard work and money but is unable to share any positive affirmations for his children. He didn't receive it, although he certainly craved love with his whole being. How would he know how to give those warm, loving words that every human needs? He'd been demeaned and discounted by his father, that poor boy Emile who raised himself and dealt with his feelings of fear and pain with more work, more money, more anger, very little joy, and certainly no parental love and affection. His parents had loved him enough to send him to America. His mother had given him love, affection and kindness, and then at nine he was left to fend for himself. But it was that early attachment that made it possible for him to survive.

One of our clients, Karen, was an absolute warrior as she

struggled with her childhood trauma and courageously battled breast cancer. She painted through her trauma recovery, diagnosis, and surgery. The first three paintings were done while she was in treatment and had started having body memories of childhood sexual abuse. Two vision boards were created while she was in treatment with our team; the last two are after breast cancer.

KAREN'S STORY:
HEALING THROUGH PAINTING

When I arrived at Judy's treatment center in 2011, I had been to treatment approximately eighteen times in sixteen years. I had a harrowing IV heroin, cocaine, and methadone addiction, and was smoking crack when I went to chemical dependency treatment for the last time in 2008. My therapist suggested that I go to treatment to address my ongoing struggles with sex addiction, an eating disorder, bipolar disorder, self-harm, and suicidal ideation. When I arrived there, I wasn't aware that I had experienced any trauma. As I came to learn the definition of trauma, and began thinking back through my adult life, it became clear that I had actually survived a great deal of it.

As other clients began recounting their stories of childhood sexual abuse, I often had profound physical and emotional reactions, but the memories had not yet begun to emerge. The therapists helped me to become aware that I often dissociated, began experiencing age regression, and frequently held my breath. They were extremely supportive, but encouraged me to just let things unfold naturally, and not to jump to any conclusions. Instead, it

was suggested that I explore the feelings I was having. I choose
the medium of art because I didn't have images or any kind of a
narrative to go along with the intense feelings I was experiencing,
but I felt that I could represent them in paintings. It also helped
me to feel more empowered. I had always loved art as a child, but
had stopped expressing myself that way by the age of twelve. The
collages and collage paintings were created very intuitively. I find it
fascinating that the memories that have recently begun emerging
mesh with the symbolism in the artwork. At the time I created them,
I wasn't even consciously aware of the meaning of many of the sym-
bols I chose. This synchronicity has served to reinforce my interest in
Carl Jung and depth psychology.

The first collage painting is titled *The Truth of Persephone*. The narcissus, in the upper
right-hand corner, is the beautiful flower that Persephone beheld, and, once plucked, the earth
opened up and she was abducted and whisked away to the Underworld by Hades to become

his bride. In many accounts of the myth, it's implied that Persephone was raped by Hades, and in some, that her father actually consented to allow Hades to do this. The pomegranate, in the upper left-hand corner, is the fruit that was given to her by Hades that stained her lips. It let her mother Demeter, and the rest of the world know, that she had tasted the fruit of knowledge and experience and was forever changed. She was no longer an innocent maiden, and so it was acknowledged that for the second half of every year, she would resume her position as Queen of the Underworld, where she served as a guide to enable lost souls to find their way home.

The spring and summer months would be spent above ground on Earth and in the heavens with Demeter, who was so distraught from the loss of her daughter that she had neglected her duties, and thus, the Earth had become barren. The spilt wine flowing from the glasses also represents blood, and the serpents at the foot of the throne have multiple meanings. I drew each piece by hand on poster board, and then cut it out, painted it, and glued it to the canvas. To me, even the painstaking process of creating these collages mirrors my own journey to discover the truth.

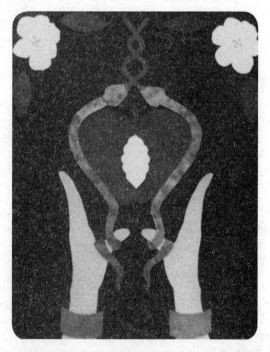

The second collage painting is titled "The Wages of Sin." It represents the story of Adam and Eve, and once again, tasting the bittersweet fruit of knowledge and experience. The apple at the center is meant to be shaped like a heart, and the bite is intended to be shaped like an aspect of feminine anatomy. I used the narcissus again; this time to represent healthy self-love.

The painting "Hearts of Darkness" was created with a background of my own blood. I literally felt the need to bleed my pain onto the canvas. The symbolic meaning of the owl, the blood, the shattered mirror, and even the story "Heart of Darkness" presaged my own journey into recovering from childhood sexual abuse. I did not know at the time that the shattered mirror with my reflection represented fragmented identity, something I would come to painfully experience.

The three remaining collages were all created in the spirit of the eternal hope for healing that resides deep within me. Judy and my therapist served to kindle this spark of hope into a burning desire to continue to persevere, heal, and uncover my truth. For that, I am so grateful because I was diagnosed with stage three breast and neuroendocrine cancer a year after my first stay there.

The collages with the women and the word "God" in the center were completed after I discovered I had cancer and had a full mastectomy at the age of forty-two. I placed "God" near images of strong women because I knew that I ultimately had to find the divine within my own heart, and I did. It was important for me, as a single woman, to reinforce the idea that I was still sexy and desirable after losing my left breast. These vision boards have continued to serve as a source of hope and inspiration. I look at them whenever I need to renew my determination to continue to fight, not just to live, but to live well.

REFLECTIVE SKETCHES

1) Interview family members, going back as far as you can, and put together a history of any trauma that occurred in their lives. See if there was depression, violence, wars, emotionally unavailable people, workaholics, unwanted pregnancy. How did this affect the family and the generations?

_____

_____

_____

2) What do you know about your family tree?

_____

_____

3) Make a list of your caregivers: parents, nannies, babysitters, etc.

_____

_____

_____

4) Identify five to six adjectives, both positive and negative, for your caregivers.

_____

_____

_____

_____

_____

5) List your siblings in order and give adjectives for them. Then identify your role in the family.

_____

_____

_____

_____

6) Identify parental and maternal grandparents and do the same thing.

_____

_____

7) If there is addiction, mental health, or behavioral issues that you are aware in any of your family please highlight those.

_____

_____

_____

8) If you are aware of trauma events, list those.

_____

_____

_____

9) Were any of your parents, grandparents, great-grandparents, or other relatives combat veterans, Holocaust survivors, or survivors of any other trauma event such as depression or natural disasters, adoption, divorce, multiple marriages, or other patterns in your family? This may be an overwhelming task, so if you find yourself in that place stop and take a breath, and then take another deep

breath. Go back to *The Trauma Heart* and fill your spirit with the triumph of those who are much the same as you are.

_____

_____

_____

_____

_____

10) What insights do you have as a result of this exercise?

_____

_____

_____

CHAPTER

5

ALL WE NEED IS LOVE: A MATTER OF ATTACHMENT

"The most terrible poverty is loneliness,
and the feeling of being unloved."

—Mother Teresa

"Loneliness is the want of intimacy."

—Frieda Fromm-Reichmann

❦

I want to talk about loneliness and the physical, emotional, and spiritual impact it has on people. I want to explore the correlation between trauma and its role in germinating loneliness and I want to explore attachment theory, trauma, developmental trauma disorder, and the ramifications of this enormous epidemic of loneliness on relationships and society as a whole.

An Epidemic of Loneliness

Originally I wanted to name this book *The Loneliest Heart* because I see loneliness at the core of a majority of my clients. There is a desperate yearning for love, connection, belonging, and a tribe among trauma survivors and those embroiled in addictions. Many who are trauma survivors and addicts have layers and layers of trauma beginning in early childhood, many times from the womb, and very often they are experiencing the fallout from intergenerational trauma. For many the loneliness seeped into their spirit before they were born, carrying the pain and sadness of their parents or grandparents.

Psychiatrist Bessel van der Kolk explained in *The Body Keeps the Score*:

> When caregivers are emotionally absent, inconsistent, frustrating, violent, intrusive, or neglectful, children are liable to become intolerably distressed and unlikely to develop a sense that external environment is able to provide relief. Thus, children with insecure attachment patterns have trouble relying on others to help them, while unable to regulate their emotional states by themselves. As a result, they experience excessive anxiety, anger, and longings to be taken care of.

Trauma and addiction are driven by compromised attachment issues and the inability to form supportive, loving relationships. Developmental trauma disorder drives compromised attachment, a vicious cycle.

This simply means that if a child is neglected, abused, ignored, or maltreated in any way, he or she finds it extremely difficult to feel loved and to feel connected. The outcome is overwhelming loneliness and a yearning for connection, often before birth.

In 1998, Jean Vanier, a philosopher, theologian, and humanitarian, wrote *Becoming Human*, an extraordinary, insightful piece that elegantly to the unloved, unwanted child. According to Vanier, "To be lonely is to feel unwanted and unloved, therefore, unlovable. Loneliness is a taste of death. No wonder some people who are desperately lonely lose themselves in mental illness or violence to forget the pain."

In the late 1950s, Frieda Fromm-Reichmann wrote about loneliness in her early work about a female patient who was catatonic.

Judith Shulevitz in *The New Republic*, "The Lethality of Loneliness,"
May 23, 2013, describes how Fromm-Reichmann begins to communicate by asking how the patient how lonely she was; this woman had
not communicated before. In response, the young woman "raised her
hand with her thumb lifted, the other four fingers bent toward her
palm," Fromm-Reichmann wrote. The thumb stood alone, "isolated
from the four hidden fingers." The analyst responded gently, "That
lonely?" And at that, the woman's "facial expression loosened up as
though in great relief and gratitude, and her fingers opened." I wonder what childhood trauma created the need to build the walls of
catatonia for protection?

Later in the article Shulevitz reports that Fromm-Reichmann
cured a schizophrenic girl. Fromm-Reichmann left Germany to
escape Hitler and was known for insisting that no patient was too
sick to be healed through trust and intimacy, and, I would add to
that, love.

This comes as no surprise to me after working with people in
despair and loneliness. Love and care from staff, from housekeeping
through clinical staff, goes a very long way in the healing process.
Kindness and compassion, empathy and hope, are essential in trauma
treatment and we can't fake it or act "as if," because trauma survivors
and addicts of all stripes are hypervigilant, intuitive, and alert to those
who are not genuine.

Within our work with trauma and addictions, research has connected multiple health issues, including mental health issues, to disease and illness triggered by the experience of trauma. The correlation
between trauma and loneliness is incredibly strong. Our understanding of the role of attachment in early childhood relationships is an
added element to this discussion.

So let's expand Judith Shulevitz's premise to include trauma, addiction, and attachment disorders as a pathway to loneliness.

Bessel van der Kolk, MD, a giant in the field of trauma and PTSD, identified developmental trauma disorder (DTD), which is described as trauma "since the egg hit the sperm," or, as Dr. Allan N. Schore, a leading expert in attachment theory, said, "trauma in the first thousand days, conception to age two." Trauma can start in utero and also be affected by intergenerational trauma.

Dr. van der Kolk hasn't received the backing of much of the "psychiatric powers that be" for his work on developmental trauma. However, I have no doubt that his findings are accurate. I have hundreds, perhaps thousands, of cases where the infant has experienced trauma in utero and that has had an enormous impact on development, attachment styles, and resilience or lack of resilience, all without the memory or words to describe it.

Relational trauma pertains to a "violation of human connection" (Judith Herman, 1992) which results in attachment injuries. Relational traumas include "a vast range of violations including childhood abuse, domestic violence, entrapment, rape, infidelity, bullying, rejection, psychological/emotional abuse, and complex grief rooted in unresolved loss of important connections." (Sheri Heller, 2015).

My experience is that many, many of our clients have six or seven out of those nine traumas. It is as though once the pain begins it is difficult to turn off the spigot. One type of trauma seems to lead to the next and, for a vulnerable child, there is no recourse. The generational patterns become passed down to one more generation and so does the overwhelming loneliness, an insatiable emptiness and disconnection, the inability to sustain supportive relationships.

Throughout this book are the stories of men and women who are survivors of childhood trauma. Although they start as victims, in treatment they begin to understand the courage and resilience it takes to walk through their trauma story to trauma resolution, and then they own the title of survivor. As the work continues, these lonely boys and girls in grown-up bodies begin to embrace the shininess of survival, creating powerful new stories of redemption and self-love. Then they become thrivers.

What are the events that create this lonely, wounded child that Jean Vanier speaks of? Abandonment and neglect comes in many shapes and sizes. They are the most lethal traumas because they create a feeling of truly being alone in the world, not good enough for the physical and emotional sustenance of their caregiver. The message is powerful and devastating: "You are not worth my time or energy; you are a zero, a burden." These and a litany of other unspoken messages are internalized by the child, who begins to operate in the world driven by those declarations.

Now please understand, most parents want to be present and available for their babies. Most parents are not malicious, but situations and circumstances can fertilize and grow the feeling of abandonment and neglect. A single mother, working to care for her latchkey children, coming home from work exhausted with very little to give emotionally, is not malicious. There is no right or wrong here, no good or bad, just what is, and everyone experiences guilt and shame. The two-parent home is often in the same situation.

DANNY'S STORY:
IT'S PRIMAL

Danny cried angrily: "You don't understand—I hate both my 'mothers!'" This last word, *mother*, virtually spat from his rage-twisted mouth. "I never knew my real mother, we never had a relationship, she threw me away when I was born."

Such pain, deep and primal. Danny felt as though he would never be able to live in this world without the insane behaviors that kept sending him back to treatment. There had always been "behaviors" that created separation and distance between him and his adopted family. He "knew" they loved him but he just couldn't connect. Alcohol and drugs, sex and relationship addiction, and lots of psychiatric diagnoses—borderline personality, ADHD, self-harm—a long list that didn't speak to the deep loneliness and alienation that he felt.

"You did have a relationship. You and your mother shared everything for nine months."

His therapist and I were intervening on this pain that screamed from his soul and looked and sounded like anger. His therapist was pregnant, a perfect storm. She and I described what a mother and child experienced together during pregnancy, what it felt like, what was going on in utero, when the baby started moving. We then asked Danny to create a body map or a trauma egg that reflected the experience that he needed, the best possible pregnancy.

Danny created a womb with a fetus that was surrounded by light and colors and music, words that said: "My mother loved music and listened to beautiful music throughout our time together, her love of bright colors made me an artist today, the cord was wrapped around my throat and now I know why I have trouble talking intimately, my mother loved me so much she gave me away to save my life because she knew I would not survive."

I can tell you that was one of the most moving pieces of work I've experienced; Danny's perspective shifted and he began to heal that primal wound.

The Primal Wound: Understanding the Adopted Child is an extraordinary book written by Nancy Newton Verrier. Verrier, a psychotherapist, speaks to the double bind of the adopted child who is wounded, possibly believing they were unwanted or thrown away, and at the same time needing, wanting a caregiver, someone to love and cherish. Mixed emotions about love and loyalty, attachment, and isolation abound. The next three stories are poignant and also filled with dreams fulfilled in the midst of a search for love.

ANDREW'S STORY:
FILLING THE VOID

I was six weeks old when my parents adopted me. Although my mom and dad were average Americans who are very loving and kind, I was a troubled child. I felt no connection or attachment. There was always a void. From a very early age I was maladjusted to the world around me through no fault of my parents. Unsure of how to handle me, they started taking me to therapists at about the age of six. This started a long process of my going to different psychologists and psychiatrists, and trying different medication or other techniques to help.

Throughout my entire life, I've suffered from an inability to form healthy and meaningful relationships with people around me. Around age fifteen I found alcohol and drugs, and by the time I was twenty I was seldom sober for twenty-four hours in a row. I was also suicidal from a very young age. I knew the way I treated my family and friends was abnormal and that the way I related to the world was flawed, but I was unable to make any meaningful changes to my behavior. Alcohol and drugs helped me cope with how I felt inside for a while, but before long the feeling would wear off and by the time I was about twenty-five it wasn't working at all anymore. I was unemployable. I was unable to spend holidays with my family because the shame and guilt were unbearable for me, and I would use so much that it was embarrassing and disappointing for everyone involved.

I asked for help and went to a detox for the second time in winter of 2005. When it was time to leave, I begged to stay because I had been released from the detox a year prior and relapsed the night I got out. I desperately wanted to stop but didn't know how. The case manager at that detox said there were only a couple of long-term treatment centers in the country that truly addressed trauma. Judy's was one of them. With Judy's and her therapists' guidance, I opened up completely for the first time about things in my life.

When I arrived, I was a difficult client. I yelled at staff, I would slam doors and leave group in a fit. Some of the staff wanted to throw me out several times. Judy Crane told them to let me stay and to just let me be. I learned later that Judy had some revolutionary concepts about how to help people like me. The first couple of weeks were tough and mostly the staff just left me alone. I remember that they were always supportive but they didn't try to push me to do things like go to group. In retrospect, the amount of patience and tolerance that Judy and her staff employed with me are still somewhat unbelievable. The time I spent at treatment completely transformed the way I view the world. Although I had some difficulties after leaving The Refuge, Judy and her family and friends have always been there for me. They continue to guide me through invaluable life lessons.

I've been clean and sober since October of 2012. Since getting sober I've gotten my GED, returned to college, and will be graduating in May with full honors. This is after a fifteen-year hiatus from dropping out of high school with failing grades, and threats from the administration of filing trespassing charges on me if I returned to their property!

I have a six-year-old daughter. Last summer I was able to be there for her when her mother was unable to continue to care for her. I never would have been able to begin to cope with this situation I was thrust into without tools and support of friends like Judy and the fellowship I've found in the rooms.

Another miracle took place last summer when my sister from my family of origin contacted me after more than a decade of diligent effort. I met my birth mother, father, and sister over Christmas break last year, and am in the process of building a relationship with them today that I never imagined possible.

For the first time in our lives, I also have a wonderful, healthy, and deepening relationship with my mom and dad who raised me. Most of my life I felt like I had a void inside me. I used a lot of different things to try and fill this missing space inside me with no useful effect. Today, I don't feel like there is something missing. Today, I'm able to have the relationships with family and friends that were missing and causing these feelings. I don't believe that any of this would have happened if it were not for the experience that started with meeting Judy and her family and staff in 2006. There are still good times and hard times but overall I am more satisfied with my life today than I ever have been. Overall I am excited to see what the future holds and I am ecstatic to continue to build these new relationships with my family of origin, my family who raised me, and with my daughter. Things have changed so much that sometimes it is hard for me to believe. All I know is that once I gave myself over to the process of recovery, it most definitely worked miracles in my life.

CLAUDIA'S STORY:
TRAUMA DOES NOT MAKE US SPECIAL

I still remember what my birth mother looks like because I see her every day in the mirror. I know the softness of her chin and the curly tendrils of her raven hair. I remember the night we spent in a shelter and how warm I felt curling up in her soft breast while we rocked in the hammock, safe in her curves. I know the stringy bristles of sugar cane and how you can chew it into a toothbrush. I love sweet plantains even though I don't know where I've had them. I also know how the darkness of an empty room for hours on end can feel like it's eating you alive. I know you can cry yourself hoarse in darkness just so you don't feel alone. Even when the light would come I didn't eagerly welcome the light of an opening door. Light was welcome but I never knew if my stepfather was coming to let me out or torture me.

I think he thought it was funny to knock me down and watch me struggle to get back up. He enjoyed watching me cry when he would grab a snake from outside and hold me down while he let it wriggle across my body or up my arm. My little baby stepsister was off limits to him, but I was fair game. I was not his child; I was worthless. I went in this fish-trapping "cage" when they weren't home and I ate last, if at all. When my sister was born my birth mom was around more and didn't disappear for what felt like days. I knew it was my job to protect my little sister, and when the house felt like it was going to burst with the loudness of fear and uncertainty, I cried less and comforted more.

The dark shadows of a corner were my solace. The day men came to our home, tied my stepfather up to a chair and beat him bloody, all I remember of the time after is only overwhelming feelings of confusion and fear. I can't recall images of men coming back to shoot my birth mom in front of me while she tried to climb out of a window; I just know it happened. She wasn't hurt badly but one of the last times I saw her she was in the clinic and I know I touched her hand. That was one of the last memories I have of her. I'd be lying if I told you I remember her dropping me off on the steps of the orphanage, although I picture her telling me to be strong and that she would always love me. These are the things I know; I don't know how I know these things or why I remember. This was my life before and what I carry in the furrows of my soul.

Like many, I have two sides of myself: my private self and the person I show the everyday world. For an individual who has experienced trauma, that private side holds so much pain, confusion, and sadness. It feels shameful and leaves me with a yearning to be understood. Other than my memories, I have nothing from my life prior to being adopted. I do not have one baby picture, or toy, or piece of clothing. I wasn't born in a hospital so I do not even have a birth certificate. It's almost as if that life wasn't real. What was real was that I had been given another chance at life. Amidst the chaos of poor life choices, my birth mother made one amazing decision and let me go.

A lawyer working for the orphanage, who was assisting in adoptions, saw me one day and took me home. He told my adoptive mother later he saw me there and "knew I didn't belong there." This lawyer decided he would help me find a family, and for the first time, I felt safe. They were a beautiful, white Ecuadorian family that had four boys. The mom was pregnant with what she hoped would be a girl, so when I came home with her husband she and her maids doted on me like I was a gift. My life was calm, predictable, and vibrant; full. I could make forts with mattresses and giggle with my foster brother Joaquin. When I was adopted at the age of about three-and-a-half years, my life seemed literally like a dream. I could grasp at moments, but they were vignettes. Small pieces of horror and a mother's warmth in a hammock, but nothing added up and nothing could compare to my new life in the United States.

A life where I wanted for nothing could never compare to being locked up in a cage like a dog when my parents couldn't take care of me. That side of me, that life before, was hard to reconcile. However, for a year or so after being adopted and before I swore off talking about my life in Ecuador, I would tell my new mother about my life before . . . before her. I told her how I got the large waxy oval scar that covered the majority of my little toddler shin, and my new mother, a teacher and trained children's counselor, gave me markers and paper. She wrote it all down and even tape recorded a few of my stories. My mother made sure she got all of it, the good and the bad. Maybe she knew one day I would need to look back at my life before, even if I needed to pack it away for now. One morning when I was five years old, I told my adoptive mother, "No more Spanish," and I never spoke another word. I couldn't. I had to learn to survive.

Despite wanting so desperately to fit in, I never really did. I always looked different and I definitely did not resemble the rest of my family. This fact often welcomed invasive questions about our family structure. "How much did you pay for her?" "Where is your real family?" and "Do you still talk to them?" Once, before Mother's Day in third grade, a friend informed me I couldn't participate in making a Mother's Day craft because I didn't have a "real mom."

My adoptive mother is in every way my mother. She told me once that she may not have given birth to me but before I was born, I was a twinkle in her eye. My mother has changed her bed when I wet it with bad dreams, she fed and clothed me, she went to every school conference, arranged every play date, stood in the rain at my sports games, sat with me through sickness, calmed me when I had tantrums, and most of all she encouraged me in every way.

My mother wanted to give me everything, not realizing it may give me a sense of entitlement. After I was adopted I did not know what it was like to need anything and not get it. I had been abused in early childhood, and I believed I was owed.

In high school, I began skipping classes, not handing in assignments, and calling myself out of school. As a flirt, I received a lot of bullying from older girls and even among friends. I switched groups frequently. My clothes got tighter, my shirts lower, and I didn't have a strong male at home to tell me to cool it with the sexiness. Surprisingly I never was sexually active in high school. My relationships were too superficial to get serious enough for sex and my mother had a tight rein on my dating. The things I focused on were what I felt I could easily control. My appearance was on the top of the list. I planned my outfits for the week and matched satin bow with the color of my shirt.

Moreover, weight control and bulimia were creeping into my mind. I felt that my breasts, which developed so early and created unwanted attention, made me look fat. Desperate to reject my curves, I dabbled with restricting, bingeing, and throwing up. If I looked "acceptable," then I thought my social anxieties would vanish. One of the few times my mother allowed me to go to a high school party, I flirted with the wrong boy and was kicked out of the party in an embarrassing scene. Similar to my reaction with friends confronting me, I swore off all future high school parties.

It wasn't until college when I really drank and started partying. There was a blithe feeling of freedom that came with drinking. The years of anxiety easily faded away. This terrible nervousness that someone would "find me out," which had always manifested in avoidance and psychosomatic pain, was now relieved easily.

When I think of the word trauma, I often would picture a large bleeding cut, a tangible open wound, not always of an experience. I knew by the way certain adults knew my story they would look at me with a sympathetic downward glance that couldn't comprehend my experiences. I knew there was something different, something that if I shared with others they would never look at me the same way again. Then again, I learned later that when I told people my story it gave me this undeniable trump card. It was manipulative. I thought no matter what they told me, nothing could compare to what I had been through. I may have always felt unique, different, and entitled as a result, but the truth is I wasn't special. For a long time my story held so much control over me I assumed it would also shut down the other person.

MICHAEL'S STORY:
MY JOURNEY

I was adopted at birth. My birth mother's name is Tracy and I forget my birth father's name. They met in Minnesota. From what I understand my father came from a wealthy family who owned a freight company and Tracy was sort of "the girl from the other side of the tracks." They were teenagers in love, or maybe lust, and Tracy became pregnant with me, I believe, when she was about seventeen years old. My birth father's family was not too thrilled about this to say the least, so from the beginning there was conflict in my life as

I lived in my mother's womb. Tracy comes from a family filled with trauma. They say this thing is generational, right? Well, her father was a volatile, abusive alcoholic, and Tracy's mom was co-dependent. At some point during the pregnancy Tracy moved to Baton Rouge, Louisiana.

My "adopted" parents were newlyweds living in Baton Rouge, Louisiana. That's the geographical connection that introduced my parents to Tracy and me.

Tracy wanted to keep me very badly, she told me this, but her mom and circumstances such as her young age and lack of a father's presence persuaded her to give me up for adoption. Tracy told me this when we met for the first time. I met her in a small south Louisiana jail when I was in treatment with Judy. She was incarcerated on drug-related charges (crack cocaine). Tracy has been in and out of jail for a number of years on predominantly drug-related charges. She became addicted to cocaine after a boyfriend introduced her to it. I think her whole life has been marred by giving me up for adoption. She has alluded to this notion a few times when we've communicated. I also have two brothers and one sister. Tracy is not in their lives; her addictions won't allow it.

So I was adopted in Baton Rouge, Louisiana. The adoption was arranged before I was born, so as soon as I was able to leave the hospital I went home to my parents. My mom has repeatedly told me that that was the best day of her life, and I believe her. My dad was actually a recovering alcoholic and was active in his alcoholism until I was about two years old. I never saw my father drink and I can thank Alcoholics Anonymous for that. That is the greatest gift my father gave me, becoming a member of AA, because it allowed him to be a father. So my dad was in and out of treatment centers for two years and his alcoholism was a concern in the adoption process.

I moved back to New Orleans when I was a year old. New Orleans is my home. I love that city with all my heart and I'm tearing up thinking about that beautiful city and its soulful people. Perhaps I'm tearing up also because I associate New Orleans with my innocence as a child.

I lived in the same neighborhood, Lakeview, a block away from my grandparents, for the first twenty years of my life. When I was about four years old I started to have some medical problems. I was bleeding rectally when I would defecate. Being so young, I didn't know the severity of the situation. I do remember seeing the blood in the toilet and being alarmed. I knew that was not natural. After many trips to a children's hospital it was established that I had colorectal cancer. Many of these procedures involved penetration of my anus. This was traumatic at the time and later I would learn led to consequences in my life.

By the time I was five years old, I had gone through an adoption where I was abandoned by the person I spent the first nine months of my life with, and was subjected to repeated invasive anal procedures where I hated being taken from my mom to have grown men violate my body.

My parents told me I was adopted when I was about nine or ten years old. I remember exactly where I was and exactly how I felt and exactly how I betrayed I felt.

Fast forward a few years and I'm thirteen years old and in high school. I had experienced some bullying in grade school and went from being in the "in crowd" to looking at that crowd from the outside just wanting to belong. I remember constantly trying to search for acceptance from them and feeling so alienated. Like I was not good enough. I did make new friends, but I always carried this sense of rejection and abandonment. Perhaps this sense of rejection was heightened by my adoption. I certainly think so.

In eighth grade, I experienced my first orgasm. I then soon discovered Internet porn. This was in 1998. From the beginning, masturbation was a regular thing and almost immediately it was aided by images either on the computer or from magazines I collected. I remember one time while masturbating I thought about how rectal stimulation supposedly feels good sexually and I decided to try it out (connection with my medical trauma).

My sophomore year of high school in 2000 was when I first started doing drugs, drinking, and had my first relationship: pot, alcohol, and a blond-haired, blue-eyed girl named Eliza. I was infatuated with her and when we broke up I remember taking that break up very hard. Again, I was confronted with the fear of abandonment. I was devastated and it took me a number of years to let go of that.

My use of drugs and alcohol continued to progress and I discovered that masturbation to Internet porn while on marijuana was a great pleasure. The computer is a Pandora's Box for sex addicts. My masturbation continued to evolve and progress, and objects inserted into my rectum became a regular occurrence. It was a thrill, a rush. Eventually I found my way to the gay chat rooms where sex was a necessity like food or water. Soon after, I met a guy off the Internet when I was seventeen years old and received a blowjob.

Over the next several years I continued to abuse drugs, act out sexually, and have relationships that failed miserably. My life was out of control. After trying several treatment centers I finally entered Judy's facility in Florida.

Judy's treatment center is unique and her treatment model is groundbreaking in that she really focuses on the trauma and accompanying process addictions that afflict many alcoholics and addicts. I saw something different in this place in my first week there. It was a peaceful environment. I remember a gentleman sharing about a colonoscopy bringing up some trauma he felt as a child and I was blown away that someone had gone through a similar experience as me—and these types of things were being talked about in treatment. Groups were small, intimate, and heavy. Real intense work was going on here.

I remember during my intake I denied having any trauma at all but eventually, over time, I began to tell my story, little by little. I fell in love with Judy's treatment center and didn't want to leave. I stayed there for four months. I eventually got to the point where I was talking openly, although reluctantly, about being HIV positive and being a sex addict. I quit fighting at the treatment center, at least when it came to my substance abuse. My substance abuse was such an overt and observable addiction that it overshadowed my sex addiction and trauma. I would say my primary addiction is sex and love addiction, with the catalyst for these addictions being my adoption and medical trauma. You get the love/abandonment/loneliness and shame piece from my adoption, and you get my sexual template/shame from my acting out through my medical trauma. I also firmly believe that my medical trauma brought up my adoption piece because I hated leaving my mom to have procedures performed. In addition, with all the medical complications I had rectally as a child, I believe that I came back to that trauma medically with contracting HIV through acting out with men.

I left Judy's treatment center in June 2009 with every intention of staying sober from chemicals and that's what I did. I was unsure of my sobriety for a few months because of my past history of relapse, but I told myself if I got a good sponsor that he would lay out some action for me to take every day that would ensure my sobriety.

My sexual addiction did not disappear. I started acting out almost immediately upon leaving treatment, and I had a mind clear of drugs and alcohol and an active relationship with God that didn't allow me to just numb the shame and pain I felt from my sex addiction. At about seventeen months sober I was bingeing in my sex addiction, completely free of drugs and alcohol, and I was miserable.

My experience with sex addiction is that it is exponentially more cunning, baffling, and powerful than alcoholism. The overt and obvious destruction that alcoholism causes really takes you completely out of life. I'm not capable of doing anything while shooting dope, it's a 24/7 affair, but with sex addiction I may act out for an eight-hour period a week and be able to go to school or work. It keeps a thin veil of shame between the world and me, and allows me to participate in life just enough to survive—but not truly live. Sex addiction is good at keeping me in bondage.

I went back to treatment with Judy in July 2010 with about a year and a half of sobriety. I focused primarily on my childhood trauma and adoption when I was there the second time. It was a really humbling experience for me to return to treatment sober. I thought I was supposed to be "healthy." It was pretty painful talking about acting out with men and sharing my experience about being HIV positive. There was a lot of focus surrounding my adoption and it was arranged for me to meet Tracy, my biological mother.

I flew down to New Orleans and met her in a small south Louisiana jail. It was pretty surreal. You could tell by her physical appearance she had been abusing crack chronically for many years, but through the wear and tear on her face I could recognize the biological, primal connection. We were only allowed a short conversation, about thirty minutes, but the time didn't matter; it was the exchanging of the senses that was twenty-six years in the making that touched my heart and soul.

I left treatment with Judy in October 2010 with more awareness and resolution on my trauma and how it relates to my addictions. I resumed taking classes to get my master's in mental health counseling and have begun a career in the counseling field. I've been in therapy for over a year now and it has been a valuable tool for me to continue the work I started with Judy. I am three-and-a-half years sober and a lot more resolution around my adoption, medical trauma, and addictions. I'm a work in progress, but it's a beautiful process. Sometimes I still feel very lonely and isolated by my HIV.

The soul wound of my traumas left a harsh scar, but I keep going. I have to. I want to get everything I can out of this gift of life God blessed me with. I know I am beautiful just how I am, HIV and all. I have nothing to be ashamed about. I . . . have . . . nothing . . . to . . . be . . . ashamed . . . about.

I was abandoned from the womb and lost in this world for quite some time, but nourished back to life by so many that I love. Thank God for love. Thank God that I can love myself today.

In her blog, *The Loneliness of Childhood Sexual Abuse*, Jasmin Cori stated, "Childhood sexual abuse is one of the loneliest experiences on the planet. It is being alone in three significant ways." The psychotherapist and author wrote that these ways are:

1) Alone with the secret.
2) Disconnected from the victimizer.
3) Disconnected from self.

I would add to that these other issues that cause significant loneliness: abandonment and neglect, bullying, alcoholism and addiction, or infidelity in the family. Any of those traumas force a child into a victim role that demands secret keeping; and puts the perpetrator in a power position to be feared. The absolute aloneness created by fear, guilt, and shame becomes a life of abject loneliness until the secret is told and the child is made to feel safe, protected, and loved.

The role of secure attachment is vital to so many areas of our lives: emotional, physical, and spiritual development; the ability to be in a relationship; and the ability to operate as a mature and competent human being. With compromised attachment, we start with a blueprint for our life that negatively impacts a lifetime of relationships; that intervene on healthy development of emotional, physical, and spiritual aspects of our life; our brains are being rewired to impaired relationships and we are ripe for trauma—a vicious cycle. Trauma creates compromised attachment, and impaired attachment invites trauma in relationships.

There are many shades to trauma, many levels to abandonment and neglect, to emotional or physical abuse, to having an alcoholic or drug-addicted parent, to domestic violence, to infidelity, and to being an adopted child in a loving home but in primal pain knowing at the soul level they have been given up. There is loneliness and despair from sexual abuse that transcends other traumas; the child takes on the shame and guilt of the perpetrator's act, and self-hatred and aloneness ensues. More than half the children in the U.S. experience trauma. Sixty percent of adults report experiencing abuse or other difficult family circumstances during childhood. You are not alone.

Remember your list of what traumas you experienced; be aware that you can acknowledge those traumas without blaming your family. But acknowledging them is vital to understanding who you are and how you operate in the world. Too often folks are resistant to identifying the traumas because of family loyalty, or the need to keep the secrets, or a real belief that "It wasn't so bad."

TRAUMA CREATES COMPROMISED ATTACHMENT AND, IMPAIRED ATTACHMENT INVITES TRAUMA IN RELATIONSHIPS.

Lonely children grow up to be lonely adults walking through their lives with a protective shield/mask. What is the shield or mask that hides your lonely little girl or boy? Or does your little one kick and scream, rant and rave, walk through the world angry and pushing people away, or is he or she needy with an insatiable search for connection?

I invite you to take this "level of loneliness" test offered by AARP. As we continue to explore loneliness, connection, attachment, trauma, and addiction, we'll begin to create a "Treatment Plan" to begin the healing process.

Take this test to measure your level of loneliness. Each question asks how often you feel a certain way by using these numbers:

1 = Never, 2 = Rarely, 3 = Sometimes, and 4 = Always.

1) How often do you feel unhappy doing so many things alone?

_____

2) How often do you feel you have no one to talk to? How often do you feel you cannot tolerate being alone?

_____

3) How often do you feel as if no one understands you?

_____

4) How often do you find yourself waiting for people to call or write?

_____

5) How often do you feel completely alone?

_____

6) How often do you feel unable to reach out and communicate with those around you?

_____

7) How often do you feel starved for company?

_____

8) How often do you feel it is difficult for you to make friends?

_____

9) How often do you feel shut out and excluded by others?

_____

Add up your responses to each question to calculate your total score. According to the UCLA Loneliness Scale created by Dr. Daniel

Russell, the average loneliness score is 20, a score of 25 or higher reflects a high level of loneliness, a score of 30 or higher reflects a very high level of loneliness.

In 2010, a New York University professor and philosopher named Ronald Dworkin wrote a paper for the Hoover Institute discussing why mass unhappiness and mass loneliness in the U.S. has triggered a rise in the caring industry. Over the past sixty years, while our general population has only doubled, the number of professional caregivers has increased more than one hundred-fold. In answering what accounts for this great change, Dworkin states that caring professionals now offer the support to lonely, unhappy people that they once found in their friends and family. He estimates half of all Americans are lonely and unhappy. Today, approximately 20 percent of the population is experiencing symptoms of anxiety and depression. As of 2004, 25 percent of Americans had no "discussion partner" of any kind—quite an increase from 1985's estimated 10 percent. As of 2010, in the U.S. there are 77,000 clinical psychologists, 192,000 clinical social workers, 105,000 mental health counselors, 50,000 marriage and family therapists, 17,000 nurse psychotherapists, and 30,000 life coaches. These numbers are a dramatic contrast to the late- 1940s, when there were only 2,500 clinical psychologists, 30,000 social workers, and family therapists numbered less than 500. Also, today most care professionals help people cope with everyday life problems, not true mental illness. People are paying for fifty-five minutes of connection, intimacy, someone to listen. Twelve years later the number of professionals has jumped dramatically to include sober companions, interventionists, educational consultants, and case managers.

Robert D. Putnam in *Bowling Alone: The Collapse and Revival of American Community* identifies a myriad of causes for the current epidemic of loneliness and isolation in the U.S.:

➡ The American family structure has changed; there is a breakdown in the traditional family unit.
➡ Where is the extended family?
➡ Changes in structure and scale of the American economy
➡ "Busy"ness and time pressure
➡ Movement of women in the paid workforce, some of necessity, some of choice
➡ Residential mobility
➡ Incredible rise in the miracle of technology

Add to this mélange the overwhelming numbers of trauma survivors, who are identifying themselves after years of secrets, lies, and isolation as a result of our industry opening the windows. There is an incredible shift in the psyche of humans today as more and more people are identifying their pain and naming the trauma that changed their lives and left them vulnerable, fearful, isolated, alone, and lonely. And if we doubt that trauma surrounds us we have only to turn on cable news 24/7.

In 2012, novelist Steven Marche extends the discussion to talk about what the epidemic of loneliness is doing to our souls and our society. Marche's report highlights:

➡ Loneliness and being alone are not the same thing
➡ Both are on the rise
➡ We meet fewer people

➡ We gather together less

➡ And when we gather, our bonds are less meaningful and less easy

➡ In 1985, 10 percent of Americans had no one to discuss meaningful things with. By 2004, it had jumped to 25 percent. And now more than a decade later?

Marche concludes that "in the face of this social disintegration, we have essentially hired an army of replacement confidants, an entire class of professional 'carers'" aligning with Dworkin's insights on the rising caring industry.

Looking to the future and the well-being of our children, psychiatrist Bruce Perry examined the disconnection between what children need to thrive and what the modern world has to offer. Today:

➡ Children have fewer healthy adults in their lives

➡ The average home today consists of fewer than three people

➡ The ratio of students to teachers is an average of 30:1

➡ TV, Internet, texting, video games dominate time and attention

Dr. Bruce Perry emphasizes the importance of human connections at early stages in life and offers tools for parents to help their children develop healthy minds, nurture friendships, and overcome traumatic experiences. The bottom line is, human-to- human, face-to-face interaction is decreasing dramatically. If adults can't regulate their time on the TV, Facebook, or iPhone, their "busyness," their "loneliness," how can we expect our children to have the resources for healthy social interaction and self-regulation?

Trauma elements create isolation and loneliness:

Trauma is a betrayal of the spirit, a soul wound: a spiritual betrayal

A feeling of brokenness which leaves the survivor feeling isolated, alone, "different"

Constant fear for their survival

Inability to trust or bond

An assault on emotional development

An infringement on social development

Hyperarousal which keeps the survivor vigilant and alert for the next onslaught, or hypoarousal, which keeps them shut down

Feelings of fear and terror, despair, confusion, isolation, sadness, separateness

To top it all off, Dr. Brian Koehler, president of the International Society for Psychological and Social Approaches to Psychosis, reports that the neuroscience of severe mental disorders overlaps with the neuroscience of chronic and profound stress, trauma, social isolation, extreme loneliness, and social defeat. This is so incredibly important for our industry to grasp. It gives great hope to those who have struggled with "mental health disorders." These are often chemical in nature but we must remember, trauma changes brain chemistry, and trauma resolution can begin the journey to healing brain chemistry as neuroscience research is showing us.

Many people come to treatment with anxiety, depression, OCD, mood disorders, and a myriad of other diagnoses. Very often those symptoms disappear when there is trauma resolution. An important question to ask clients when presented with a list of diagnoses: "When did you first experience anxiety, depression, etc.? What was going on in your life at that time?"

Oxytocin:
The Cuddle Hormone

*O**xytocin* is a soothing hormone produced in the brain. Often called the "love hormone" or "cuddle hormone," it creates a powerful feeling of connectedness between mother and baby. Purely on an ancient survival basis, oxytocin creates the maternal instinct, which drives Momma to care for her precious child. Oxytocin regulates childbirth and breastfeeding, and serves the propagation of the species.

Oxytocin is also released when people snuggle, hug, or are bonding socially. High levels of this snuggle hormone are found in couples in their first six months of relationship; it may increase romantic attachment and empathy. I tell my clients that the true test of a relationship is what you have created that is sustained after the first six months. So this powerful hormone that we experience at our own birth and when we give birth is one of the driving forces of skin hunger. We'll die without touch. Unfortunately, many people suffer in silence, desperately needing to be held.

In my first position as a therapist, there was a wonderful housemother who would rock our clients who would come in the evenings asking to be held. Miss Marcia taught a lot of women how to be loved. I've held many people in my lap and rocked them, and the tears often just stream down their face. And I have an amazing therapist, a big sensitive man with a lovely Jamaican accent who also rocks our clients. Recently at an intensive, one of our clients did some very powerful, painful work. Her therapist asked what she needed. This woman who had been sexually abused asked for "John" to hold her. He was another client who was the essence of a safe grandfather.

My experience is that those who need to be held will often go to massage parlors just to be held, or put themselves in dangerous situations to have their needs met. As therapists, we must always ask permission and also be certain that it is in the best therapeutic interests of the client.

Skin Hunger: Do You Need a Hug?

Could the Beatles be right? All we need is love? From the first breath we need, crave, ache, and cry for love, connection, nurturing, life-fulfilling attachment, and for our needs to be met. More than that, we will wither away and die without attachment to another: our mother, our caregiver, the source of our life. And if our body doesn't wither away, surely our soul does, our spirit.

Look into the eyes of a newborn, there is a question, a searching for the truth: "Will you care for me? Will you love me? Can I trust you?" It is instinctual, built into our survival toolbox. Babies are cute and cuddly, wonderful to hold. We coo and babble and make fools of ourselves for those little bundles of joy. That is a survival mechanism hardwired into our humanness, into creation.

In 2012, yoga teacher Marcus Julian Felicetti said, "Love is a miracle drug," in his *Mind Body Green* article, "10 Reasons Why We Need at Least 8 Hugs a Day." His research found that "a deep hug had a powerful impact on healing as well as loneliness, sickness, depression, and stress." Felicetti discusses the benefits of a hug that include: building trust and a sense of safety, boosting oxytocin and serotonin levels, strengthening our immune system, boosting self-esteem, releasing tension in our bodies, balancing our nervous system, teaching us how to give and receive warmth and love, connecting us with our heart and feelings in the moment, and encouraging empathy and understanding, which translates well in relationships.

Love, belonging, acceptance, and purpose are the basic needs of every human spirit. Let me tell you a story that may resonate with you, and offer hope and healing. It's not an uncommon story. A little girl, four years old, along with her two older brothers, six and eight years old, are abandoned by a single mom, taken by child protective services, separated, and left to the foster care system. We read it in the newspapers, see it on the news. So sad! And we move on.

Well, like all such children, that abandonment becomes the most devastating trauma, the separation of siblings painful beyond understanding. As trauma is measured, abandonment and neglect far outweigh all others, even the most violent of traumas. The message is clear. You are nothing, zero, you are a throw-away child, you have no value, not worthy of time or attention. Or they are battered daily with the messages: "I wish you weren't born, you ruined my life, you are stupid, fat, worthless, lazy, ugly, helpless." These and a litany of other messages become ingrained in the consciousness and spirit, and drive all future choices and behaviors. If you unravel the trauma story, all the behaviors and choices make sense. Follow me and I will show you.

JENNY'S STORY:
SKIN HUNGER

For one little girl, let's call her Jenny, these negative messages created a craving for love, for nurturing, for caring, a hunger for human touch that overwhelmed her whole body.

Can you relate? *Skin hunger* is an ache for touch, not sexual touch, but loving, connecting touch, touch that validates our worth. Infants die without touch. Adults whither without touch, rage without touch, become depressed, or anxious, or seek touch—any touch—in unhealthy, dangerous ways.

For Jenny, the little girl, it was a craving as intense as any addiction. After being taken into the first of many foster homes, she was sexually abused between the ages of four and seven years old by several foster caretakers and an older foster child. This attention gave her the message "You are special." Even though it was brutal and came with so many other negative messages; it was attention that Jenny craved.

Then, when she was seven years old and very ill with pneumonia, Jenny was taken to the hospital where the nurses really cared for her. They bathed her, fed her, touched her, talked to her, listened to her, and comforted this little girl in ways she had never experienced before. After that, there were many trips to the hospital where she got much care and concern from the nurses and doctors. Everything felt like love; she had nothing to measure it against.

The medical folks couldn't understand the bruises, the broken bones, or the wounds on her body. It was unfathomable that they could be self-inflicted—but for Jenny, the trade-off was worth the pain. Her need for love, attachment, and connection was so huge that for many years she purposefully hurt herself, creating wounds that brought her repeatedly to the loving arms of the nurses.

When I met Jenny, a bright but wounded woman of twenty-eight, it was very clear how she had damaged herself physically, and how she had been damaged by others emotionally and spiritually. So Jenny, all grown up with children of her own, reacted in every other way like a seven-year-old broken, wounded, and very needy little girl.

The healing of Jenny and those like her require clinicians to be loving, compassionate, empathetic, non-judgmental, patient, and, most of all, available to "listen and witness." After a lifetime of brokenness, of course the process of trauma resolution is often slow with many steps forward and back, like a magical dance.

Bright and Shining Spirits

When I was a little girl there was a bright and shining spirit that coursed through my whole being. I knew I was born for something very special and important, and God whispered that to me every moment. Anyone else out there have that feeling that you knew you were born for something special and glorious?

I was sick and home from school one day. It seemed I always had a lot of tonsillitis and ear infections. My mother would say I had big tonsils that caught every infection.

I had a special rapport with my kindergarten teacher, Ms. Dyer; she had been my mother's teacher twenty years before me, and she also taught my sisters. Well, on that particular sick day, my teacher sent me a bouquet of tea roses from the florist. Wow! That kindness spoke volumes to me at six years old. It told me Ms. Dyer was a kind and loving woman, for her to make that gesture told me I was important and special. That was a huge gift to my identity.

Sixty years later, it's still pivotal. We never know how what we do or say affects another human spirit, especially children. Attention, connection, attachment, and respect are the building blocks of a child's life, along with many loving hugs, touch, and caring, sincere words. I think the world suffers from skin hunger so deep that it contributes to the pain, despair, fear, and anger in the world.

Tea roses, kind words, applause for a child's performance, cheering and supporting a child through special events, lots of tender hugs, lots of "You are loved" in intent, words, and actions can lead to solid self-esteem. This helps children have a resilient spirit, and gives them a feeling of safety and well-being.

On the other hand, neglect, abandonment, derision, negative and hateful words, and angry and fearful or selfish actions tarnish and destroy that shining spirit each of us is born with. With trauma survivors, we often must communicate with that little child within first, showing love, kindness, and good parenting.

REFLECTIVE SKETCHES

1) What were the common themes of the three adoption stories?

_____

_____

_____

2) Describe three ways that Andrew, Claudia, and Michael were resilient.

_____

_____

_____

3) Can you relate to anything in their stories?

_____

_____

4) Are you getting eight hugs a day and, if not, why not?

_____

_____

5) What happens when you smile at a stranger? Does it make a difference?

_____

_____

6) Do you speak to the cashier at your local store? Would it make a difference? How does it make you feel? How do you think it makes them feel?

_____

_____

_____

CHAPTER

6

RUNNING
INTO THE FIRE

Resurrection

It is the time of resurrection,
The time of eternity,
It is the time of generosity, the sea of lavish splendor.
The treasure of gifts has come, its shining has flamed out.
See, the rose garden of love
Is rising from the world's agony.

—Rumi

❧

Who are the people who run toward the pain, the catastrophe, the chaos? Who are those people whose DNA or family mantra determine their role and their talent to solve the problems, salve the wounds, unravel the chaos? Who can put out the fires, put the house and lives back in order, soothe the wounded heart and soul, or sing a lullaby and put a child's fears to rest?

If over the years of your life your first response is to run toward the fire, take a breath and resolve the catastrophe or chaos, and you are talented at that role, if it comes naturally to you, then I suspect that you are the nurses, doctors, teachers, police, therapists, and caretakers of all kinds. I applaud you and thank you for your service!

My experience, however, is that there are enormous numbers of courageous, compassionate, and committed people who serve others, often at the expense of themselves and their families. I would like to explore the lives of these people, who "run into the fire."

STACY'S STORY:
WITNESS TO THEIR PAIN, BECAME HER PAIN

I fell in love with Africa *the minute I stepped off the plane in Freetown, Sierra Leone in 1995. From that moment I was hooked. Africa was in my blood: the smells, the feel of the air, the feeling of sacredness, the people, oh, the people. I am still awed by how these wonderful people can go through such hardships and still laugh, be gracious, generous, kind. I loved working with the local nationals. Most of our work staff was made up of a large number of host country nationals. Later, when I worked in Afghanistan, I loved the work, but my true love was and always will be Africa.*

Stacy is a delightful, charismatic woman, filled with energy and an all-consuming passion for whatever life puts in front of her. I first met Stacy in 2016 when she joined a five-day intensive retreat that we hold monthly through our treatment and training program, Spirit2Spirit. The venue was a glorious lakeside bed-and-breakfast on Lake Weir in Ocklawaha, Florida. The venue is important because the trauma work we do during those five to ten days is very deep, experiential, intimate, and very emotional. Intimacy is created as a result of the depth and honesty that is felt in shared pain and joy. As we learn to trust, we're able to risk telling our story, and be open to all possibilities for a healthy future.

Stacy attended our intensive retreat to explore ways she could let go of the pain of her inability to cure her daughter of her drug addiction and trauma history, which was emotionally, physically, and spiritually overwhelming her. Stacy's daughter had been in multiple treatment centers and had many near-death overdoses.

At the beginning of an intensive we ask, "What would you like to happen for you this week?" Stacy's response was to help her daughter "achieve recovery, or find a way to let go." Stacy is petite and bubbly, enthusiastic and passionate at her best. At the beginning of this intensive and for the next two sessions Stacy's most common response was "Roger that"—the lingo of her field of work.

"Stacy, can you describe your daughter?"

"Roger that."

"We're going to break for lunch, would you like a sandwich?"

"Roger that!"

As light-hearted as I make it sound, those responses were the immediate reactions from a woman who worked for twenty years in war-torn countries, part of the support personnel for peacekeeping missions all over the world. In other words, she was essentially a soldier without a gun.

Stacy reported that she and her sister grew up in a family dedicated to service for others. Raised in Port Arthur, Texas, during a time of racial strife, the sisters were taught that their life's purpose was to help others less fortunate to have better lives. Her father was a newspaper editor and her mother was a reporter. Their editorials and articles condemned segregation and supported equal rights.

After one such editorial, a brick was thrown through a window of their home. Threats were made and the girls were terrified, but they were expected to go to school the next day and brave the bullying and taunts.

When asked what dinner was like in her family, Stacy said, "We talked about politics, justice—or rather the injustice—and civil rights!"

Now let's unravel the elements of a first-responder's life. It comes as no surprise to me that Stacy would ultimately devote her life to others, "a soldier without a gun," a mother without a how-to guide for single parenting, and without an understanding of the breadth and depth of family trauma. Stacy was born and bred to serve. She had an amazing upbringing, but focusing on service to others often leaves no focus on self. The automatic reply of "Roger that!" in the "real world" (i.e., back home, outside of a war zone) spoke to me of burnout, numbness, and undiagnosed PTSD.

Stacy was asked to put her daughter's "work" on the side, and dive into her own story. The people at this intensive were from different regions, cultures, and socio-economic backgrounds. However, the commonalities were the depth of their isolation, personal grief stories, inability to be in truly intimate relationships, the need for validation, low self-worth. Each person was either emotionally erratic or numb. In short, this was a perfect group for healing, as group members can be the instruments for each other's healing.

Stacy was truly numb to the events in her life that she had been experiencing for the last twenty years and, as do many of us in the caring professions, she often reverted to "dark humor" to alleviate the stark reality of a situation. Witness her caption to her collage.

Flat Chick Bridge

The story is that in April 1996, fighting broke out in Monrovia and Monrovian citizens scaled the embassy wall for protection. Thousands of people were sleeping on the grounds of the embassy. The embassy ran out of water so it was my company's job to make the water runs. The water runs took us across the bridge; on the other side we had to fill the water truck. During the water runs we had to radio in our location so that when we got close to the embassy they could open the gates for us. We had to give landmarks. One of the landmarks on the way back was "Flat Chick Bridge." There was a woman shot on the bridge and she died there. The bridge is narrow and we had no option but to continually drive over her body. Hence, "Flat Chick Bridge." I call this survivalist humor, which many will not understand unless they lived it. Otherwise, it was just too much too take in, and we would fall apart—and to fall apart meant life or death. The last landmark was "Dead Man's Curve." When we radioed this in, they would know to open the gates because this was right outside the embassy.

I have thought about this woman on the bridge for years. Judy gave me an assignment; she asked me to give her a name and think of her story. I named her *Aminata*. Judy asked me to show Amanata how I wanted her life to be. In the collage I show the environment around her and what it was like during the fighting. There was shooting on the bridge and she was trapped. However, I show her rising up and continuing to walk home with the water she has for her family on her head. Aminata was put to rest by this assignment and I was able to have peace around her.

Flat Chick Bridge is symbolic of the many ways that we ratchet up our capacity for layers and layers of trauma, until the tiniest bit of stress can bring us to our knees praying for relief.

The body, mind, and spirit experiences stress and trauma at the sensory, cellular, and visceral, level so we cannot discount our own trauma as "not so bad." When we judge our own trauma experience, we do so at our own peril.

The Babies of Darfur

One day in Darfur we had to go out to a village that had been attacked by the Janjaweed (Sudanese government militia). The Arab Sudanese were eliminating the black Sudanese: genocide. We landed at the village in the helicopter. Some of the *tukels* (round, thatched huts) were still smoking. We could smell charred wood and flesh. I'll never forgot the smell. There were several dead, including children. All the time I was walking through the village I wanted to pick up the charred skeletons of the babies, but I couldn't; we could not disturb the scene because it was being investigated. We spent several hours in that village.

During an intensive, we did breath work. This is where you breathe deeply for about an hour and music is played. I thought this would be silly but I was willing try. *Whew*, was I wrong. Images started appearing to me during the breath work. They were of this village, something I had forgotten for a long time. The baby skeletons appeared and all I wanted to do was pick them up. Much to my embarrassment, I started saying over and over, "The babies, the babies, the babies." Visually, I was able to pick up those charred tiny skeletons in that village and put them to rest the way they deserved. I knew I could not bring them back but they deserved dignity.

I had held these stories inside me for twenty years and had not shared them with anyone. Through these intensives I have not only brought the stories back to myself, but also to the Universe. These people who suffered in Africa deserve for their stories to be told.

The collage depicts the Janjaweed (men on horseback) and the burning village, the dead. The pictures of the living, smiling children I have around the dead, to me, are the spirits of the dead living on. The picture of me laying the bones is an event I was involved in on the National Mall where volunteers lay millions of "bones" from the Capitol to the Washington Monument to represent all that died in genocides. It was a very healing process.

This woman, who bravely steps onto bloody ground, is living her life one day at a time without imagining that there is anything extraordinary in how she's lived her life. Stacy is following the family theme, repeated at dinner, "How are we going to save the world today?"

And so she finds herself in Liberia, Sudan, South Sudan, Afghanistan, Washington, DC, in the fifth Family Week at another treatment center to be there for her daughter, or at her mother's bedside—following the family job description of "doing" for others.

That is an amazing gift, the ability to organize and solve problems and walk through one crisis after another, however, when she finally stood still and breathed, her life began. When Stacy stops and really breathes, she *experiences* her extraordinary life.

She and her daughter, Kenzie, have done tremendous work together and separately. They are now able to not be co-dependent (well, not nearly as much) on one another, accept each other where they are, and enjoy life. Kenzie is sober and expecting a child in the fall. Now, is that not living?

We each have a story and if we stand still and breathe in and out, slowly and consciously, we can be brave and experience our story with all our senses and all of our emotions, and not be afraid to welcome the variety of the guests who come to our door throughout our story. We are no longer hostage to our trauma story and can embrace our survival, triumph, and grace, and create a glorious story of our choosing.

Our stories are the stuff of Tom Clancy, Nicholas Sparks or John Grisham. These trauma and addiction survivor stories are to be celebrated because they inspire us to our very core.

WICO'S STORY:
A HERO'S STORY

"Woohoo Wico! Yay Wico! We're so proud of you!"

These were some of the hoots and shouts for Wico, an 82-year-old Dutch Indonesian-American hero. Wico was an integral part of a trauma intensive at The Refuge along with twelve other people from nineteen to eighty-two years old, from twelve very different backgrounds, but with a dozen very similar responses to their histories, their trauma stories.

Wico, the oldest of the group, was referred by his incredibly loving daughter and son-in-law, who recognized the extreme emotional pain, sadness, and depression that had overwhelmed him. After a life of love and joy and apparent success, Wico was on the brink of despair and was suicidal. Wico's son-in-law David approached me with the thought that perhaps a trauma intensive would help to save this beloved man. David is a colleague in our industry and recognized the imperative need for an intervention. Wico and his beautiful wife Evie were so willing to try.

I've been blessed to work with many war veterans, but Wico's life moved me in a way that demanded that I share some of his story with the permission of his family. Wico did not volunteer to go to war; he was violently thrown into the tumult and terror of the Second

World War as a child of ten in Dutch Indonesia. So, although it wasn't his choice, Wico is one of my heroes who "ran into the fire."

Research shows that the huge numbers of veterans of all countries in the coalition forces of Iraq and Afghanistan who are committing suicide as a result of wounds of moral injury (discussed in Chapter 3) are far outnumbered in ratio by the number of suicides by WWII veterans, now in their eighties and nineties.

There is no doubt that this silent, great generation came home as heroes but never discussed or shared their deepest pain, sadness, and remorse about the war, and how it impacted who they were, and how they survived. Their reluctance to share their pain and secret wounds trickles down through the intergenerational matrix, seemingly without rhyme or reason for behaviors. For instance, my silent, brooding grandfather—I don't know his history, his pain, what silenced him. What silenced my three brothers-in-law, all veterans of Vietnam?

Wico also kept silent about the despair that began to envelop him, as his long-term memory became louder than his short-term memory, as the horror of being a fourteen-year-old prisoner of war became much more in the forefront of his heart.

Wico became intimate with his group, younger men and women who were fighting their demons in the here-and-now, also consumed by the secrets of their past. I am always amazed at the intimacy that transpires in five short days, the trust and courage to share the deepest and the darkest in order to be and live free. That's what happened for Wico and his peers in pain and trauma. They each shared their stories through experiential exercises, telling their stories in many different ways through art, psychodrama, Somatic Experiencing, and adventure therapy.

The power of the group experience is in my estimation much more effective than individual work, and that's what I witnessed with Wico and his group. This brave man wanted to live more than he wanted to die. So he took a leap of faith and trusted his secrets with these men and women, who showered him with love and celebrated his courage by sharing their secrets and pain as well.

Wico has written his life story and it is poignant and intense. He blessed me with a copy and gave me permission to share his story. And I would like to share some of it with you now. His story deserves its very own book, perhaps even a movie.

I regret that I cannot begin to do justice to Wico's incredible story but I will give you pieces and pray that his whole story can be published because his survival story is a gift.

WICO'S STORY • 1928–1931:
WAR THROUGH A CHILD'S EYES

My father took a ride in a sidecar of a motorcycle. While riding it, the sidecar got disengaged from the motorcycle. It crashed against a tree. At the time they never heard of wearing helmets, so my father hit his unprotected head against the tree. He was for a long time hospitalized and the best doctors in the Dutch East Indies (now Indonesia) couldn't help him. He had to go to Holland for treatment. My mother and father went to Holland on two of their furloughs, which they were entitled to once every three years, but the best doctors in Holland couldn't help him either. In the meantime, his *personality changed by the day. He became violent and very moody. According to Hetty [Wico's older sister, Wico being the youngest of six] he argued with my mother about everything.*

Today we would diagnose Wico's father with traumatic brain injury (TBI). Wico was born after the accident, so he never knew his father as anything but violent and moody. Wico's parents were divorced as a result and Wico was raised by his father and a servant, Min. Wico believed that he was born to try and save the marriage but to no avail. His two brothers moved out before Wico could know them They were in a camp as part of an effort to reclaim the jungle in New Guinea. This would later become a battleground for his two brothers and many other young soldiers.

There was a difference of eight years between Wico and the next youngest child, Carlos. Wico shared that at six years old he, his father, mother, and Min, moved by ship, the *Kapul Puti* (White Ship) to New Guinea. Wico describes Min "as a second father to me; (he) stayed with us through thick and thin." Wico describes a game that he and another boy who he became friends with, played on the ship.

One of our games was going to our mothers and pulling a string of hair to see which was stronger. I always won, because my mother had strong, thick hair. Another game we did is put a piece of paper at the end of yarn and use it as a kite on the stern of the ship. We had just simple toys. I remember, that I always made homemade toys.

Wico goes on to describe moving into their house:

Our two-story house was built with gedek walls, had a bamboo ladder to get to the second floor, and a hard, earthen floor with no plumbing and electricity. The reason for the second floor is for the torrential rains we sometimes got. The flood could be almost knee deep in the "living room," but fortunately, it usually only lasted for one day. We had also no bathroom or toilet, not even an outhouse!

I was happy, even without all the luxury we had in Java. I now wonder is this why those Papuan [indigenous people of New Guinea] were happy too, just as I was living in this adventurous world? The end for me came more or less when my parents divorced. I don't agree with some people, including professionals, who say sometimes it's better to get divorced for the children's sake. The children will always suffer no matter what, some indeed more than others. I think it's up to the parents to keep their disagreement to themselves, even if it hurts them doing so.

My father spent a lot of time with helping me with my school work. It had probably taken a toll for me losing a mother, moving back from New Guinea to Java, moving three times to different addresses in Java, going to three different schools, and this all within one year between the ages of six and seven! In that time, it was a big deal to advance to a higher grade. It's not unusual that the failure rate can be as much as 15 percent. I was in fifth grade before World War II and never stayed down.

At this point in Wico's trauma story he describes common themes for survivors: family discord, divorce, health issues, multiple moves, financial and material insecurity, and emotional instability. He also describes elements that create resilience, such as having a steady care-taker in his father, additional loving support from Min, and a joy for play and the world around him.

December 8, 1941–August 15,

The war in the Dutch East Indies started when Pearl Harbor was attacked by the Japanese on December 7, 1941, which was December 8, 1941 Dutch East Indies local time. The Dutch government, in exile, declared war that same day on the Japanese. I remember my father being glued to the radio and taking in the bad news, one story after the other. I saw his gloomy face, especially after the announcement of two English battleships, the Prince of Wales and the Repulse, that were sunk by the Japanese in the first days of the Pacific War. We were told to glue strips of paper on the windows to avoid them from shattering if we were bombed. The children must carry at all times a small bag and an eraser to bite on and earplugs, to be used if there was an air raid. If this happened during school time we had to go to the nearest trench, which were dug in many places including school grounds. Many trenches were used by kids as swimming pools during the rainy season!

War is a horrifying experience for anyone, but for children the fear and terror are multiplied a thousand-fold. The remnants of our family history, both known and unknown, continue to drive the patterns of behavior, communication, the condition and style of our relationships, what we share and don't share with the people we love, and who love us.

Our ability to be truly intimate depends on how deeply we are willing to share our truths with one another. This journey of exploring our family history allows us to open up to the possibilities of who we are and who we can become.

On my last visit with Wico, his wife of sixty-one years, Eveline (Evie), Ingrid, his daughter, and David, his son-in-law, there was such joy and love and I felt so honored to be audience to Wico's storytelling, Evie jumping in with additional insights. They have been through so much history together and have raised a family who love and respect and care for them without reservation.

Wico's willingness to put his ghosts to rest has given a gift to his family as well. The next pieces I want to share are more difficult to hear; our role is to witness for one another and grow and embrace our common pain and our common joy.

Overall, I didn't have a pleasant youth, but the years 1942 through 1947, up to seeing my siblings after my release from prison camp, were the worst of my entire life. No doubt also, that some events, that I remember and some I don't, such as not remembering visiting my father held by the Kempeitai (Japanese Military Police), will probably affect me for life. My problem was more emotional in my later life, looking back at what happened in those earlier years, when I was fourteen. (I am now seventy-seven in 2008). I have never ever told anyone in detail what happened to me in those years, only a bit here and there of some events. Since I haven't felt good for almost two years, I thought to tell my family doctor about those troubled years. The doctor referred me to a psychiatrist. The diagnosis I got from the psychiatrist was severe post-traumatic stress trauma and I'm being treated for this.

As you can see, Wico held his secret pain tightly wound inside his soul and his heart for sixty-three years, never telling anyone until he had no choice. Writing his life story was the beginning of saving his wounded heart. I met Wico four to five years ago and as he and his family reported to me, so much changed; suicide was no longer a solution. Sharing his story, and experiencing it with others is what healed him.

So to continue, Wico speaks of his father and nine other men being picked up by the Japanese Military Police. Later he discovers that only two men survived; his father died.

Wico did not go to school from 1942–1947, a huge loss to this young boy who thrived in a teaching environment. He survived by being part of a community that looked after each other and he developed extremely good survival skills, but he was just a boy, who like so many others over the decades and centuries had to do whatever it took to survive.

Wico and the other boys were drafted for indoctrination classes called *seinendan,* part of the Japanese youth movement. The boys marched with bamboo spears to "defend from invaders," watched war movies, and learned how the Japanese would win the war on the ground, in the air, and on the sea.

> The occupation and oppression had changed all of us, in security and fear, especially around the Kempeitai [Japanese military secret police]. Casual friends could not be trusted. On September 17, 1945, Dutch citizens began being picked up. The police ordered me to go with them for interrogation, which actually meant that they never release you afterwards! I was ushered into a prison cell with at least fifty other inmates, a cell probably intended for fifteen or twenty inmates. I was issued a 2x6 tikar (palm mat) and told to find a place.

Wico goes on to describe his surroundings and I've watched enough movies to be able to envision this horrifying scene. What is overwhelming to me is to imagine my one-year-old grandson or fifteen-year-old granddaughter having this same God-awful experience, the kind of hell that Wico and so many endured, and so many endure even as I type these words.

More horrifying to me is, even knowing the resilience and strength of character my children and grandchildren have and that they would endure, they would still be changed forever. That is the lesson of trauma survivors; we are changed forever by our life experiences, but we are capable of turning the trauma experience into a life of purpose as well.

I haven't taken a bath in over a year! Having dysentery is like a death sentence for them (patients frail and weak after being held in Japanese camps and rearrested). One died even on my watch! Can you imagine how I felt as a fourteen-year-old kid? I was so afraid I would get the same disease. I still don't understand how I didn't get sick in prison . . . someone must have watched over me. My father? No soap to wash my hands with. Eating out of bedpans used by dysentery patients. The toilet always had a wet floor and was dirty. None of us had shoes, except maybe two or three older guys. We ate with our hands— we had no utensils—and we went to bed dirty. We slept on the tikar on the concrete floor. The tikar was infested with bedbugs and we had a constant battle with the lice that lived in our clothes and hair. Every time I thought how miserable life was, I always thought it was better than having dysentery. There was another boy in my cell, probably one or two years older than me. His father had dysentery and died later. Can you imagine how he must have felt? I thought how lucky I was, even without any family in prison with me, but at least I have my father.

Not knowing of course, that he died a year earlier in a Kempeitai
camp. It must have been at that time that I became a thinker,
that is, if I feel bad, there were always people worse off than me.
If I was in pain, I compared it with worse pain I had in the past.
The only time this comparison didn't work was when I was passing
kidney stones forty years later.

Wico, the "thinking" man, had created a resilience dialogue, a positive outlook that has saved many survivors and certainly saved him. He had the ability to look beyond the present event to a time of hope. And Wico had other survival skills, the child in him continued to create games that kept his mind active and engaged and relationships.

One positive thing I got from my imprisonment was that I think
it made me a better person. We picked up pebbles and sticks (on
our half-hour break) that we used for playing checkers and chess. I
remember playing cards and checkers with my father at age seven
and I thought I was playing checkers very well by beating him a
couple of times. Later, I found out that he was the best checkers
player in the family. We had a champion checkers player in our
midst in prison. In my eyes, he was an "old guy" of twenty-seven.
He beat us for months until I found a strategy to beat him all the
time. My strategy has always worked for me. I was using it thirteen
years later in the Air Force against the base champion. The first
play ended in a draw, but I won the following two games. Beating
the guys in checkers in prison did me good, because the winner got
the banana peel with the strings still attached.

I can almost see the twinkle in Wico's eye as he shares his triumph —that spirit, the innate joy of life shining through.

One day, we received an American Red Cross package that we had to share with four persons. Later we found out, that we were supposed to get one package for every person! Everybody who reads this, please donate every time you see an American Red Cross person asking for a donation at Christmas time. I have never seen since that time how meticulously we divided everything in four portions. What I liked most was the cheese, corned beef, and chocolate. It was almost like a ritual how we split the chocolate bar in four pieces. We first cleaned the concrete floor as best we could, then one was chosen who was going to attack the bar, then when we all got our share, we would hoom-pie-pa (rock-paper-scissors). The winner got the crumbs, but they were so small, that licking of the concrete floor was the only way to get it all. Remember how the part about going to the toilet on the filthy wet floor on bare feet?!

In my mind's eye I can envision this boy, fourteen, adapting to this world, just as Victor Frankl described in *Man's Search for Meaning*:

Everything can be taken from a man but one thing; the last of the human freedoms—to choose one's attitude in any given set of circumstances, to choose one's own way.

The worst thing for me that happened at this time that I will never forget is the death of one of ours. He had reached the end of a venereal disease. He contracted the disease before he was interned. Without any medicine, he must have had a terrible pain before he died. The screams from the pain, especially at night before his death was unbearable to hear. I was so afraid that one of us I shared a room with, would get any kind of disease especially dysentery and also die from it. I got my first sex education at that time from the guy that slept next to me. He told me that he too had another kind of a "woman" disease. Hearing all of that, no wonder that women were considered to be evil, causing all those problems. Needless to say I had negative feelings against women.

After the death of this other prisoner, Wico and his mates were moved several more times and then finally, two years after that last move, they boarded a train.

The train ride brought us after almost three long days to free-dom! I'll never forget the time seeing the Dutch flag again waving in the wind, after not seeing her for so many years. We all cried and even now writing this down I still get emotional.

Wico's beautifully emotional story continues as he meets his Evie, Eveline, whom he would marry and celebrate sixty-one anniversaries together.

I had passed by the van Ommerens' house and I saw Evie playing in the street. We didn't have time to talk. Can you believe it? She was thirteen and I was sixteen. This was the first time I saw my future wife, wow! I went to the Red Cross, as so many of us also did. I found out that Hetty (my sister) and Carlos (my brother) were in Surabaya and Teddy (my brother) in Bali. They couldn't give me information about my parents and my other brother, Ewald. I later knew why; they didn't make it through the war. Hetty told me that my father died in a Kempeitai prison. The Kempeitai were notorious for their cruelty. He died April 18, 1945 after being tortured. My father was buried in Semarang honor cemetery which is maintained by the Dutch government, comparable to Arlington National Cemetery.

My mother died October 1944, when she and others were moved to another prison camp and had to walk through the jungle of New Guinea, weak from malnutrition. She was left somewhere in the jungle. We don't know how and we don't know the date she died. She wasn't buried anywhere. Ewald, my brother, died also in New Guinea's jungle December 31, 1942. Teddy and Ewald were guerilla fighters during the Japanese occupation in New Guinea. They received the highest medal one can receive from the Dutch government. There are three books written (in Dutch) about their ordeal fighting in the guerilla war in the jungle.

Wico's story is a prime example of intergenerational trauma, and a wonderful example of survival and resilience. His was a life well-lived as the patriarch of his family, a Dutch citizen and a great American, a success in all areas of his life, and a trauma survivor who asked for help and renewed his spirit as he shed his secret pain. Wico, I love you and I bow to your shining spirit.

Wico passed away November 5, 2016, in Ocala, Florida. Born January 14, 1931, in Java, Indonesia, he was a 1954 graduate of the Royal Netherlands Military Academy, the Netherlands and the U.S. Air Force Flight School, class of 1954. He flew F-84F fighter-bombers under the name "The Flying Dutchman." He and Eveline immigrated to the U.S. on January 7, 1961, under the shadow of the Statue of Liberty, and raised three children. Wico and Evie settled into Oak Run and enjoyed a retired life of tennis, line dancing, shuffleboard, and regular visits from their children and grandchildren. They traveled the world together, became U.S. citizens, and visited all fifty states. Wico lived life to its fullest after surviving POW internment camps and the horrors of WWII in Indonesia.

Wico was at The Guest House, welcoming and greeting each arrival and entertaining them all. He was guided in his life by each trauma and sorrow, but lived to embrace the fullness of his life. I honor Wico and his family, their love, care, and courage, and I'm excited for the generations that follow.

The final experience of our intensive is the "leap of faith," a ropes course challenge. Each group member gets into a harness (safety first) and then climbs what is essentially a telephone pole, and then they stand on the top of the pole, about twelve inches across. They take a deep breath, jump into the air, and grab the trapeze across a six-foot space. *Woohoo!* The climb and the leap can be a life-changing experience, moving through fear, making a decision, taking a breath, and then jumping off to the hoots and hollers and support of your new tribe, who know the deepest and darkest of your pain and encourage you to leave it behind you now.

Tremendously exhilarating and terrifying at the same time, this challenge is a perfect drumbeat to these folks who have faced their trauma story, unraveled the story, and are at the beginning of changing their lives forever in a positive way. Because he was an eighty-two-year-old on kidney dialysis, Wico could not climb the pole. But his group was adamant that he should fly, so they harnessed him and hooked him to a pulley, and together they pulled him up to the top of the pole, yelling and cheering and applauding as he hung in the sky, making his own leap of faith. Woohoo, Wico, well done!

FATHER JOE'S STORY:
MIRACLES HAPPEN HERE

Father Joe created a lovely memorial to his trauma resolution and self-forgiveness on the Memorial Trail at my former treatment center, the Refuge. He made these scripture panels as part of the trail. Father Joe spent five months working through his years of pain and moral injury. From the depth of Joe's trauma story, you'd be forgiven for believing that he couldn't heal. However, Joe had an overwhelming desire to have the life he deserved, the life he dreamed of. I've spoken to and seen Joe over the years, but more than anything I've reveled in Joe's life as celebrated on Facebook. So I e-mailed Father Joe and asked if I could use his story and his beautiful memorial and he said "Of course." Here's Father Joe's list he sent in an e-mail:

LIST OF MY TRAUMA HISTORY

➡ Molested by my dad as a toddler

➡ Near drowning at age three

➡ Growing up in a home dominated by Dad's alcoholism and rage

➡ The death of my brother, who was seventeen, and my aunt, from an auto accident, when I was thirteen

➡ Eight years of being sexually exploited by a priest during my high school and college years in seminary.

➡ The pressure to stay closeted as a gay man my first fifty years of life.

➡ An array of betrayals by church officials and the institution of the church during my one year of seminary and my twenty-four years of ministry.

- Ten years as a diocesan official having to help defend the church in the midst of the sex abuse scandals and lawsuits, as well as being called upon as a change agent in implementing reforms for child and youth safety.
- Seventeen years of active alcoholism.
- Extensive history of compulsive behavior.
- Overeating

"My lunch hour is almost up," Joe concluded in his e-mail, "so I'll need to follow up with my time at the Refuge and life in the six years since."

The most amazing thing about Joe is his trauma history list. Not only did he complete it on his lunch hour, but there was no longer a "charge" or "energy" to his trauma overshadowing Joe's life.

When our guests come to treatment this "list" ruled their lives in multiple ways. Often the "list" was a series of secrets that are "stuffed away in a box," "pushed down deep, "there is "no memory," "just a feeling of yuck."

Often the list drives or "creates" every behavior—the self-destructive behaviors, such as the addiction—in order not to feel the overwhelming feelings. So when Joe can reel off his list of traumas, it speaks volumes. It means there is real trauma resolution and the past no longer consumes Jim's present. It means that today, tomorrow, each day can be lived fully in every moment and in healthy, joyful, loving relationships.

Joe is no longer a priest; he courageously relinquished his collar to live in his integrity. I saw Joe live in faith, start over without a job or role that defined his purpose. I watched and experienced Joe grow in his spirit and grace and find purpose that has him continuing to run into the fire and help others.

He's joined the Gay Men's Chorus, he blossomed in his relationships, embraced true love and commitment, and found and married his soul mate. It is delightful to see the joy and playfulness in his life today. Joe's experience proves that there is life after trauma resolution. I love the power of healing, and Facebook gives me joy every day. I am continually reminded why I love this work . . . it's because *miracles happen every day* when we can, as Rumi invites us to, "Welcome and entertain every arrival of each new guest, a joy, a depression, a meanness, a crowd of sorrows, who violently sweep your house empty of its furniture."

And that's what happens when our guests come to the work with hope for healing and a willingness to do and feel whatever it takes to reclaim your life. We "treat each guest honorably." Because "He may

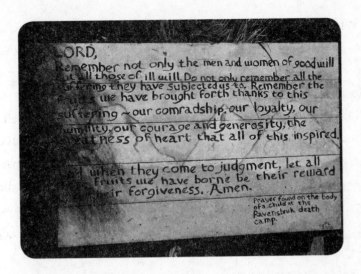

LORD,
Remember not only the men and women of good will
but all those of ill will. Do not only remember all the
suffering they have subjected us to. Remember the
fruits we have brought forth thanks to this
suffering ~ our comradship, our loyalty, our
humility, our courage and generosity, the
greatness of heart that all of this inspired.

And when they come to judgment, let all
the fruits we have borne be their reward
and their forgiveness. Amen.

Prayer found on the body of a child at the Ravensbruk death camp.

be clearing you out for some new delight." And this is exactly the work that Joe did and the miracle happened:

> "The dark thought, the shame, the malice,
> meet them at the door laughing and invite them in.
> Be grateful for whatever comes,
> Because each has been sent
> As a guide from beyond."

REFLECTIVE SKETCHES

1) Reading these stories, do you see yourself in the way you care for others over yourself?

_____

_____

_____

2) What family messages did you receive as a child that play out as you live as an adult?

_____

_____

_____

_____

3) As you read these stories, what ways do you envision yourself changing?

_____

_____

_____

_____

4) Did you ever reach a breaking point in your care for others or for causes where you just had to put it all down and put yourself first?

_____

_____

_____

_____

5) What are five ways that you relate to Stacy, Wico, and Joe?

_____

_____

_____

_____

_____

6) What are the ways you see resilience in Stacy, Wico, and Joe?

_____

_____

_____

CHAPTER
7

SPIRIT2SPIRIT: HEALING TRAUMA

"Ask not why the addiction, but why the pain."

—Gabor Maté

❧

always envision the partnership of healers and the wounded walking through pain together into our authentic selves.

This vision of partnership is dyadic, which is defined by *Merriam-Webster* as, "a socially significant relationship." This is a vital concept because of the isolation and loneliness created by trauma events, the insecure attachment that is created by early childhood trauma, and impaired attachment styles that families share through the generations of their own unhealed trauma.

Trauma survivors seeking help often don't comprehend that there truly is a path to healing. Creating a therapeutic relationship that is trusting, genuine, empathetic, compassionate and authentic is the beginning of creating the ability for our clients to learn to be in relationships that can mirror trust, genuineness, empathy, compassion, and authenticity.

One of the ways people feel safe after a traumatic experience is in the presence of another human being. This connection to someone whose nervous system is calm informs our own nervous system that the danger has passed. We encourage and create opportunity for that with the entire staff—including chefs, housekeepers and ancillary staff—being present and aware, bearing witness, and providing calm support.

For example, when a client gets angry, belligerent, and demanding, staff is aware that this is not a "here and now" response but rather a reaction to a moment or a situation that triggers an old trauma response. This is a teachable moment for everyone. When staff stays calm and present, they recognize that this raging person in front of them is not an adult but a raging six-year-old. It provides an opportunity to know that this behavior is not resistance or denial but a fear response to a very old and painful trauma event.

Research has shown the biggest predictor of successful treatment is the viability of the therapeutic relationship. The dyadic therapeutic process has many elements: the trauma therapy healing process, the attachment healing process (healthy relationships), and assisting our client to find a life of meaning and purpose as described by Viktor Frankl in *Man's Search for Meaning*.

Frankl survived multiple concentration camps after losing his whole family because he found meaning with every day of his survival. A neurologist and psychiatrist, Frankl created logotherapy around the concept of a meaningful life.

At the core of good trauma therapy is the ability for therapist to assist our clients to create a life of purpose beyond the trauma history. I believe that is why there is a preponderance of therapists and other healers who have found their purpose by being available for others.

So our approach may best be described as long term, intense, experiential, dyadic developmental therapy. Our clients build healing relationships with therapists, their small group, the therapeutic community, the outside community (often twelve-step recovery or a like-minded community) and, ultimately, can reunite and heal with family and their larger world.

We think and work outside the box, seeing each client as an individual. Trauma is centered in the nervous system, and what one client responds to another might not. We have a very large toolbox with many modalities and interventions. We use many experiential modalities. Psychodrama, for instance, creates a story on a stage where the client can see their life in action before them. Group process is a very powerful tool where clients come together, facilitated by a therapist, to share their pain, their stories, and their triumphs through assignments such as body maps, time lines, masks, collages, and letters, to name a few. The common denominator in a group process is diminishing the feeling of aloneness, uniqueness (no one has experienced what I have), empathy, and compassion. Group is one of the most powerful tools we have.

We also rely heavily on the somatic tools because trauma is centered at the cellular, visceral, and sensory levels. Those modalities are: Somatic Experiencing™ created by Peter Levine; equine therapy; art and music therapy; ecology therapy (working in the gardens or caring for the animals); ropes course and adventure therapy; yoga; meditation; drumming; breath work (an incredibly powerful modality that creates a breath connection to the body and the spirit through music and a breathing pattern).

It's my belief that attachment is at the core of our ability to handle trauma, and that being aware and creating opportunity for healthy attachment is key to healing. The therapeutic bond between client and therapist is key to successful treatment; we're expanding that concept. This is why our alumni are so strong and connected. In essence, we provide a place of safety until they create another for themselves. This is much like what twelve-step meetings do and have done successfully for decades.

There are a number of keys for trauma treatment to be successful.
It:

- ➡ Must be visceral
- ➡ Must be sensory
- ➡ Must be cellular
- ➡ Must build trust
- ➡ Must create safety
- ➡ Must not judge
- ➡ Must witness
- ➡ Must build community
- ➡ Must create intimacy
- ➡ Must demand integrity
- ➡ Must and should include the family
- ➡ Takes time, sometimes a long time

Disasters such as tornadoes, earthquakes, transportation accidents, or wildfires are typically unexpected, sudden, and overwhelming. For many people, although there are no outwardly visible signs of physical injury, there can nonetheless be an emotional toll. It's normal for people who have experienced disaster to have strong emotional reactions. Understanding responses to distressing events can help you cope effectively with your feelings, thoughts, and behaviors, and help you along the path to recovery

Consider these common reactions and responses to disaster: people frequently feel stunned, disoriented, or unable to integrate distressing information. Once these initial reactions subside, people can experience a variety of thoughts and behaviors. Common responses can be:

Intense or unpredictable feelings. You may be anxious, nervous, overwhelmed, or grief- stricken. You may also feel more irritable or moody than usual.

Changes to thoughts and behavior patterns. You might have repeated and vivid memories of the event. These memories may occur for no apparent reason and may lead to physical reactions such as rapid heartbeat or sweating. It may be difficult to concentrate or make decisions. Sleep and eating patterns also can be disrupted; some people may overeat and oversleep, while others experience a loss of sleep and loss of appetite.

Sensitivity to environmental factors. Sirens, loud noises, burning smells, or other environmental sensations may stimulate memories of the disaster, creating heightened anxiety. These "triggers" may be accompanied by fears that the stressful event will be repeated.

Strained interpersonal relationships. Increased conflict, such as more frequent disagreements with family members and coworkers, can occur. You might also become withdrawn, isolated, or disengaged from your usual social activities.

Stress-related physical symptoms. Headaches, nausea, and chest pain may occur and could require medical attention. Preexisting medical conditions can be affected by disaster-related stress.

Fortunately, research shows that most people are resilient and are able to bounce back from tragedy over time. It is common for people to experience stress in the immediate aftermath, but within a few months most people are able to resume functioning as they did prior to the disaster. It's important to remember that resilience and recovery are the norm, and prolonged distress is not.

How to Cope

There are a number of steps you can take to build emotional well-being and gain a sense of control following a disaster.

Give yourself time to adjust. Anticipate that this will be a difficult time in your life. Allow yourself to mourn the losses you have experienced and try to be patient with changes in your emotional state.

Ask for support. Social support from people who care about you and who will listen and empathize with your situation is a key component to disaster recovery. Family and friends can be an important resource. You can find support and common ground from those who've also survived the disaster. You may also want to reach out to others not involved who may be able to provide greater support and objectivity.

Communicate your experience. Express what you are feeling in whatever ways feel comfortable to you: talking with family or close friends, keeping a diary, or engaging in a creative activity (e.g., drawing, molding clay, etc.).

Find a local support group led by appropriately trained and experienced professionals. Support groups are frequently available for survivors. Group discussion can help you realize that you're not alone in your reactions and emotions. Support group meetings can be especially helpful for people with limited personal support systems.

Engage in healthy behaviors to enhance your ability to cope with excessive stress. Eat well-balanced meals and get plenty of rest. If you experience ongoing difficulties with sleep, you may be able to find some relief through relaxation techniques. Avoid alcohol and drugs, because they can be a numbing diversion that could detract from as well as delay active coping and moving forward from the disaster.

Establish or reestablish routines. This can include eating meals at regular times, sleeping and waking on a regular cycle, following an exercise program, etc. Build in some positive routines to have something to look forward to during these distressing times, like pursuing a hobby, walking through an attractive park or neighborhood, or reading a good book.

Avoid making major life decisions. Switching careers or jobs and making other important decisions tend to be highly stressful in their own right. They're even harder to take on when you're recovering from a disaster.

Suppose you experienced Hurricane Katrina, one of the most devastating natural events to hit the United States. Now suppose that before Katrina you had been abandoned by your father, neglected by family, emotionally and physically abused, moved multiple times, and lived in fear every day. Those layers of trauma can impede resilience, and Katrina becomes synergistically 200 times more devastating.

This is the reality for many people, layer upon layer of emotionally exhausting and impactful life events that leach into the emotional, physical, and spiritual landscape of their spirit. All their spirit craves is soothing and relief. At that point, it's difficult at best and for many virtually impossible to incorporate the above suggestions; immediate soothing and relief become the imperative.

Spirit2Spirit™ Clinical Model—
Dr. Tom Antonek, licensed psychologist

As a licensed psychologist with over thirty years of experience in the field of mental health and addiction treatment, I've worked with dozens of treatment centers across the country. I have had the fortune to have worked for a number of illustrious and gifted clinicians and mentors at treatment centers that provide competent and compassionate care. I am convinced that there are many other treatment centers that continue to exist with the mission of being a part of the solution to those who are dying from the horrific disease of addiction. That being said, what makes Judy's treatment center so different?

Judy's treatment model and center is the byproduct of her dream and vision. She has the mysterious ability to attract an array of clinicians from all walks of life that come together in their differences with the common bond of committing to their own work and personal journey. This organizational culture permeates her treatment center in an effort to maximize the clinician's potential when being invited into the lives of courageous clients who come to Judy for treatment and healing. In this regard, the clinical staff has had the privileged benefit of being personally trained by Judy as Certified Trauma Therapists (CTT). Subsequently, the interventions and treatment plans developed to treat various addictions (alcohol, drugs, sex, food, and gambling) are built upon the foundation of uncovering the trauma bonds that hold clients captive to their addictive coping strategies that imprison them to their own pathology.

Most of Judy's clients have been severely victimized and the historical reality of the victimization can't be erased. However, the relentless self-destructive maintenance of addiction that the traumatized individual is consumed by can be arrested. The phenomenon of the transformation to becoming rehabilitated and whole is a wonder to behold to which many alumni are all too willing to attest.

This is my experience: the sickest of the sick seem to find their way to this treatment center created in a forest. Many clients have been to multiple treatment centers over the course of many years of treatment, yet they continue to be tormented by their thoughts, brutalized by their own self-destructive behaviors, and hanging on to what little life or willingness to live is left in them. These souls find solace in this place from the environment, the skill of clinicians, the compassion of staff, and the legacy of miraculous healing that is transformative and modeled by Judy herself.

JESSICA'S STORY:
FINDING HER VOICE THROUGH ART

So many trauma survivors struggle with the words to share their story. The cellular, visceral memory, however, runs deep. We know that each guest in our program has a pathway to the story; the task for the therapist, the group, and the survivor is to find the path.

Jessica found it impossible to speak about her sexual trauma, but found her voice through art and photography.

Towering Tree

This is a photography piece I did around my grief and anger. I use the tree because to me it symbolizes a foundation for growth and life. I put the girl in the middle on the train tracks to symbolize my inner struggle through my growth of wanting to give up and my suicidal ideations. But the tree grows around the girl anyway, surrounding her with strength, life, beauty, and love. Trees have been a source of strength for me and help me feel connected.

Seen and Unseen

This is an assignment I did while in treatment with Judy around my sexual trauma. It helped me let those demons out. I couldn't speak about it, but when it came to art, I found a way for me to release my pain so I and others could understand.

Red Scream at 4 AM

This is one I did at four in the morning when I could not sleep. My head was spinning. I felt paranoid. So I used my materials and this is what came from that.

Trauma Therapist Sean's Perspective

Between the world of academia and professional mental-health counseling, I've received a lot of training. It wasn't until I finished graduate school that I realized school taught me a lot, but I needed to really focus my attention on certain skills and techniques with which I'd become proficient. I immediately noticed that all trainings and certifications were not created equal. Some left me walking away with real and definitive skills, while others left me feeling overwhelmed by cost and the plethora of hoops to jump through (usually each hoop had yet another additional cost attached to it). Furthermore, on top of the before-mentioned overwhelm, there was often a feeling of underwhelm when I would be given lots of theoretical rhetoric, yet an in-depth and experiential process was often nonexistent, or so sterile and generic it had little to no practical application. The level of real-life application, in-depth experiential understanding, and the emphasis on being willing to do the things we ask our clients to do is the hallmark of my experience being trained by Spirit2Spirit!

We've all heard, probably hundreds of times that the most important factor in a client's success in their therapeutic journey, is the relationship between said client and their therapist. However, what fosters that rapport? What fosters that relationship which then becomes the foundation for interpersonal growth? Recently I was speaking at a conference where a renowned professional in the field of trauma and sex addiction discussed his research into this relational process between client and therapist. What he reported was that the most indicative factor to indicate whether a client perceived a therapist as trustworthy and safe to connect to was the perception that the therapist did, or would be willing to do, the things they ask of their clients. Essentially, practicing what we preach!

Trauma survivors are very perceptive; they had to be to survive, and they can tell if we are comfortable holding space with them. I've worked at one of the premier trauma resolution and addiction treatment centers in the world for the past five years, and I've seen many therapists come and go. The reason they go is rarely because the work is too "heavy," and almost never because of issues within the organization. Instead, the biggest reason we often hire three therapists to fill one position is because many therapists still have way too much unfinished business, leading them to struggle greatly and almost immediately. They'll be unable to hold space and unable to take the client where they need to go. Fancy degrees will not give us the ability to help a client navigate the dark forests we ourselves are too afraid to explore! While getting my certified trauma therapist certification (CTT), I was given both the skills and the knowledge to effectively work with trauma at a high level. But the most valuable piece for me was learning the practical application of the approaches being taught and being given the opportunity to explore my own darkness, thus ensuring that it would not limit me personally or professionally with my clients.

The training was a beautiful mixture of experiential and didactic. Amazing speakers from all over the country and from the top programs and practices would come in and give us a diverse array of perspectives on top of the already incredibly knowledgeable and skilled Spirit2Spirit team. When I describe the training to other professionals, I often say it was a fifty/fifty training: half the time we'd be learning why something worked and the other half of the time we'd be doing it! We'd be learning the science and rationale behind the "why and how" of the modality and/or intervention tool, and the second part of the day we would be seeing and feeling the impact of real comprehensive trauma work at a core level. This journey would take place within the already small group, and sometimes even smaller breakout groups to make room for further exploration and understanding. I've been to numerous trainings where there were literally not enough seats for all the participants, but the trainings with Spirit2Spirit were small and intimate. When I wanted a question answered, it was never ignored; instead I was given individual attention that often turned into a lively group discussion and debate. Due to the size of the training group, my peers became friends and professional colleagues. That contributed just as much to my personal and professional development as anything else. (I still collaborate and consult with many of them on a regular basis years after completion.)

After I completed my trauma therapist training, I joined the high intensity trauma and addiction treatment program, and I expected to be support staff for at least a year. However, what I found was that my training had me years ahead of most of my post-graduate school colleagues. I found myself intuitively knowing how to handle clients and situations that seemed to baffle some of my peers. It was an amazing experience to realize that I had an arsenal of therapeutic tools to call upon when working with my clients, and most of the skills I had came directly from the training.

On top of discovering that my CTT prepared me regarding my skill and technique with clients, I found that it helped me to feel more comfortable, even when sitting with some of the saddest stories and most intense pain one could imagine. I found myself being able to develop rapport with clients who had long histories of being kicked out or running away from treatment: the "difficult" clients. I believe that I was able to meet these clients, many of whom had such severe attachment disorders that their brains were now literally *wired* not to trust, with an authenticity that they may not have received in previous programs.

I consider my experience with Spirit2Spirit™ to be one of my greatest personal and professional experiences. It has undoubtedly made me a better therapist and helped me to understand not just my clients' wounds, but my own wounds as well. As a result, I'm able to help clients see the beauty in their lives, not in spite of their past trauma, but because of it.

Once Upon a Time

One assignment we offer often is called a fairy tale because that's what it is. Clients must begin with "Once upon a time," and end with a happy ending. This is a great assignment for someone who has a secret they're afraid to tell because of perceived consequences or old family rules. For instance, many trauma survivors who have been abused in any way or those holding a family secret such as parental infidelity or addiction or domestic violence are terrified to put voice to the secret. However, in a fairy tale you can share the secret safely.

Colleen is an extraordinary young therapist who completed this assignment during an S2S training. In these trainings, therapists participate in doing their own trauma work while learning the process. Growing up she felt like the forgotten one, inconsequential in the family. It was a very painful childhood and it impacted her ability to trust and to be truly intimate. During one training she participated in, I repeatedly forgot her name. There were twenty other attendees and I remembered every other name. I call this a God shot—the universe creating just the right therapeutic situation. All she needed to heal was love, but she had to first speak out for herself and believe that she deserved it.

This young lady's response to my repeated forgetting her name each time was, "It doesn't matter, I'll answer to anything, don't worry about it."

DON'T EVER SETTLE FOR LESS THAN YOU DESERVE.

I finally insisted that she touch the truth of her feelings of loneliness and hold me and others in her life accountable. Don't ever settle for less than you deserve; and know that you deserve the world.

This fairy tale is the result of that assignment. And she has spoken her truth.

COLLEEN'S FAIRY TALE:
THE SPIDER QUEEN

Once upon a time, in the kingdom of spiders, the queen spider that watched over the whole spider kingdom, making sure that all was well and peaceful and alive, saw that something was missing. The spider queen loved her kingdom and worked to see that everything needed for it to be well and peaceful and alive existed. The queen's only job was to oversee her kingdom and do anything she could to make sure all the spiders were happy and thriving. So when she saw that something was missing, she grew even more

passionate and loving and creative for her kingdom to make everything right again.

The queen went into her inner web and invited her inner circle
of trusted spiders responsible for supporting the queen's work to
join her. For days and nights, they carefully and excitedly made a
plan to solve the missing piece of the kingdom. After a long while,
the queen and her inner circle came out to address her kingdom of
anticipatory spiders, who knew the long while she had spent plan-
ning and thinking and creating what was needed to restore what
was missing in the kingdom.

The spiders loved their spider queen and thrived in her love.
They knew and trusted that whatever her plan involved, it would be
something to celebrate. The queen unfolded her plan to the spiders
by selecting an unknowing spider mom and dad to join her in front
of the spider kingdom. Loud enough for everyone to hear, the spider
queen explained to the chosen mom and dad that they had been
carefully picked to nurture the next addition to the spider kingdom.
The spider queen handed a small but sturdy and well-built pouch to
the chosen spider mom and dad. She told them the pouch con-
tained a growing spider baby that had been specially crafted and
created by the queen and her inner circle. She explained that the
spider baby would bring elements of aliveness, creativity, and an
ability to share and grow the important connections in the spider
family communities. The spider baby would also add enthusiasm
and joy to all the lives of the many spiders.

The spider kingdom celebrated the queen's spider baby and
threw an enormous party for the spider mom and dad in preparation
for the new baby spider. And so the day soon came when the baby
spider emerged from the pouch and was received with enormous

happiness in the spider kingdom! The queen declared that her kingdom had been restored and was well and peaceful and alive, again. And they all lived happily ever after.

Laura was in the first group trained by our staff in the S2S model. Initially she was a bit reticent about sharing so personally with peers, however, that changed when she observed the powerful impact on others of her group. The alumni of S2S are a close-knit group from all over the country, and they often work together on various projects and intensives. Part of what brings them together is that our therapists experience exactly what our clients experience, especially the trust and intimacy of sharing their story.

LAURA'S FAIRY TALE:
IN THE PURPLE PALACE

Long ago, in the year 1980, a lovable, smiling little girl was born. The whole town loved her. She lived in a beautiful purple house overlooking the sea, surrounded by palm trees. Little Laura was adored by her daddy, but he was very busy doing all those things daddies do that allow for Laura and Laura's mommy and big sis to live in their purple palace with all the big and beautiful palms. Even though he was very busy and important, he still played with Laura all the time. But he never noticed his queen. Queen Syphilis was sometimes very mean and critical toward his baby girl Laura.

Syphilis didn't realize she was mean to Laura either; she just didn't know better.

Laura had a pet donkey named Baboo. Baboo was gray and brown with big white teeth. Syphilis wanted Laura to have a beautiful golden pony, but Laura only wanted Baboo, who she loved unconditionally. Laura loved Baboo with everything she had.

One day Baboo and Syphilis disappeared. Lucky for Laura, she had her big sister to play with her and take care of her. Laura was so sad though; she missed Baboo so much, but it was nice not to have Syphilis around to make her feel ugly and "less."

Meanwhile, a few miles away, Baboo had taken Syphilis against her will and locked them both in a room with one bed, a toilet, a mirror, and enough food and water to last seven days. Baboo told Syphilis that she had a lesson to learn but would not tell her what it was. If Syphilis didn't learn it in seven days, they would perish in the room together never to be heard from again. If she learned the lesson, all would be well, and they would return home, and Laura and her daddy and sister would have no memory of their being gone.

Syphilis cried and whined, "Why me? I'm so perfect and beautiful and skinny and my outfit is just impeccable. I don't deserve this!" Baboo prepared food and water for her and gave her Kleenex to dry her tears but said nothing.

Back at the purple palace, Laura and her sister and daddy loved each other and supported each other, and every night when little Laura went to bed, Daddy said, "I love you just the way you are." The three missed Syphilis. Daddy searched far and wide, but something made him believe it would all be okay so he never left Laura and her sister. He listened to them. He validated their feelings, and he apologized for not seeing what his queen was doing to them.

Back down the road, Syphilis still ranted and raved. She would look in the mirror all day hating how her gray hair was starting to show and lamenting her imperfect makeup. But after a few days, she realized how kind and gentle and compassionate Baboo was being. She still hated to look at him and thought him to be hideous, but her heart was opening to him a little bit as the days passed. Syphilis missed her purple silk sheets and her fancy friends and her telephone that she used to spend hours on at the expense of playing with little Laura. However, she realized, as the days passed, that there were other things that made her happy and even feel a little fulfilled. She started to love the quiet, the trees outside the one window, and the way Baboo talked about how wonderful baby Laura was. She realized she didn't know Laura, the daughter she claimed to love so much, at all.

Day seven was rapidly approaching and Syphilis, while scared, was feeling more at peace than she ever had. She liked not spending two hours every day trying to be beautiful and perfect and focusing on all her friends' fancy clothes, designer crap, and silly gossip. She realized that she didn't need to make mean comments when everyone around her didn't look just so. She even realized Baboo was much more adorable than she had ever realized. She even pet his gray and brown fur and didn't try to comb it so that it looked how she thought it should look. Syphilis had even stopped compulsively looking in the mirror. She started talking about things that mattered, about love and life and inner beauty. Just when Syphilis was resigning herself to perishing with Baboo and had entered a place of acceptance, Baboo then magically opened the door.

The two walked back to the purple palace and Laura ran out to

Baboo, hugging him with all her might. Laura was scared because her hair wasn't brushed and she wasn't wearing her perfect purple dress, but Syphilis scooped her up anyway and said, "I've missed you so. You are perfect just as you are."

Little Laura went on living her life secure in the knowledge that she was loved and accepted just as she was by the people who mattered most. She surrounded herself with loving, amazing people, and even if Syphilis would slip into her old ways every now and then, Laura had enough confidence, inner strength, and self-love to empathize with Syphilis and know that all that meanness and criticism had nothing at all to do with Laura.

At Spirit2Spirit Consulting we do five- or ten-day intensives and I go to families and do intensives for them. I set up intensives where people come together and do group therapy with us; the work done there is wonderful. And then I go out and train other therapists. These consist of five modules over year-long period where you have to do your own work to get the certified trauma therapist designation.

We have a *responsibility* to do our own work. I invite you to find a way to do that work of yours, because if you don't, you're going to be facing a client who is going to bring up all your stuff and your response isn't going to be pretty; it's going to be dangerous. Harry's story below depicts a therapist doing his own work.

HARRY'S STORY:
PLAYING HIS CARDS

Getting sober in 1982 was the last thing on my mind; staying out
of jails and institutions was in my prefrontal cortex, back then I
called it my brain. I had a criminal record that would not let me
into the interviewing process; my applications were thrown into
the garbage. An associate at the halfway house, way before they
were known as sober living environments, told me about a roofing
company that was hiring. Background check to be a roofer in South
Florida is an oxymoron. If you are moronic and begging for a job,
roofing is the answer.

Somehow, God got me to be in the right place at specifically
the right time, and my life changed with me just showing up and
being a vulgar NYC street urchin. There were others like me in
Delray and they loved my uncivilized ass because at one time they
were me. Life changed. Sober was cool. All my junkie friends who
were as nuts as I was went to these meetings and it was fun, cool.
It was cool that people sought me out to hang with, not for what
I could get them or to help them commit some crime that I was
stupid or desperate enough to do prior to my sobriety. Like Sally
Field said when she picked up her Oscar, "You like me!" They liked
me for being me without drugs; if I had a personality it was not in
my conscious thoughts. Work, friends, and Jean came into my life,
and I learned that to keep these people I had to really change, not
con them. Change was weird. Sober led to right decisions which
led to my own business because of my clear head. What I learned

was that there are a lot of dope fiends in the world; some have never smoked coke or stuck a needle in their arm. They have a unique word for their manipulating dope-fiend mentality: business. I learned quickly and was better at it than them; I made money, and lots of it. Sobriety with money is very cool. I traveled and even had some culture leak into my "concrete" addict/alcoholic mind. I found myself enjoying going to the theater, ballet, Broadway, and museums.

Life was good, ego was bad; relapse after fifteen years and the old me was still around. I gave away everything I loved; hurt does not do the feeling justice. Before that, I was sponsoring knuckle-heads and for the most part they listened to me. At one point roofing got slow, I went to college to keep sane and took a psychology course and an English course. The relapse was long and I hurt many people. My so-called friends bailed on me. "TF," who was always around, scooped me up, brushed me off, and loved me for me again. He told me I had it, but chose the wrong road and friends; money can make you do that, if you let it. Jean was divorcing me; threats were real in my head. She told me I had to leave, start again, and she would join me.

Jail, treatment, and another halfway house led me eventually to Judy Crane. God and Judy Crane—I'll be damned, he was talking to her also.

Judy was waiting and eventually offered me a job. The job turned into a love that turned into a career that turned into a passion. At least that is my chronological thinking; any of those pieces can be moved like checkers and put in many different orders. I work at a treatment center that gives me almost as much pride as my six children. I am available. I am available to my wife, children, grandchildren, friends, and classmates. And I'm available to any client at Judy's treatment center who thinks I might be of some assistance in helping them untangle their lives. I have a life and being available is part of it. Husband is part of it, father is part of it, grandfather is part of it, student is part of it, and so are my clients.

While working with Judy and clients I learned some stuff of which I had no previous experience, thinking more along the lines that life was the hand you were dealt so play the cards! Abandonment and neglect came into my vocabulary and at my age I really didn't want to mess with them, but that was my start. Loneliness led to drugs.

When I was twelve years old, a guy on a Greyhound bus got to me, started to fondle me in the middle of the bus, in a seat. Why I didn't jump and say something? Fear kept me quiet and I never told anyone until I began to work with Judy. It fit and I didn't like it. I would rather be a junkie thief than a wounded little boy whose mom didn't love him. Play your cards.

Sometimes I thought I won; only now do I know I always lost with those cards dealt to me.

I'm available. Homeless, married, bad conduct discharge, prison, heroin, junkie, thief, methadone, alcoholic, jail in four states, divorce, father of six, grandfather of four, loving husband, sober, businessman, homeowner, Caribbean traveler, lover of the arts and culture, relapse, shame, guilt, liar, hurt, wounded, victim, survivor, student with a master's degree at sixty-five, and a human being with a terrible use of the English language. This is not who I am; this is what I have to share with clients. I am a sober man.

Why Doing Your Own Work Makes You
a Better Therapist

I love clinicians and folks who work in our field. When I speak I always ask, "How many of you work with trauma?" Most people raise their hand and I feel so good that our industry has acknowledged the importance of trauma treatment.

The second question I ask is, "How many of you are trained in trauma treatment?" And most folks raise their hands and share that they have been trained in EMDR, DBT, CBT, or another powerful modality. So then I ask, "How many of you understand sex addiction, eating disorders, self-harm?" I ask this question because all of those diagnoses are created by trauma. I challenge clinicians to fill their tool box with somatic experience, psychodrama, hypnosis, and a multitude of other experiential and body-centered modalities, as well as in-depth understanding of process addictions. If you're working with trauma, you must understand sex addiction, relationship addiction, eating disorders, and self-harm. Sexual, emotional, and physical abuse are at the core of these diagnoses. Finally the last question I ask is, "How many of you have done your own work?" Most raise their hand and I challenge that. My presentations are visceral, sensory, and cellular just as trauma is; after those presentations, it becomes very clear that many folks in the audience need more and deeper personal work.

I believe we have an ethical responsibility to do our own trauma work and that we must be willing to go to those places that we lead our clients into. Many clinicians come to my treatment center in the forest to do trauma work because, although they may be sober a long time, they have become emotionally vulnerable and often have suicidal ideation or are in the shadow of burnout. It is the greatest gift that you can give yourself, your family, and your clients.

When I train therapists in our model of trauma treatment, every participant becomes a client initially, sharing their life experiences and completing all of the exercises, experientials, and process groups that we expect of our clients. As a result of this training, clinicians immediately do treatment in an intense, experiential, and more powerful way—and they heal.

What becomes very clear is the level of pain created by unhealthy or nonexistent attachment, abandonment and neglect, and abuse of any type. The messages that those "little t" traumas create driving the voices in our head repeat, I'm not good enough, or It's my fault, or I will always fail, or I deserve to be abused.

Every therapist completes a *trauma egg* which identifies the layers and patterns of trauma and negative life experiences. There is power for therapists to share in a safe setting with other therapists; often we may intervene or identify secondary trauma which is setting in our hearts. We see many sources of trauma: adoption, divorce, abandonment and neglect, abuse of every kind, fires, accidents, medical issues, mental illness in the family, death of family members, substance abuse in the family, multiple moves, and bullying. The list is long with trauma affecting everyone differently, I'm always so proud and excited for everyone who works toward trauma resolution because life changes. There can be extraordinary freedom for individuals and families as our lives begin to make sense and as our choices change, life can become juicier.

Let's look at behaviors that may be creating discomfort for you and perhaps in your relationships. I invite you to identify those that you relate to. Now you may be tempted to identify behaviors for someone else and that's fine, but don't neglect yourself. I guarantee that you are part of the equation. I shout from the rooftops: if you work in this industry, are a first responder, ER doctor, nurse, or police officer, serving in the military, or are on the front lines of child or elder abuse as a social worker, please tell your story to a qualified trauma therapist and find resolution.

Every day that you continue in your career you are adding multiple new layers of trauma and your soul needs healing!

Teresa is an S2S alumna who, after many years of recovery, experienced multiple devastating traumas and came to the forest to examine the layers of new trauma that had stirred up her old trauma. Two years later, she added the S2S credential to her long list of credentials, CTT, certified trauma therapist.

TERESA'S STORY:
CALMING THE WINDS
OF THE TORNADO

The year was 2010. My life had been swept up into a tornado and I felt as if I had lost total control. In December 2009, my ex-husband died of an overdose to methadone and alcohol, and I had to tell my daughter. I am a social worker and have worked in the field of addiction for twenty-two years, yet I was unable to help my family. My daughter had moved out and was living with an abusive man and was also using. After his funeral, my mama bear came out and I began a Marchman Act* on my daughter.

---

* Temporary detention for individuals requiring substance abuse evaluation and treatment in the state of Florida.

The months that followed were pure hell on my mind, body, and spirit. I was working as a psychotherapist in private practice, and going to court to try to get my daughter into treatment. The feelings of my daughter becoming my drug of choice was painful and more painful than my own addiction. I was holding on to twenty-five years of being sober and keeping my support system strong, attending Al-Anon, AA, and NA. And then it began. I stopped eating, I stopped sleeping, and the feelings of not wanting to live began to creep in as depression was wrapping around my mind. Yet I would wake up every day and go to the office, and I would go to the courthouse to try to convince the court that my daughter needed treatment.

The tornado started spinning faster the day that I spoke at an AA meeting to center myself after a court day. I walked out of the meeting feeling centered with the thought I can let go, she will be able to find her own higher power and I am getting support. That night I was on the back of a Harley-Davidson without a helmet or the proper gear. We hit a woman crossing the street, and the last thing I remember as my face slid across Congress Avenue was the voice of my daughter: "You never speak to me anymore except when we are in the courtroom."

As the paramedics began to cut off my clothes, I asked for my phone to call my sponsor and my brother. The gentleman driving the motorcycle had a brain injury, the woman we hit was killed, and I was the only one who was coherent. When I looked at the woman lying on the pavement I did not see an African-American woman; I saw my mother. The pain and the guilt of the death of this woman haunted me, and the pain and the remorse of my daughter never coming to visit me in the hospital haunted me even more. I lay in the trauma unit for three days and prayed for peace. I remember my brother and my sponsor sitting over me and telling me it is time to let go and take care of yourself.

The tornado took another spin four weeks later, on the day that I received the phone call April 3, 2010, from my brother Michael telling me he was going to see his daughter. I told him to "fly safe" while also asking if he needed to fly today. Twenty minutes later I received the call that my brother's plane had landed in Lake Osborne and he didn't make it. The tornado was spinning so fast I could not breathe; yet the voices in my head said that I needed to handle this. The day turned into a media circus at my sister-in-law's house and fear took over my body.

What I did not know about was the fight-or-flight response that was going on in my body. My body was so full of energy and the messages in my head were my father's (who had passed away twenty-five years before) telling me to "take care of this." The questions were overwhelming, and as I scanned the room with the family sitting on the sofa, everybody looked like they were in shock. Finally, a friend of my brother's, a retired CIA agent, put his hands on my shoulders and stated, "I got this." I sat down as he handled the press. I scanned the room and felt alone. My daughter was not there and I waited for my brother's daughter to arrive. The next few days felt like a nightmare and I moved like a robot. I knew I wanted to take my brother's ashes home to Ohio and have a service with the family there also, so that is what we did.

Still trying to calm the tornado, I took my niece to Ohio to spread my brother's (her father) ashes to all of the places that had meaning to them, and to share with her the memories of her father. She had few memories of hearing about his childhood so we decided to spread his ashes in some favorite childhood places, as well as with mom and dad. We had a small service with the family up north, which helped give me some closure. What I didn't realize was that I was not honoring my own body, mind, and soul. I was still taking care of everybody else. I realized I was traveling with the ashes of my brother, and Motrin, Robaxin, vitamin C, and medication to be able to go to the bathroom. I had lost over forty pounds and was not eating, surviving on Ensure, yogurt, and drinking aloe to coat my stomach. I made it look like the tornado was calming down, yet the tornado inside of me was getting much worse. I had just perfected the mask that I had worn, the beautiful mask of the caretaker, the hero, the one that everyone asked me to be, the one that I enjoyed being, and the one I hid behind. On the flight home from Ohio, my first home, I felt lost, scared, and the mantra began: Everybody is dead, Mom, Dad, and now my brother.

Upon my return to Florida I returned to my chair in private practice and began to see private clients. My workaholism went into full effect. I continued to balance work, meetings, and the Marchman Act proceedings for my daughter. Then my daughter never showed up to the treatment center, and within two weeks she was arrested for some of her consequences, and the reality was I had lost her, too. My mind shifted into, "they are all dead." I sat in my big over-stuffed chair in my private office and wept. I did what I did best, and I hired an attorney to help my daughter, and I then decided to go home.

Later that afternoon I walked over to my balcony and stood there for a few minutes. I lit a cigarette and I thought about the last few months of my life. The phone rang and it was a client, but I could not speak to anyone at that moment. I was done, I had nothing else to give. The hero was gone. She was dead; everybody was dead. For the first time in my life I knew what it felt like to want to die. I wanted to jump. I wanted to be with everybody else that had already gone before me. I had nothing left inside of me for me. As a therapist, I'd given it all away, as a mom I had nothing else to give, and as a human being I was done.

I made the phone call to Judy Crane and she told me to "Get out of the chair." My first thought was I got this, yet as I explained to her, every time I drove to my office I couldn't get my body to calm down. I had to drive by where the motorcycle accident happened. No matter what I did by going to meetings or talking about it, I could not get my body to relax. I would shake from my head to my feet, and I would just continue to go to the office and do therapy.

It was the beginning of June and my daughter was pregnant and safe. Mom was dead, Dad was dead, my brother was dead, my ex-husband was dead, and my daughter was gone. I was lost. I packed my SUV and headed to Judy's treatment center. I still am not sure how I drove that late afternoon; I felt as if I was not even in my own body. I referred my clients to my colleagues and other therapists in the area before closing down my practice. I had turned my home over to my adopted daughter to take care of for a while.

The feelings that whirled in my body were foreign to me; I had never let go like this nor have I asked for help like this since I had asked for help twenty-five years ago when I surrendered to my disease of addiction. The difference was I had my brother, I had my father, I had a different support, and today I had me. I was a shell this day as I drove; I was empty.

I remember as I turned onto the dirt road I saw a bear on the left-hand side of the road and thought to myself, protection. I drove down the long dirt road with a sense of peace and freedom, yet fear of what was about to happen. Even though I felt vulnerable, I had some sense of safety as I knew a few people who worked at the treatment center.

The next morning, I felt overwhelming fear and sadness as I was embarking on my journey to come out of my tornado. I remember screaming through the forest, "Everybody is dead, everybody is dead!" The pure shock that I had landed in such a surreal place and the safety around me was too much for me to handle. I, the therapist for over twenty years, could not handle the visceral feelings and the things I was seeing around me at the time.

My masks began to engulf me and the feelings of "I have to hide" became overwhelming. I walked through this beautiful forest and began to meet my peers, yet the little girl inside of me was so scared. I was assigned a therapist and masked my fear with anger and arrogance. I remember asking her, "Where did you get your degree, online?" I was beginning my journey of hurting people because I was so hurt. I did not know this slogan at the time. I was in so much pain as I sat in the groups; my mind was racing with so much critical thinking. I did not know how to turn it off—even though I had taught this so many times to others.

I remember the moment that I sat in a large group with Judy Crane, when she was showing her slide presentation on "Nuts and Bolts." I sat in such shock and disbelief of what trauma was and is. I had been a therapist for over twenty years and thought that I had been doing a good job. Not until then did I realize that I had just begun to look at such core issues in this disease of addiction, relapse, and trauma. I sat in awe of the content that was presented. I was in shock with what was going on inside of my body, and the knowledge expanding inside of my head. My first reaction to Judy was one of anger, I'm sure. I was in such disbelief that here I sat with twenty-five years clean and more than twenty years working in the field of addiction, needing to re-learn everything about me and the world of addiction.

What a wonderful yet scary place to be.

REFLECTIVE SKETCHES

❦

Spirit2Spirit™ Treatment Plan

Objective: To expand understanding of trauma.

1) Read *In the Realm of the Hungry Ghosts* by Dr. Gabor Maté to increase understanding of the connection between addiction and trauma.

_____

_____

2) Read *Waking the Tiger* by Peter A. Levine to expand insight to the somatic experience of trauma.

_____

_____

3) Gather as much information about your family history for as many generations as far back as possible.

_____

_____

_____

_____

_____

4) Have a "Celebrate Our Family" gathering, inviting your guests to bring family pictures, and historical papers such as birth, death, marriage, and divorce papers. Include diplomas and medical histories where available.

_____

_____

_____

5) Put together a family history that can be shared and kept for
younger generations.

_____

_____

_____

6) Find a therapist who specializes in trauma/PTSD, substance, and
process addictions.

_____

_____

7) With the help of your therapist, locate a trauma group or a healing
intensive.

_____

_____

8) Make a collage of what you would like your life to look like in six
months, one year, and five years. Dream big! This is especially helpful
when you are in the middle of trauma resolution.

_____

_____

9) Keep your collages in a place where you can view them regularly.
Take note of what is manifested.

_____

_____

CHAPTER
8

WE
REWROTE
OUR
STORIES

*"Owning our story can be hard but not nearly
as difficult as spending our lives running from it.
Embracing our vulnerabilities is risky but not nearly
as dangerous as giving up on love and belonging and joy—
the experiences that make us the most vulnerable.
Only when we are brave enough to explore the darkness
will we discover the infinite power of our light."*

—Brené Brown

❧

R esilience is built when any life event or situation changes you and your vision of yourself in the world in a positive way. Our clients come in and they have survived the most incredible traumas, layers and layers of trauma. It isn't just one car accident; it's a series of events that started in childhood, or in utero, or intergenerationally. And they have survived that. My goal as a clinician is to tap into what it is about that client that made it possible for them to survive.

The Role of Resilience

W hen we talk about resilience, we're talking about what made it possible for someone to cop drugs every day and come up with the kind of money he or she needed to be an addict. What kind of brain power said, "I'm going to manage this and I'm going to do this"?

As addicts of all stripes, whether process addictions or substance abuse, or whether we are survivors of anxiety and depression, we have talents and skills that far surpass most normal people. When we address our trauma and PTSD, we find joy and healing, but in order to get there, we have to walk through that Black Dot of pain. We have to be able to say, "I'm willing to stay here in the middle of this ugly place for as long as it takes, until I can walk through it." And we do that in partnership with our therapist. That's the model we created; that's the model that works.

Most of us relapse as a result of getting to that place and saying, "Oh no, I can't bear this pain." Pain is part of being human but we'll medicate in any form to avoid it. Yet the medication is much worse than the pain in the end—the pain we just have to be able to bear.

When we experience grief, the depth of our grief is really honoring the depth of our feeling for that person, place, thing, or situation. The depth of grief says that was meaningful in my life and I need to be able to honor that and experience it until I don't have to experience any more at that depth.

With treatment, trauma doesn't go away; it just gets easier to bear. It doesn't have that impact on us when we finally do that work; when we finally allow ourselves to experience what it was like when we were children, when we experience whatever it was that harmed us or hurt us.

Behaviors clients exhibit are the behaviors they know. They don't know how to cope with life so they're using the behaviors they have.

When I opened my treatment center, we didn't discharge easily. I've heard questions from those in the industry asking me why I was letting clients stay when they relapse. Why are you letting clients who get into relationships stay? Why are you having people there who continue to cut?

My answer: because we haven't given them another coping mechanism yet. And why should I take away what is working for them and has worked for them for a period of time, until I've been able to work with their trauma and help them work through that? So we don't discharge easily. I hope that in this industry it has begun to change–I think it has. I think it's crazy for us to assume that people come in and they're going to change that day because they no longer have drugs in their system, or because they have a really good mood stabilizer. Well, that's just not how it works. What I want you to know is that my favorite clients are the really tough ones; those who break the rules, the ones who are going to fight and rebel—because when they get it, they really get it.

Those are the people that I get so excited about when I see them on Facebook because they've made such dramatic changes. They've been there and they've tapped in to their resilience. They've accessed those places where they have these crazy ideas that work and they know how to operate in the world. How many of your clients come in and test you, and test you, and test you? Ask yourself, "What is it about this client that I can work with?"

In my own life, I didn't think for a minute that I was ever going to get sober. When it happened, it was such a shock to me. I didn't get sober until I was forty-two years old—that's a long time to be in pain. And then I started to realize how much of that was around trauma work. The truth is that when we're in that place of relapse, when stuff comes up, we have a couple of choices: we can go crazy, we can commit suicide, or we can relapse. Of these choices, the truth is relapse is the sanest option if trauma resolution isn't being considered or pursued.

So, when we're looking at people who are chronically relapsing, our job is to find out what is it that triggers that relapse. What's going on in your life, what event is mimicking your trauma that stirs up that emotional need to have some soothing? Until we give our clients other soothing mechanisms, they're going to continue to relapse or, God forbid, commit suicide. Suicide has been huge this year in our industry—bigger than any year I've experienced. Add to that, deaths from heroin overdoses have grown in the last ten years. It's horrifying what's happening to our folks. We live in a world that is absolutely filled with trauma and PTSD.

Trauma is the breeding ground for survivors of all stripes and behaviors. They're often described as exceedingly bright, creative, maddening, extraordinarily driven, and talented in a multitude of ways, sensitive well beyond the norm, vigilant and aware of all around them, and astute in reading what's going on around them in danger-ous situations. We survive by our wits and learned behaviors that have given us relief from overwhelming angst and pain.

Certainly in the midst of active addiction and alleged psychiatric diagnosis or PTSD it takes cleverness and great talent to maintain the insanity. How many of us keep waiting to be "found out"? We believe that we are "faking it," that others have the secret of living in their own skin while we are still seeking the key to the mystery of life.

Our diseases, our traumas, have become incredibly beneficial to the world. I can work with any client because when I look at that person, I look at whom they started out as. Then I want to know what events, what series of events, created the behaviors that we're looking at. Behaviors always make sense when you understand the story: beginning, middle, and the end, when they arrive in treatment.

Creating a Lifetime of Resilience

My goal is to try and help families sort out that their loved ones are not stuck in bad behavior, they're in survival behavior. And my question to the families is, why? What are they attempting to survive? Our clients come in feeling shame, guilt, and remorse because of behaviors they've done or been a part of. And it's only been part of them being able to survive. Now is that fair? Can you see that? I want this book to be read beyond the clinical and therapeutic communities. I want people to be able to read this book and say, "There's nothing wrong with my child, he or she is just trying to survive." So they understand that in response to these behaviors we're not going to point a finger and say, "Bad kid."

I don't know how you operate with your clients or family or friends, but I know how I operate with my people. I'm always going to look at them to find the goodness in them. What is it about that person that was so incredibly magnificent before it got shot down? What creates resilience in these little ones as they grow into trauma survivors?

The American Psychological Association says the factors in resilience and developing resilience are part of a personal journey. Some variations may reflect cultural differences, life experiences, the level and quality of or lack of support systems. The primary predictors of levels of resilience are relationships that create love and trust, provide role models, and offer encouragement, reassurance, and solace. The one thing I'm very proud of is that, when we opened our treatment center, it came from a place of our own authenticity, who we are as human beings: loving, compassionate, empathetic. We never give up.

We did not create guilt or shame in clients, because number one, it's wrong. We tapped into these places of resilience and what was wonderful about them. We would have clients come in and I'd say to them, "You're so amazing, you're so bright, so talented. You have something wonderful waiting for you."

Then I would have to ask them, "What did you just hear me say?" Because so many of them would say, "You just told me I am a complete failure and I will never amount to anything."

Because those messages are so engrained, we are a ninety-day program. This is vital because you can't change those messages in thirty days. You have to be consistent in the verbiage and in the actions that you show the client: that you don't give up on them, that you do believe something wonderful will happen for them. I hope that's what your model for life is as well, because that's what works.

BJ is a young lady with a long addiction treatment history—multiple treatments—and so she thought she knew her way around a treatment program. What she didn't expect was to be loved and cared for in spite of her "acting out" behaviors; she didn't expect to be able to tell her story and find the causes and conditions for her relapse history. What BJ found was that she was lovable and worthy of love and caring.

BJ'S STORY:
SURVIVAL WITH THE LOVE
OF JUST ONE PERSON

BJ was in treatment in the forest. She was not an "easy" client, she broke all the rules, and kept the community and staff in upheaval with her old behaviors, however, when she truly connected with someone it was powerful. When she describes breaking her compact mirror for a suicide attempt, she stops because she thinks of Caroline, of her therapist Angela, of program director Bella, and she couldn't do it!!

There had been many attempts. So why was this different? To me it's simple, no matter what, these people loved her and no matter how hard BJ tried to push them away with her old acting-out behaviors, they never gave up on her, loved her in spite of behaviors, loved the wounded little girl inside, no matter what . . . And they honored the woman she would/could become.

BJ's history of early childhood trauma had created a compromised attachment style. She had no healthy relational caretakers; her social, emotional, and spiritual development was impaired as a result of neglect, abandonment, and abuse. BJ's saving grace was the love of her gramma. Her trauma created very little love in her life and yet she was able to have love from a staff that went beyond the automatic response of I love you, that is too often given without real depth. Gramma and a loving, compassionate staff were providing reparative experiences. All she needed to survive was the love of just one person, and all she needed to heal was the love and hope she got from three very different staff members who loved her unconditionally, set boundaries, and offered hope.

The love of just one person provided the road map to building resilience, the beginning of belief that she might be worthy of love and that her history of hurt, abuse, and pain did not diminish the light that still flickered in her spirit. Healthy attachment was slowly being built.

> Attachment is defined as an enduring relationship with a specific person that is characterized by soothing, comfort, pleasure, and safety. It also included feelings of intense distress when faced with the loss, or threat of loss, of this person. (Perry, 2010)

The primary attachment figure is usually the mother. In the absence of that healthy attachment as babies, our systems, brain, body, emotions, and socialization are impaired and our attachment style is impaired. Our attachment style, developed from the womb through early childhood, holds the blueprint for all of our relationships in life. So if we start out with dysfunctional or no attachment, unless there is repair, we are impaired in many areas.

When clients would leave the forest, the client evaluation of their treatment experience overwhelmingly spoke to the hope that they felt, along with unconditional love and the fact that staff would never give up. Even when discharge became an option, the clients/ alumni overwhelmingly reported that staff kept up with their care and concern for them.

I believe that's an imperative of the treatment experience. Too often these folks have been abandoned and neglected, offered no hope, and limited unconditional love which is very different than conditional love.

Conditional love says as long as you behave well I will love you, as long as you follow our expectations we will love you. Unconditional love says I/we will love you unconditionally no matter what you do even when we don't approve or agree with your behaviors. You are not your behaviors. That reparative experience is what can/should happen in the very best trauma treatment.

Factors That Create Resilience

Make connections—secure attachment. One of the biggest, most horrendous things about trauma is that there is an attachment disorder. Relationships just don't work, they're wired for survival; they're not wired for love, not to give it or to receive it. And sex doesn't count.

Avoid seeing crises as insurmountable. Help change the perceptions of our clients – that there are solutions and we are a team/partners and that we are going to do this together.

Accept that change is part of living. All is surmountable.

Move toward your goals. We accomplish one thing, one day at a time. We help our clients change one thing and be able to support them in that change.

Take decisive action (act, not react). In recovery our job is to help our clients to start to act and not react. Reaction is about fear—and our clients are always reacting and our job is to get a handle on their reactions and to start acting.

Opportunities for self-discovery. We find new strengths from our events. What's amazing to me is our clients come in and they have forgotten what they have done in their life—they've forgotten that they've traveled in the world, they've forgotten that they played instruments. We forget that we have this other place in our life where we've succeeded and done well. We forget because everything that's been horrible and dark overwhelms us and we forget. My job as a therapist is to help our clients remember who they are authentically at their level.

Nurture a positive view. As a therapist I help my clients to take the negative they're looking at and turn it into a positive. Anything I did out there in my disease I can turn into a positive. How else could I be here today where once I was a manipulator and now I'm a motivator? So I invite you to try and change the language for yourself and your clients. Because they need to hear that. There's great talent and skill in being an addict or an alcoholic and an anxiety, depressive or OCD person.

Perspective Hopeful Outlook Self-care. I always make sure people have the opportunity to do self-care.

Working Toward Trauma Resolution

The role of the therapist in the healing process involves dyadic attachment—providing the opportunity to create an environment for healthy social engagement. The most important thing we do is witness. We create a safe space where our clients can begin to do this dark, healing work that has to be done; that's our job. We are a warm, compassionate, empathetic role model to assist in the opportunity to develop new social skills. We're teaching our clients how to communicate, how to be present, how to be available; and then when we get in a small group that gets remodeled again within the group.

A relationship that engenders trust will lead to a wider community of trust and acceptance. We do a lot of trust and community-building exercises because our clients don't know how to have a relationship. That's why ninety days is so important. It's not just about acquiring life skills; it's learning how to live.

I want to share with you a previous client's trauma recovery. She came to us for treatment many years sober but trauma had made her life unmanageable. The tattoos on her face were to express her internal pain and abuse. As she got well she had them lasered off. The core of her trauma was enormous abuse; loss of relationships; inability to be in healthy relationships. There was no secure attachment relationship, yet her level of resilience enabled her to survive incredible pain. However, surviving was not enough. She wanted more and begged for help, love, and compassionate acceptance.

CHLOE'S STORY:
REMOVING OLD SCARS

It was March 2007. I was sitting in a jail cell, the first time I was ever arrested in my life. My face was covered with blood from being in a domestic fight. I stood up, trying to keep myself together as mug shots were taken and I was booked. I was shackled like a criminal. I had a list of three felonies, one misdemeanor, and was looking at up to six months in jail. I had hit rock bottom in my life. I was an active cutter and I hated myself and what I had become. I hated life and could no longer hide the deep pain and anger inside of me. I felt like I was in a deep hole, with no way out. I felt trapped in a cycle of self-destruction.

The next morning, they took me in front of the judge. With my charges, he was going to sentence me to serve time. I called out to a God I hardly knew, and in tears begged him to get me out of jail, that if he knew me, I would literally die in jail. The judge who was supposed to show up was absent, and instead I got another judge. She took pity on me and disagreed with the prosecution regarding going to jail. She sentenced me to three months of anger management and treatment in Florida with Judy Crane. At the time I was living in Vermont where it was cold and snowy, so to me this was nothing but heaven-sent. I packed one suitcase with as many of my belongings as I could fit in.

March 2007

Present–2015

When I first stepped into the treatment center in the forest, I was weak, tired, and done pretending. When people looked at me, they saw someone scary and strong, while on the inside all I wanted was someone to hug me and tell me that I was okay and that I was loved. In treatment with Judy I had an opportunity to re-evaluate my life, find out what my triggers are, and where my hurt came from. The first time I met Judy she opened the door and her eyes were compassionate and understanding without any of the fear I had been so used to because I am covered from top to bottom with tattoos. I don't personally think they were quite prepared for me because I looked very different on paper than in person. I remember Judy asking me why I tattooed my face the way I did. I told her that it defined the pain and shame that I was feeling on the inside. That was my first day on the road to recovery; the first glimpse of hope for my life.

For the next three months, I worked hard on my issues; the death of my parents, abandonment issues, and my fears. I started to see the positive side of my life. I left treatment with tools, the love of Judy and the staff of the treatment center, and my heart was beating again. The deep pain was gone and for the first time in my life I was at peace. Also for the first time, the scars and tattoos left on my face no longer matched how I was feeling on the inside. Shortly after trauma treatment I got laser treatment to remove the old scars from my face. I am no longer that same person; by the grace and mercy and forgiveness from my God, and the people who saved my life and taught me how to trust again. They loved me when I couldn't be loved, and spent numerous hours listening to me. Thank you, thank you! You gave me my life back. I have since been blessed. I have physical scars that will never go away, yet they remind me who I was, and who I never want to go back to being. It is one day at a time, one moment, knowing today that I have all the tools I need to cope and the hand of God to catch me when I fall.

MELANIE'S STORY:
CRUSHING COKE CAN GRANDMA

Melanie came to the forest so very depressed, not knowing exactly what was wrong. A young woman of twenty, she was described by her therapist as a workaholic who was struggling with a blanket of depression. Melanie was truly anxious to be well and to understand why she found herself in this space. She breathed into the work and before long her cellular memory began to assert itself. She was able to recognize that there had been abuse as a small child from her grandmother. Melanie was brimming with righteous anger and pain when she came to me and said:

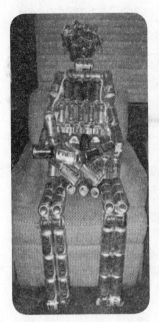
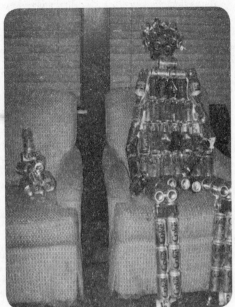

"Fine, so now I know without a doubt there was abuse, what am I supposed to do with it?"

"This is a process," I said. "I'm not sure what form it will take, maybe a letter, a collage, a psychodrama, but something around your grandmother to clear the space. You will know inside."

A few days later Melanie asked to show me her project and there, in all her glory, was *Coke Can Grandma*. Wow! Inside each can was a note that described the negative messages internalized by the abuse, quite an enormous undertaking to process the trauma.

I asked, "Melanie what do you want to do with *Coke Can Grandma?*" Grandma was life-sized, after all.

Melanie answered, "Run her over with your golf cart!" And that's exactly what Melanie did, drive over *Coke Can Grandma*

repeatedly, to the cheers and support of her group and therapist.
It was an extremely cathartic experience.

Then Melanie cleaned every one of those cans, took out the
negative messages, and created Coke can flowers for each of
the therapists. True trauma resolution. Melanie also was able to
confront her abusers and be a driving force for healing throughout
her family.

TAYLOR'S STORY:
HEALING AT THE CELLULAR LEVEL

Taylor is a wonderful young woman who came to us at eighteen
months sober, however, she had continued to self-injure throughout
that time. Sober but still in emotional pain and struggling with relationships. She experienced great shame about the self-harm but
was compelled to continue to self-harm. This was a soothing behavior that helped to keep flashbacks and memories of early childhood
trauma at bay. It took many months for this woman to share the
physical wounds and the story of her childhood pain.

She was much loved by clients and staff, and when trauma
resolution came, it was a culmination of developing faith, trust,
and rapport with staff; telling her pain through art and many other
modalities; and hard work that included: psychodrama, process
group, equine therapy, and ropes course. The breakthrough came as
a result of Somatic Experiencing, which her very special therapist
provided. I witnessed this.

Taylor's body trembles and shakes off its visceral response to her trauma. This lasted for thirty minutes as the cellular level, the viscera, threw off the body's memory of the trauma. It was one of the most extraordinary healing experiences that I've witnessed. It took months of multiple modalities to move Taylor through her trauma, along with lots of love and compassion.

Besides Somatic Experiencing, Taylor used art to express her pain and angst.

Taylor's Painting

The observer can absolutely feel the intensity of self-harm and how very visceral and sensory the experience is. It's important to understand that cutting and burning is a form of relief for many. Others who are frozen in their pain find the ability to feel through self-harm. Taylor struggled greatly with relationships, but today she is married and joyful, healthy, and living her dream.

BRADFORD'S STORY:
THE MANY MASKS OF HEALING

Mask 1: When Billy asked me to do a mask that would represent who I am and who I want to be, this was the theme for the who I want to be. Yes, there are a lot of sayings and phrases on this mask, mainly because they represent how I want to believe. If I can only live in a world where all of the people live in harmony, I want the courage to rope an alligator and tame him to be nice. I want a world where physics won't always apply. If I use an umbrella, who's to say that I can't fly? The greatest emphasis of this mask is the point that no one dictates how my belief system is going to be—but me!

Mask 2: Billy asked me to do a mask on "Surrender." Being from the South and still living on the farm that my Confederate forefathers owned, I grew up always hearing that the term "surrender" was a huge taboo in our family . . . we never surrender! I was a different breed. I wasn't racist at all, like many of the family, and was always considered "liberal" or "grossly open-minded." I struggled with the term *surrender*, mainly because I thought it meant just giving up. However, with help from Billy and others, I came to believe that the only way I could truly grow or let go of my past/ addictions/bad behaviors, was by surrendering to "something/any-thing *greater than myself!* Shit, I ran the show, and it certainly was a mess. So in this mask the angel has the addict/alcoholic in her arms, gently carrying him out of the flames of addiction. In those flames, you'll find alcohol bottles and syringes for dope. The addict

(me) in this mask is completely exhausted. It is very tiring trying to be the ring leader, main attraction/main act, admissions taker, and clean-up crew all at one time. My circus was a one-man show!

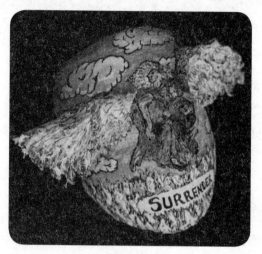

Surrender

The following is from a man who struggled for most of his life with multiple addictions. In treatment, this giant of a man, nearly seven feet tall, bright, compassionate, and a born leader, learned the whys and wherefores of his chronic relapses and his deep well of emotional pain. This alumnus continues his trauma work, joined a men's group, and has attended five-day intensives with our team at Spirit2Spirit trauma training. As he went even more thoroughly into the trauma, he had physical and emotional releases so that those old soothing behaviors will not be a choice. He's replaced those survival behaviors with healthy relationships, community, and the ability to have compassion for that little boy so wounded, terrified, and confused. He has offered the gift of his story.

CRAIG'S STORY:
FINDING A LIFELINE
THROUGH OTHERS

One day your life is moving along at its own pace. Everything is falling into place like it has been for so long. Some things are good. Some things are bad. And most things find their way somewhere in between. In an instant, none of those things matter anymore. Nothing is good. And nothing will ever be the same again.

In my life that's how I viewed trauma. Sudden. Unforeseen. Shocking. Tragic. My story didn't have any occurrences that fit that description. Why then did my outlook on life come with such fear and confusion? Why was I so easily obsessed with the notion that if I could only achieve enough wealth, be with the right woman, get high enough, that I could be happy? Why wasn't I happy already?

In the forest I learned that the things that happened early in my life had a huge and negative impact on the way I viewed myself and the world that surrounded me. Growing up with a violently abusive sibling I learned fear of harm. Having been molested by several different babysitters, I learned to not trust people from whom I should have been looking for guidance and growth. Having a mother dying of a dreadful disease, I learned that the closer I allow someone emotionally, the more likely I was to be devastated by loss. Not having the tools to overcome these emotional flaws, I searched for external sources of comfort and peace; sources that only served to propagate the painfully uncomfortable confusion that brewed inside me.

I didn't learn these things in a classroom with lessons and tests. I learned by watching. It impacts each individual differently. But the behaviors of trauma survivors are amazingly similar. I owe so much of my peace of mind to the brave people who came to face their demons, face their fear, anger, shame, and guilt. Finding confidence in their ability to do so by watching their fellow survivors walk that difficult path. And awakening to the reality that they are not alone. That awakening helped me to accept the challenges that I faced in my search for happiness.

It was by chance that I came to the treatment center in the forest a little over one year ago. I had rejected the notion that I needed residential treatment. But I was crippling myself with active addictions to alcohol and cocaine. I was at the point that I knew that I was not going to escape the grasp of my addiction without help. I checked myself into the detox program, expecting to stay only seven days or so. But after meeting some of the clients I decided to give it a try. It was the best decision I had ever made.

One of the things I'm most proud of in my lifetime is that I was able to protect my children from the traumas of my youth. My son recently graduated college and my daughter is in her senior year of high school; I unapologetically live vicariously through them. Not through their accomplishments, but through the wonderfully beautiful people that they are. I see another life for myself in them. What my life could have been had I not faced the challenges that I did. And I'm not sad about it. It's a great source of pride for me.

My son and I were in a major city a few hundred miles from home, a little over seven months ago. He had recently signed a contract to play professional basketball in Japan. He and I were there together having some father-son bonding time a few weeks before he left.

He was working with a personal trainer. And I was tagging along with a permanent smile painted on my face. What a wonderful start to his adult life!

One evening I looked at the date and realized that I had a monthly anniversary in my sobriety. When I told him he looked at me and said he was proud of me and that he loved me. Wow! That really sunk in quickly. He knew that I had been going to AA meetings regularly; that I was taking my addiction and trauma recovery seriously; and that this time it looked as if I was through with trying to find peace in very unpleasant places. I went off to sleep feeling better about myself than I had in a long time.

At 5:30 the next morning I awoke to him waking from a nightmare. He asked me what was going on. I jumped in his bed with him and hugged him from behind and told him that everything was okay. I told him that I had him and to wake up so we could go get some breakfast. It wasn't a nightmare, though—he was in cardiac arrest. He had an enlarged heart that had gone undetected. My son died in my arms that morning.

Things in my life were moving along in a great direction. Things were falling into their own places at their own paces. I was allowing life to unfold in front of me instead of me trying to piece it all together with my own expectations attached. It was working. Then, suddenly, nothing mattered anymore.

Nothing was good. And nothing will ever be the same again. The last seven months have been riddled with one example after another of the most challenging moments I could have ever have imagined. And I don't expect that to stop anytime soon. Some of my

Refuge brothers and sisters have been through the same tragedy. During my time there I witnessed them dealing with their trauma. Their strength and love were an inspiration to me then; their experience and love are a lifeline to me now. I talk to my son all the time. Like that night a lifetime ago, I tell him that I am sober. I tell him that that run of monthly anniversaries was not interrupted by his passing. And I hear him tell me that he loves me and that he's proud of me. I owe my life to The Refuge.

ABBY'S STORY:
USING HER SENSES TO FIND HER WORDS

She sobbed in my arms. This tiny little three-year-old, so lost and afraid, her incredible huge turquoise eyes brimming with tears and overwhelmed with terror; not fear, pure terror. Her breathing came in rapid gulping breaths, trying to survive the horror she was experiencing. Smells were overwhelming her. Gasoline and oil, garage smells, the noise of someone else's rasping cough; more than she could bear. It had started with the rattling of coins in someone's pocket, which was the sound of the monster as he walked down the hall to her bedroom.

Curled in my lap, hanging on for her life, afraid that she would die as I rocked her and continued to hold her gently. I touched her hair and cooed, "It's going to be okay, you are safe, I'm here with you, it's Judy. I'll protect you Abby, no one is going to hurt you. I promise you, you are safe Abby, you are safe." And we rocked and rocked and rocked and held on.

"No, no, he's hurting me, please get away, get off me, no." Then those screams, the screams and wailing of a little girl. I kept pulling her back to the present. "You're safe, I have you Abby, hang on, I'll protect you Abby. I'll protect you. Feel my heart beating Abby, it is beating with yours, breathe." My heart was hurting for this little girl and what had been done to her by this monster with her uncle's face, her favorite uncle. She knew it must be her fault. She was a temptress, a tease, she "wanted it." Shame, it's your own fault. *Momma said it was my fault.*

My fault, not the monster's. He's a good man, it must be you.

I continued to soothe her with words and the feeling of being held in a loving way. And we rocked and rocked.

Slowly the sobs turned to hiccups, and then just tears running down her face, and finally calm breathing as she uncoiled into her twenty-six-year-old five-foot-seven-inch body, protected and held by my five-foot body. Abby, this gorgeous, sometime fragile, always resilient, woman/child. I had Abby look around the room, and asked: "Tell me five things you see." She said, "You, Judy, the door, Tommy, my group, four group." I asked her to describe things she heard, two things she smelled, and finally things she felt. "Sad, small, sort of safe." This is a centering exercise for clients who are experiencing flashback or dissociation to bring them back to the here and now.

This could not have been a more perfect storm to unmask the monster that held her hostage . . . the smells of the garage and the rasping cough of one of the men in the group, and the sound of coins rattling, triggered the memories in a very visceral way. Abby had been feeling "yuck," never understanding her behaviors. Always filled with a huge veil of shame. Searching for love and acceptance and at the same time pushing loving relationships away and never understanding why. When you unravel the story, all of the behaviors make sense.

Abby had no memory of this time in her life, just the feelings, which overwhelmed and confused her. They didn't make sense to her, she couldn't explain them to anyone; they just were. Then came the sound of the coins and the garage smells; the perfect combination to trigger the memories. It makes pre-verbal sense to me. At three, this little girl had no words to explain what she was experiencing and when she tried to seek protection she was shushed and pushed away. There was no one to protect her and it happened over and over again until she was nine years old. Somewhere around five it started to feel good. She was special, chosen. In her family, which was so chaotic and violent, those were the moments when she felt most safe. In kindergarten she was very, very quiet, beyond shy; oftentimes not present. Teachers wrote that she daydreamed; they suspected a learning disability. They put her in special education classes. She rode the short, yellow bus and the other kids taunted and bullied her. More fear, more pain, so alone.

At six, teachers decided she must be depressed. She would cry and bang her head on the desk, many times drawing blood and frightening the other children and teachers. She must be depressed, anxious, and ADHD. So the child psychiatrist prescribed Ritalin. Only in treatment did Abby finally understand that she had been a child suffering from PTSD. That all of her behaviors made sense as a result of her story. That she is not "bad" but "wounded." Only then could she heal from the moral injury and trauma—and heal she did.

I have always had good ears. I listen and watch and intuit what
people are really saying, what they are feeling. Folks usually see
Momma in me; good Momma, bad Momma, indifferent Momma,
abusive Momma sometimes. Whatever they need to heal, I think
because I feel safe and I won't judge.

Images of Resilience

The families of my people, as most families, are secret-keepers.
The secret is to protect someone or a reputation or a way of life.
Often, when the secrets are finally told, the pieces to a puzzle fall into
place. Many times the acknowledgement of the secrets is followed by
a huge cleansing breath—it finally makes sense.

Here's an example: Carol, at forty-two years old, was in treatment
again, crack and alcohol and any other drugs, and men. There was
always a relationship. She was born to a privileged family; Nana ruled
the family. Carol felt lost and unloved most of her life. Nana was cold
to her, verbally abusive, dismissive, and she alienated Carol from the
rest of her family. This began when she was very young.

Carol tried to avoid the pain even in treatment by "acting out."
Some clients "act in" but almost everyone experiences relapses in
behavior while in treatment to avoid re-experiencing the pain. It's
not surprising and provides a juicy therapeutic opportunity. What
we discovered was that Carol already had the puzzle pieces. She had
found her parents' marriage certificate dated after her conception.
Well, in her rigid, fundamentalist, Southern grandma's world, this
made Carol a bastard child who created a moral dilemma for the

family. Consequently, all of grandma's rage and disappointment was loaded onto the poor little girl. And that poor little girl never understood why she felt shame and never understood that it was not hers to own. And all the drugs or men would never change that. Now the healing could begin.

GENEVA'S STORY:
CHOOSING TO STAY IN THE LIGHT

As I looked at my reflection, I no longer recognized the face staring back at me. The vivacious soul that once dwelled behind my green eyes was gone. I stared at a stranger; one who was hiding something dark and ugly within her. I wanted to break the glass and set myself free, but I know that doing so would release the demons of my past. I was terrified. Fear had kept me incarcerated for many years and I had lost control of my own life. The more I tried to escape the memories that haunted me, the further I fell in an abyss of misery. I began to try to escape in other ways—drugs and alcohol became my new gods and I looked to them to save me from the pain.

Before I knew it, I was held captive by my addiction. My world quickly crumbled around me. The girl I once knew vanished. Then I began taking hostages. Those I loved suffered, too, as I transformed into a monster. My dear family and friends felt the wrath of my long reign of terror. Countless times they showed me unconditional love while I treated them with cruelty like never before. Disgusted with the girl I had become, I began to wonder where this behavior originated. That fateful day, alone in the mirror, I decided something had to change. The miracle came when I made the choice to delve into my traumatic past and seek help to rebuild the girl that fear and addiction had dismantled. I had nothing left to lose and I was finally ready to fight for my life.

First, I had to let go of my escape plan. The drugs and alcohol weren't improving my situation, so with the support of many professionals and loved ones, I turned away from the substances. This was by no means easy. In fact, it was one of the most difficult things I had ever done. Every time I thought they were gone, my former gods beckoned me to return to my life with them. I ignored their desperate pleas and instead dove headfirst into my past. It wasn't pretty; many tears were shed as I retold my traumas to therapists and trusted friends.

Over time, the weight of my pain lightened as I released all that had been trapped inside me for so long. I had hope again. I began to feel pure joy. My laughter and smile reappeared, and I once again recognized the girl in the mirror.

I came from the depths of hell back to a life that wasn't always perfect but I was truly living again. My fight will never end because I refuse to go back to that dark place. I continue to work with others and take the steps necessary to maintain a life rich in beauty and joy. The dark will always be there waiting for me, but with the help of others and my newfound strength, I choose to stay in the light. Recovery from trauma and addiction is the best gift I have ever received. It takes effort, support, and courage, but is truly worth it. I chose to fight and today, I can look into the mirror and like the woman with those green eyes—now full of love and hope.

JANE'S STORY:
FREAKIN' AWESOME!

I couldn't understand why after working the Twelve Steps with a sponsor and being active in the AA community in Delray, I felt more alone than ever. A few months after I received my one-year chip I tried to end my life. I couldn't understand why I was sober and miserable. I got sober at twenty years old and thought not drinking would solve my problems. I had heard about Judy's treatment center from a friend and called to find information. I was picked up by sober escorts the next day. My life has been forever changed.

I realized I was being held back from recovery by childhood trauma. I was sexually abused when I was eight years old by my stepbrother and it was pushed under the rug all my life. Going through my early years, I self-medicated with self-harm, alcohol, and abusive relationships. I was opened to a whole new level of self-awareness. Most importantly, I found my voice! At family week I got to confront my mother and tell her my feelings about the abuse while reading a letter to my perpetrator in the circle. My therapist gave me a shirt to wear that said "I am freakin' awesome." From that day on the seed was planted: I am freakin' awesome! While in treatment with Judy I got to learn how to have relationships with people and to look up instead of down while walking. Now I look at people in the eyes when they talk to me. I found a higher power whom I lean on in the darkest of times.

Since I left treatment I have only grown stronger and my life has gotten even brighter. Don't get me wrong, there has been heartache but my tool kit is full of coping skills and beautiful people I can call day and night.

I moved home to the Midwest and live in an apartment with my best friend. I am fully self-supporting and work as a manager at a gym, with college plans. I can look at myself in the mirror and smile at the woman I have become. I'm able to offer other women the love and compassion that was so freely given to me. I am eternally grateful to Judy Crane for making such a beautiful place where for the first time ever in my life I knew I was not alone.

MEAGAN'S STORY:
FINDING HER SPIRIT

I was born in Azlec, Texas. My parents had recently moved to this town to take over the family business following the death of my paternal grandfather who was killed in a car accident. When I was six months old, they sold the business and we relocated to Seattle. Justin, my younger brother, was born three years later.

My early childhood was blissful and idyllic. I was a happy, sweet, confident little girl with a wonderful imagination. The relationship I had with my mom was especially close. She balanced being a stay-at-home mom with her career as a concert bassoonist and pianist. My dad, an environmental lawyer turned real estate developer, was a workaholic and not a reliable presence, but a loving father nevertheless. He did his best.

My parents strove to give my brother and me the best of everything. We ate organic, watched only PBS, and took classes in art, horseback riding, gymnastics, pottery, skiing, swimming, astronomy, ballet, tennis, and whatever else we showed interest in. We attended the best private co-op kindergarten, preschool, first, and second grade.

What happened when I was about seven years old was no one's fault. It could have been avoided, though. We had a babysitter who was the son of my dad's friend and business partner. He was young, maybe fourteen years old, a neighborhood boy. The babysitter began molesting me. It was painful, but I pretended nothing was happening. My brother was sometimes in the same room too. I was so young, innocent, confused, and scared. Yet for some reason, I didn't feel comfortable enough to tell my parents. In fact, I didn't want them to know what was happening. To protect myself from him, I started wearing several pairs of tights under my ballet leotard and pants over everything. That didn't prevent the abuse from continuing though and eventually he raped me. I couldn't get out of bed for several days and pretended I was sick. After this, I told my mom I didn't want him to babysit me anymore, though I didn't tell her why.

Somehow (the details are foggy), the babysitter was confronted and confessed. My mom wanted to go to the police, but she told me recently my dad said he'd divorce her if she did. I went to a social worker with my mom and I also went to see my pediatrician, but I was still pretending nothing happened. I wore two bathing suits and wouldn't take them off for my pediatrician.

Soon after this, my memories of the abuse "vanished" from my consciousness for several years. I had no recollection of any molestation or rape. However, I was not at all the same person.

My loss of self was the most tragic and devastating conse-
quence of the abuse. I literally, with all my heart, believed that
Meagan's spirit was gone and dead. I thought that I was a bad,
guilty, and deceitful spirit—an imposter—living in her body and living
out her life. Worse, I took responsibility for whatever happened to the
"good little Meagan" who was gone.

In my early teens, I was sexually assaulted by the father of a
friend and his colleague, which resulted in a terrifying pregnancy
and abortion. The subsequent PTSD and its debilitating afflictions
had plagued me for too long.

As a little girl, the sexual abuse I experienced was so devastating to my self-perception that I believed I was a different person
entirely. Therefore, I became a different person. Since I felt bad,
guilty, disgusting, angry, scared, and unworthy of anything good,
I acted accordingly. When I disclosed a fragment of my trauma
by the babysitter to my parents, they sought counseling for me.
From age eight through twenty-eight, my mother and father
referred me to countless psychologists and psychiatrists. However,
twenty years of weekly therapy sessions were futile because I was
too ashamed and frightened to reveal the sexual abuse and its
repercussions.

Victims of sexual abuse frequently medicate their trauma with
eating disorders. I was no exception. Everything in my world felt out
of control, but restricting and punishing my body through anorexia
and deprivation created an illusion of control that was dangerously
enticing.

Growing up, since my sexual abuse and anorexia were con-
secrated secrets, the therapists hoping to help me were ineffec-
tive. Instead of PTSD, I was diagnosed with bipolar disorder and

borderline personality disorder along with depression and anxiety. At the age of twelve, I started on a course of Prozac, followed unsuccessfully by a multitude of antidepressants, antipsychotics, lithium, and clonazepam. By age seventeen, I felt so hopeless that I was seduced by suicidal ideations. One morning, I decided to end it all and swallowed over 300 Tylenol. After I recovered from my overdose in the adolescent psychiatric ward, my parents sent me to Provo Canyon School, a psychiatric and behavioral modification center in Utah. Once I completed six months of harrowing and highly medicated treatment, I returned to Seattle, graduated from high school, and enrolled at Franklin University Switzerland on the other side of the world, where I hoped to escape myself and my past.

To my surprise, many years later while working at Museo Cantonale d'Arte in Switzerland, I discovered that to be painted, teased, bitten, and chased by autistic children was infinitely more rewarding than my chosen career curating art exhibitions. The passion and joy I experienced facilitating art therapy at the museum for boys and girls with special needs first inspired my interest in social work. After graduating with a bachelor of arts in art history from Franklin University Switzerland, I studied practical art therapy and art instruction at Scuola di Rudolph Steiner and Universit Svizzera Italiana and began exploring MSW programs.

After seven years of living, studying, and working abroad in the fairy-tale beautiful Swiss Italian town of Lugano, I returned to my hometown of Seattle. I completed my studies in Eastern medicine to become a certified practitioner of Jin Shin Do Acupressure while I worked at Microsoft as an Italian translator. My ambition to become a social worker was nurtured by volunteering at the Crisis Clinic and Lifelong AIDS Alliance. Nevertheless, I had personal issues begging

to be addressed, and conceded to help myself before embarking on
a career helping others.

On October 12, 2008, I admitted myself to The Refuge, a residential treatment center in the swamplands of central Florida. I was
determined to confront myself, my anorexia, and my post-traumatic
stress disorder. Just before I entered The Refuge, I weighed less
than seventy-five pounds. I was dying from malnutrition and immi-
nent heart failure. Additionally, I been numbing with alcohol, drugs,
and unhealthy relationships for years.

For a few years, free of medication and buoyant with optimism,
I excelled emotionally, socially, and academically. Eventually though,
the familiar sense of anxiety, depression, and overriding fear
from my unresolved trauma returned. Furthermore, medical issues
resulting from years of unnecessary and traumatic dental work due
to dental malpractice, and stress-induced epileptic seizures took
their toll in every facet of my life. From my transcripts, it's clear
that I struggled academically my last few years at Franklin. To
tackle the issue of my faltering scholastic career, I took a semester
off and stayed in Seattle to focus on restoring my health. While
I was home, the healing success I experienced with acupressure
inspired me to learn the practice myself. Before I returned to Switzerland to complete my education at Franklin University, I began
earning my degree in Jin Shin Do Acupressure. My academic
success improved dramatically after my hiatus. At USC, I expect to
exceed my previous scholastic performance since I have grown more
disciplined, responsible, committed, wiser, and self-aware since my
early twenties.

The Refuge taught me to heal myself through seven months of
intensive cognitive, dialectical, experiential, and traditional therapies

combined with breathwork and twelve-step groups. Through this process, I discovered I did not actually have any mental illness or mental disorder. In fact, I had been suffering from PTSD and all its manifestations, including anorexia Thankfully, since I completed my treatment at The Refuge five years ago, I've been relieved of all signs or symptoms of PTSD, and I have never again acted out on my eating disorder.

REFLECTIVE SKETCHES

1) Why did you read *The Trauma Heart*?

_____

2) Did *The Trauma Heart* give you what you needed?

_____

_____

3) What emotions did you feel reading *The Trauma Heart*?

_____

_____

_____

4) Did the book help you look more deeply into your story?

_____

_____

_____

5) Did reading the book lead you to the result you wanted?

_____

_____

_____

6) Did the intention you made at the beginning of the book materialize?

_____

_____

_____

REFERENCES

Bretherton, Inge. "The origins of attachment theory: John Bowlby and Mary Ainsworth." *A Century of Developmental Psychology*. (n.d.): 431–71. Web.

Beattie, Melody. *Codependent No More*. Center City, MN: Hazelden, 1986. Print.

Carnes, Patrick, PhD. *The Betrayal Bond: Breaking Free of Exploitive Relationships*. Deerfield Beach: Health Communications, Inc, 1997. Print.

Cleave, Chris. *Little Bee*. New York: Simon & Schuster, 2009. Print.

De Victoria, Samuel Lopez, PhD. "Emotional Trauma in the Womb." *World of Psychology*. N.p., 30 June 2010. Web.

Deveraux, Jude. *The Invitation*. New York: Pocket Books, 1994. Print.

Diaz, Luis. "Cellular Memory Release," n.p., n.d. *www.cellularmemory.org*. Web.

Drescher, Kent, David Foy, Caroline Kelly, Anna Leshner, Kerrie Schutz, and Brett Litz. "An exploration of the viability and usefulness of the construct of moral injury in war veterans." *Traumatology*, 17, 8–13. 2011. doi: 10.1177/1534765610395615. Web.

Dworkin, Ronald W. "The Rise of the Caring Industry." *Policy Review*. Hoover Institution, 1 June 2010. Web.

Eliot, T. S. *Four Quartets*. London: Faber and Faber, 1944. Print.

Felicetti, Marcus Julian. "10 Reasons Why We Need at Least 8 Hugs a Day." Mind Body Green, 10 Aug. 2012. Web.

Felitti, Vincent J. "The Relationship of Adverse Childhood Experiences to Adult Health: Turning Gold into Lead." *Journal of Psychosomatic Medicine and Psychotherapy* 48.4 (2002): 359–69. Web.

Frankl, Viktor. *Man's Search for Meaning*. Boston: Beacon Press, 1959. Print.

Hari, Johann. Chasing the Scream: *The First and Last Days of the War on Drugs*. New York: Bloomsbury, 2015. Print.

Heller, Sheri, LCSW. "Healing the Traumatized Child." *Psych Central Professional*. N.p., 27 Jan. 2015. Web. 12 Aug. 2015.

Herman, Judith Lewis. *Trauma and Recovery: the Aftermath of Violence, from Domestic Abuse to Political Terror*. New York: Basic Books, 1997. Print.

Hurley, Dan. "Grandma's Experiences Leave a Mark on Your Genes." *Discover* May 2013: 664–81. Print.

Koehler, B., M.D. "Psychotic Disorders: From DNA to Neighborhood." *The American Psychoanalyst* (2011): 13–16. Web.

Levine, Peter A., PhD. In an *Unspoken Voice: How the Body Releases Trauma and Restores Goodness*. Berkeley: North Atlantic, 2010. Print.

Levine, Peter A. *Waking the Tiger: Healing Trauma*. Berkeley, Calif: North Atlantic Books, 1997. Print.

Lopez De Victoria, Samuel, PhD. "Emotional Trauma in the Womb." *Psych Central*, 29 June 2010. Web.

Maguen, Shira, PhD and Brett Litz, PhD, "Moral Injury in the Context of War." National Center for PTSD. Web. Marche, Stephen. "Is Facebook Making Us Lonely?" *The Atlantic*. Atlantic Media Company, 19 Feb. 2014. Web.

Maté, Gabor. *In the Realm of Hungry Ghosts: Close Encounters with Addiction*. Toronto: Vintage Canada, 2012. Print.

Mellody, Pia. *Facing Codependence*. New York: HarperCollins, 1989. Print.

Northrup, Christiane. *Mother-Daughter Wisdom: Understanding the Crucial Link Between Mothers, Daughters, and Health*. New York: Bantam Books, 2006. Print.

Putnam, Robert D. *Bowling Alone: The Collapse and Revival of American Community*. New York: Simon & Schuster, 2000. Print.

Quinton, D. "A Poem from a Granddaughter about Her Grandmother." Class Assignment, The Cornerstone School. 2012.

Reichmann, Frieda Fromm. "Loneliness." *Psychiatry: Journal for the Study of Interpersonal Processes* 22.1 (1959): 1–15. Web.

Rūmī, Jalāl Al-Dīn. *Rumi: the Book of Love*. Trans. Coleman Barks. New York: HarperOne, HarperCollins, 2003. Print.

Rūmī, Jalāl Al-Dīn. *One-Handed Basket Weaving*. Trans. Coleman Barks and Mary Louise Laird. Berkeley: Quelquefois Press, 1993. Print.

Russell, Dan, Letitia Anne Peplau, and Mary Lund Ferguson. "Developing a Measure of Loneliness." *Journal of Personality Assessment*: 42.3 (1978): 290–94. Web.

Russell, Daniel, PhD. "How Lonely Are You? Take Our Loneliness Test—AARP The Magazine." *AARP*. AARP The Magazine, 24 Sept. 2010. Web.

Scharnberg, Kirsten. "Women GIs and Post-Traumatic Stress Disorder." *Military.com*. DefenseWatch, 28 Mar. 2005. Web.

Schnurr, Paula P., PhD, Matthew J. Friedman, MD, PhD, Charles C. Enge, MD, MPH, Edna B. Foa, PhD, M. Tracie Shea, PhD, Bruce K. Chow, MS, Patricia A. Resick, PhD,

Veronica Thurston, MBA, Susan M. Orsillo, PhD, Rodney Haug, PhD, Carole Turner, MN, and Nancy Bernardy, PhD. "Cognitive Behavioral Therapy for Posttraumatic Stress Disorder in Women A Randomized Controlled Trial." *Original Contribution* 297.8 (2007): 820–30. *Jama.ama-assn.org.* Web. 1 Feb. 2012.

Schore, Allan. PhD. *"The Most Important Years in Life: Our Beginnings."* Presentation at Oslo and Akershus University College of Applied Sciences, Oslo Norway, September 28, 2014.

Shulevitz, Judith. "The Lethality of Loneliness." *New Republic*: 13 May 2013: n. pag. Web.

Solomon, Marion Fried., and Daniel J. Siegel. *Healing Trauma: Attachment, Mind, Body, and Brain.* New York: W.W. Norton, 2003. Print.

Tanielian, Terri, Lisa H. Jaycox, Terry Schell, Grant N. Marshall, M. Audrey Burnam, Christine Eibner, Benjamin Karney, Lisa S. Meredith, Jeanne Ringel, and Mary E. Vaiana. "Invisible Wounds." *RAND Corporation.* N.p., 08 Apr. 2008. Web.

Van der Kolk, Bessel, MD. *The Body Keeps the Score: Brain, Mind, and Body in the Healing of Trauma.* NYC, NY: Penguin Books, 2015. Print.

Vanier, Jean. *Becoming Human.* Toronto: Anansi Press, 2008. Print.

Weaver, Ian C G, Nadia Cervoni, Frances A. Champagne, Ana C. D'alessio, Shakti Sharma, Jonathan R. Seckl, Sergiy Dymov, Moshe Szyf, and Michael J. Meaney. "Epigenetic programming by maternal behavior." *Nature Neuroscience* 7.8 (2004): 847–54. Web.

Weller, Francis. *The Wild Edge of Sorrow: Rituals of Renewal and the Sacred Work of Grief.* Berkeley, CA: North Atlantic Books, 2015. Print.

Williamson, Marianne. *A Return to Love: Reflections on the Principles of a Course in Miracles.* New York: Harper Collins Publishers, 1992. Print.

Winfrey, Oprah. *What I Know for Sure.* New York: Flatiron, 2014. Print.

Woititz, Janet G., EdD. *Adult Children of Alcoholics.* Deerfield Beach: Health Communications, Inc., 1983. Print.

Wood, David. "Moral Injury: The Grunts–Damned If They Kill, Damned If They Don't." *The Huffington Post.* TheHuffingtonPost.com, 18 Mar. 2014. Web.

Diagnostic and Statistical Manual of Mental Disorders: DSM-5. Arlington, VA: American Psychiatric Association, 2013. Print.

Diagnostic and Statistical Manual of Mental Disorders, Fourth Edition: Primary Care Version: International Version with ICD-10 Codes. Washington, DC: American Psychiatric Association, 1996. Print.

Houston PBS. "Dr. Bruce Perry, Childhood Development on LIVING SMART with Patricia Gras." *YouTube.* YouTube, 15 Mar. 2010. Web.

HELPFUL ORGANIZATIONS AND INFORMATION

International Institute for Trauma and Addiction Professionals
IITAP.com
This organization also has a focus on multiple addictions including process addictions such as sex and relationship, gaming and gambling disorders, eating disorders, self-harming behaviors, and financial disorders. Explore the therapist directory.

National Board of Certified Counselors
NBCC.org
Explore this website and find therapists in your area with a specialty in trauma and addictions. Interview prospective therapists from any of these sites. Obviously, some are more qualified than others.

Psychology Today
Psychologytoday.com
This site has a wonderful therapist-finder section and is also a great resource for ongoing information in the field of trauma and addiction.

The Guest House Ocala
Theguesthouseocala.com
We can provide additional information about treatment in your area.

RECOMMENDED READING

Angelou, Maya. *I Know Why the Caged Bird Sings*. New York: Random House, 1970.

Brown, Laura S. *Your Turn for Care: Surviving the Aging and Death of the Adults Who Harmed You*. CreateSpace Independent Publishing Platform, 2012.

Carnes, Patrick, PhD. *The Betrayal Bond: Breaking Free of Exploitive Relationships*. Deerfield Beach: Health Communications, Inc, 1997.

Levine, Peter A., PhD. *In an Unspoken Voice: How the Body Releases Trauma and Restores Goodness*. Berkeley: North Atlantic, 2010.

Levine, Peter A., and Maggie Kline. *Trauma through a Child's Eyes: Awakening the Ordinary Miracle of Healing: Infancy through Adolescence*. Berkeley, CA: North Atlantic Books, 2006.

Levine, Peter A. *Waking the Tiger: Healing Trauma*. Berkeley, Calif: North Atlantic Books, 1997.

Maltz, Wendy. *The Sexual Healing Journey: A Guide for Survivors of Sexual Abuse*. New York, NY: William Morrow, 2012.

Maté, Gabor. *In the Realm of Hungry Ghosts: Close Encounters with Addiction*. Toronto: Vintage Canada, 2012.

Schiraldi, Glenn R. *The Post-Traumatic Stress Disorder Sourcebook: A Guide to Healing, Recovery, and Growth*. New York, NY: McGraw-Hill Education, 2016.

Siegel, Daniel J. *Mindsight: The New Science of Personal Transformation*. New York: Bantam Trade Paperbacks, 2011.

Siegel, Daniel J. *The Mindful Brain: Reflection and Attunement in the Cultivation of Well-Being*. New York: W.W. Norton, 2007.

Siegel, Daniel J. and Marion Solomon, PhD. *Healing Trauma: Attachment, Mind, Body and Brain*. New York: Norton, 2003.

Van der Kolk, Bessel, M.D. *The Body Keeps the Score: Brain, Mind, and Body in the Healing of Trauma*. NYC, NY: Penguin Books, 2015.

Van der Kolk, Bessel, Alexander C. McFarlane, and Lars Weisæth. *Traumatic Stress: The Effects of Overwhelming Experience on Mind, Body, and Society*. New York: Guilford Press, 2007.

SUGGESTED MOVIES

Trauma/Trauma Resolution

- Good Will Hunting (1997)
- Antwone Fischer (2002)
- The Fisher King (1991)
- Lars and the Real Girl (2007)
- Defending Your Life (1991)
- About a Boy (2002)
- The Brothers Bloom (2008)
- Billy Elliot (2000)
- Penelope (2007)
- The Book Thief (2013)
- Dallas Buyers Club (2013)
- Gravity (2013)
- Her (2013)
- Nebraska (2013)
- Philomena (2013)
- 12 Years a Slave (2013)
- All is Lost (2013)
- August: Osage County (2013)
- Blue Jasmine (2013)
- The Kids Are Alright (2010)
- Delivery Man (2013)

Family Systems

➡ The Great Santini (1979)
➡ Ordinary People (1980)
➡ Lars and the Real Girl (2007)
➡ A Thousand Acres (1997)
➡ Dead Poets Society (1989)
➡ On Golden Pond (1981)
➡ Parenthood (1989)
➡ Penelope (2007)

Addiction/Alcoholism

➡ The Basketball Diaries (1995)
➡ The Shawshank Redemption (1994)
➡ Clean and Sober (1988)
➡ The Fisher King (1991)

Grief

➡ Billy Elliot (2000)
➡ Antwone Fischer (2002)
➡ The Fisher King (1991)
➡ Ghost Town (2008)
➡ Dallas Buyers Club (2013)

Suicide

➡ Harold and Maude (1971)
➡ About a Boy (2002)

Social Anorexia

➡ Lars and the Real Girl (2007)

Co-Dependence

➡ When a Man Loves a Woman (1994)
➡ The Nanny Diaries (2007)
➡ Ghost Town (2008)

Questioning Sexuality

- Trembling Before G-d (2001)
- In & Out (1997)
- Torch Song Trilogy (1988)
- Transamerica (2005)
- Boys Don't Cry (1999)
- Chasing Amy (1997)
- Brokeback Mountain (2005)
- Billy Elliot (2000)
- Dallas Buyers Club (2013)

Courtship Disorder

- Runaway Bride (1999)
- Pretty Woman (1990)
- Benny and Joon (1993)
- Lars and the Real Girl (2007)
- As Good as it Gets (1997)
- About a Boy (2002)
- Penelope (2007)

Love Addiction/Love Avoidance

- When Harry Met Sally (1989)
- Addicted to Love (1997)
- An Officer and a Gentleman (1982)
- Torch Song Trilogy (1988)
- High Fidelity (2000)
- Her (2013)

Fantasy and Romance

- Don Juan DeMarco (1994)
- In & Out (1997)
- Breakfast at Tiffany's (1961)
- Torch Song Trilogy (1988)
- Her (2013)

ABOUT THE AUTHOR

JUDY CRANE has over three decades of experience working in both residential and outpatient settings. She founded a treatment center The Refuge—A Healing Place in 2003. This facility became one of the country's leading centers specializing in trauma, PTSD, and addiction. In 2008, Judy established her company Spirit2 Spirit, hosting weeklong, group setting, and intensive therapy sessions and also offering training in trauma therapy. In 2013, Judy sold The Refuge, and most recently she co-founded The Guest House Ocala, a boutique treatment facility.

Judy earned her BA at Rutgers University and her MA from the New York Institute of Technology. She is a Certified Trauma Therapist, Certified Sex Addiction Therapist and a Certified Hypnotist.

Judy lives in Ocala, Florida, and spends her time providing healing therapy at The Guest House Ocala and doing speaking engagements around the world.

For more information about Judy and her work, please visit *www.theguesthouseocala.com.*

Key to The Guest House. (See "The Guest House," page 7.)

1

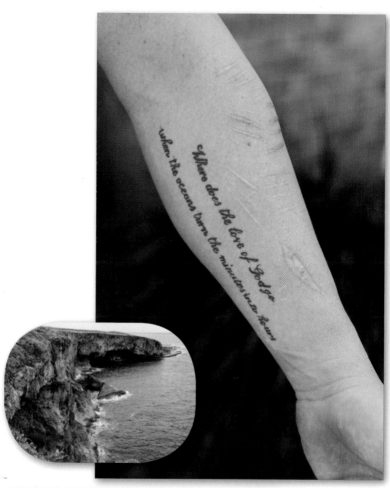

Zac's healing scars. (See Zac's Story, page 9.)

A client painted her way through a trauma resolution. (See page 48.)

*"The Chameleon,"
Cheryl's collage.
(See Cheryl's Story,
page 69.)*

*"Rising from the Ashes"
by Cheryl.*

4

Burn baby burn. (See Getting Off the Sofa, page 84.)

Bradford's timeline. (See Bradford's Story, page 96.)

Kate's "Masks of Courage." (See Kate's Story, page 112.)

Delaney Rose, Judy's granddaughter.
(See "A Granddaughter's Poem to Her Grandmother," page 150.)

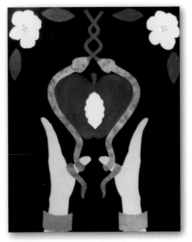

Karen's "The Truth of Persephone" and "The Wages of Sin."
(See Karen's Story, page 170.)

Karen's "Beautiful Dreamer."

Karen's "Love" collage.

Karen's "Sexy" collage.

Stacy's trauma resolution collages, depicting scenes from Liberia and Darfur.
(See Stacy's Story, page 222.)

Father Joe's trauma resolution. (See Father Joe's Story, page 242.)

Jessica's "Towering Tree," "Seen and Unseen," and "Red Scream at 4 A.M."
(See Jessica's Story, page 259.)

BJ's trauma resolution artwork. (See BJ's Story, page 295.)

*Chloe's tattoo, "Bruises and Scars" (left)
and with them removed, trauma resolution.
(See Chloe's Story, page 300.)*

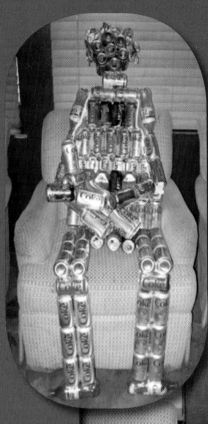

Melanie's
"Coke Can Grandma."
(See Melanie's Story, page 302.)

13

Taylor's expression of pain and angst.
(See Taylor's Story, page 304.)

Bradford's trauma resolution mask "Who I Want to Be."
(See Bradford's Story, page 306.)

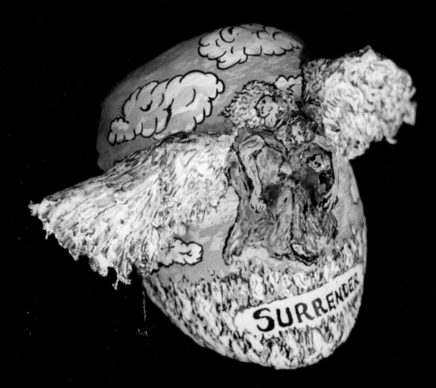

Bradford's trauma resolution mask "Surrender."